CHILD ABUSE

BANFF INTERNATIONAL BEHAVIORAL SCIENCE Series

SERIES EDITORS

Kenneth D. Craig, *University of British Columbia*
Keith S. Dobson, *University of Calgary*
Robert J. McMahon, *University of Washington*
Ray DeV. Peters, *Queen's University*

Volumes in the **Banff International Behavioral Science Series** take the behavioral science perspective on important basic and applied challenges that confront practitioners working in the fields of the social, psychological, and health services. The editors invite leading investigators and practitioners to contribute because of their expertise on emergent issues and topics. Contributions to the volumes integrate information on themes and key issues relating to current research and professional practice. The chapters reflect the authors' personal, critical analysis of the topics, the current scientific and professional literature, and discussions and deliberations with other experts and practitioners. It is our intention to have this continuing series of publications provide an "expressive" early indicator of the developing nature and composition of the behavioral sciences and scientific applications to human problems and issues. The volumes should appeal to practitioners, scientists, and students interested in the interface between professional practice and research advances.

Volumes in This Series:

CHILD ABUSE

New Directions in Prevention and Treatment Across the Lifespan

David A. Wolfe
Robert J. McMahon
Ray DeV. Peters
editors

B̶ANFF I̶NTERNATIONAL B̶EHAVIORAL S̶CIENCE SERIES

 SAGE Publications
International Educational and Professional Publisher
Thousand Oaks   London   New Delhi

For information:

SAGE Publications, Inc.
2455 Teller Road
Thousand Oaks, California 91320
E-mail: order@sagepub.com

SAGE Publications Ltd.
6 Bonhill Street
London EC2A 4PU
United Kingdom

SAGE Publications India Pvt. Ltd.
M-32 Market
Greater Kailash I
New Delhi 110 048 India

HV
6626.5
.C4957
1997

Printed in the United States of America

Child abuse: New directions in prevention and treatment across
    the lifespan / edited by David A. Wolfe, Robert J. McMahon, and Ray DeV. Peters.
        p. cm. — (Banff international behavioral science series; v. 4)
    ISBN 0-7619-1095-6 (cloth: acid-free paper). — ISBN
0-7619-1096-4 (pbk.: acid-free paper)
        1. Child abuse. 2. Child abuse—Prevention. 3. Child abuse—
Treatment.   I. Wolfe, David A. II. McMahon, Robert J. (Robert Joseph), 1953–   .
III. Peters, Ray DeV., 1942–   . IV. Series.
HV6626.5.C4957   1997
362.76'7—dc21   97-4856

This book is printed on acid-free paper.

97 98 99 00 01 02 03   10 9 8 7 6 5 4 3 2 1

Acquisition Editor: Jim Nageotte
Editorial Assistant: Kathleen Derby
Production Assistant: Denise Santoyo
Cover Designer: Candice Harman
Print Buyer: Anna Chin

Contents

Preface

This volume brings together experts in both physical abuse and sexual abuse, who discuss innovative approaches to treatment and prevention. Although these two areas of trauma and abuse are logically connected in many ways, this is one of the few volumes that has addressed both topics under one cover. The result is a compendium of information that has seldom been shared between these two fields.

The emphasis throughout the volume is on prevention and treatment approaches for physical and sexual abuse. This emphasis is accompanied by current psychological perspectives concerning the causes and treatment of different forms of child maltreatment. Each chapter offers a critical review of current findings and discussion of emerging theories, applications, and future directions related to various aspects of child physical and sexual abuse. The information is intended for researchers, practitioners, and students in behavioural sciences and should be of special interest to persons involved in various levels of intervention, such as social workers, clinical psychologists, psychiatrists, and other mental health professionals.

The book is divided into two sections for the purpose of highlighting both physical and sexual abuse. This division is relevant to the organization and presentation of the material, allowing for similar issues and themes to be presented in the same section and for greater emphasis on the dual nature of the book.

Part I, "Prevention and Treatment of Child Physical Abuse," begins with a chapter by E. Mark Cummings, who introduces the volume with an overview of the way marital conflict, child abuse, and other major family events can affect the ongoing development of children and youth. He considers themes pertinent to marital conflict as a familial process related to abuse and proposes new directions for the conceptualization and study of the impact on children. In Chapter 2, Joel Milner and Cynthia Dopke provide an overview of child physical abuse offender characteristics as described in controlled studies in the literature. These characteristics are discussed in relation to major theoretical models that aid in the formation of treatment planning and services for children and parents. In Chapter 3, Marlies Sudermann and Peter Jaffe review the progress that has been made in recognizing the effect of witnessing domestic violence on the life course of children and adolescents. They describe and confront myths about wife assault and dating violence and present an integrated community response to preventing violence in marital and dating relationships.

Treatment and prevention approaches aimed at physical child abuse and relationship-based violence provide the focus for the remaining half of Part I. In Chapter 4, Sandra Azar uses a cognitive-behavioral framework to explain both the etiology of child physical abuse and the developmental disturbances observed among affected children. Parents' maladaptive role "schemata" regarding children and parent-child relationships, negative attributional biases, and poor problem-solving ability form the basis for a documented treatment program for this population. Chapters 5 and 6 each provide practical discussions of ways that child maltreatment interventions can be integrated into broader intervention and educational services involving children and youth. David Wolfe and colleagues describe their youth-centered educational program, based on the premise that adolescence offers a prime opportunity to educate about issues concerning healthy, nonviolent relationships. After describing their risk model of the development of violence in relationships, they present a competency-enhancement, proactive strategy to promote healthy, nonviolent relationships, along with initial evaluation findings. Turning to the early parent-child relationship, David Olds reviews the procedures and outcomes from two large-scale evaluations of their early intervention program for mothers and young children and reports on current efforts to expand the project for use in broader intervention efforts. This important project was designed to prevent a host of maternal and child health problems that create substantial risks for child abuse and neglect and later crime and delinquency. Current findings from Olds's ongoing randomized clinical trials support the significance of this approach.

Part II, "Prevention and Treatment of Child Sexual Abuse," presents recent findings related more specifically to child sexual abuse, extending and further integrating the previous section on the causes and treatments of physical abuse. Several insightful developments in the delivery of early intervention and prevention services are discussed, such as programs for violence prevention in schools and communities and preparation of children who must testify in court.

In Chapter 7, Lucy Berliner reviews treatment outcome with children who have been sexually abused. Strategies to develop treatment goals for child victims are developed from cognitive behavioral therapy, including gradual exposure, stress inoculation training, corrective information, cognitive restructuring, and the teaching of positive coping and social skills. The nature of sexual abuse treatment for children poses particularly complex evaluation difficulties, which are also addressed in this chapter. In Chapter 8, John Briere describes a theory of abuse-related symptom development and outlines a specific psychotherapy for adults severely abused as children. The psychosocial difficulties of abuse survivors are examined in the context of post-traumatic stress, dissociation, long-term alterations in self-functions and capacities, and ways to cope. William Friedrich continues the discussion of treatment methods in Chapter 9, presenting an informative perspective on the nature and course of psychotherapy with sexually abused boys. Particular consideration is given to gender and social issues pertaining to the treatment of sexually abused boys and adolescents. The treatment model that Friedrich presents addresses areas of attachment, dysregulation, and self-development/perception, each of which has relevance to treatment.

Edward Connors and Maurice Oates next describe the emergence of sexual abuse treatment models within First Nations communities, where the sexual abuse of children has become a serious concern. During the last 15 years, First Nations have evolved models of healing that combine therapeutic knowledge from nonnative society with healing approaches from traditional practices. This chapter reviews the historical development and effectiveness of these models of sexual abuse treatment within First Nations communities, which have important relevance to many communities. Finally, Louise Sas, in Chapter 11, looks at current developments in many communities concerning the interface between abuse victims and the court system. Recent legislative changes in North America's criminal courts are discussed in relation to the treatment and reception of child sexual abuse victims who appear in court as witnesses. Sas presents a detailed description of court preparation techniques, including ways to empower the child witness, reduce their stress and fears, and help them resist suggestions on the stand by being assertive and direct.

The Banff Conferences
on Behavioural Science

This volume is one of a continuing series of publications sponsored by the Banff International Conferences on Behavioural Science. We are pleased to join Sage Publications in bringing this series to an audience of practitioners, investigators, and students. The publications arise from conferences held each spring since 1969 in Banff, Alberta, Canada, with papers representing the product of deliberations on themes and key issues. The conferences bring together outstanding behavioural scientists and professionals in a forum where they can present and discuss data related to emergent issues and topics. As a continuing event, the Banff International Conferences have served as an expressive "early indicator" of the developing nature and composition of the behavioural sciences and scientific applications to human problems and issues.

Because distance, schedules, and restricted audience preclude wide attendance at the conferences, the resulting publications have equal status with the conferences proper. Each presenter at each Banff Conference is required to write a chapter specifically for the forthcoming book, separate from his or her presentation and discussion at the conference itself. Consequently, this volume is not a set of conference proceedings. Rather, it is an integrated volume of chapters contributed by leading researchers and practitioners who have had the unique opportunity of spending several days together presenting and discussing ideas prior to preparing their chapters.

Our "conference of colleagues" format provides for formal and informal interactions among all participants through invited addresses, workshops, poster presentations, and conversation hours. When combined with sight-seeing expeditions, cross-country and downhill skiing, and other recreations in the spectacular Canadian Rockies, the conferences have generated great enthusiasm and satisfaction among participants. The Banff Centre, our venue for the conferences for many years, has contributed immeasurably to the success of these meetings through its very comfortable accommodation, dining, and conference facilities. The following list documents conference themes over the past 28 years.

1969 I
Ideal Mental Health Services

1970 II
Services and Programs for Exceptional Children and Youth

1971 III
Implementing Behavioural Programs for Schools and Clinics

1972 IV
Behaviour Change: Methodology, Concepts, and Practice

1973 V
Evaluation of Behavioural Programs in Community, Residential, and School Settings

1974 VI
Behaviour Modification and Families and Behavioural Approaches to Parenting

1975 VII
The Behavioural Management of Anxiety, Depression, and Pain

1976 VIII
Behavioural Self-Management Strategies, Techniques, and Outcomes

1977 IX
Behavioural Systems for the Developmentally Disabled
    A. School and Family Environments
    B. Institutional, Clinical, and Community Environments

1978 X
Behavioural Medicine: Changing Health Lifestyles

1979 XI
Violent Behaviour: Social Learning Approaches to Prediction, Management, and Treatment

1980 XII
Adherence, Compliance, and Generalization in Behavioural Medicine

1981 XIII
Essentials of Behavioural Treatments for Families

1982 XIV
Advances in Clinical Behaviour Therapy

1983 XV
Childhood Disorders: Behavioural-Developmental Approaches

1984 XVI
Education in "1984"

1985 XVII
Social Learning and Systems Approaches to Marriage and the Family

1986 XVIII
Health Enhancement, Disease Prevention, and Early Intervention: Biobehavioural Perspectives

1987 XIX
Early Intervention in the Coming Decade

1988 XX
Behaviour Disorders of Adolescence: Research, Intervention, and Policy in Clinical and School Settings

1989 XXI
Psychology, Sport, and Health Promotion

1990 XXII
Aggression and Violence Throughout the Lifespan

1991 XXIII
Addictive Behaviours Across the Lifespan: Prevention, Treatment, and Policy Issues

1992 XXIV
State of the Art in Cognitive/Behaviour Therapy

1993 XXV
Anxiety and Depression in Adults and Children

1994 XXVI
Prevention and Early Intervention: Child Disorders, Substance Abuse, and Delinquency*

1995 XXVII
Child Abuse: New Directions in Prevention and Treatment Across the Lifespan*

1996 XXVIII
Best Practice: Developing and Promoting Empirically Validated Interventions

1997 XXIX
Stress: Vulnerability and Resiliency

We would especially like to thank Philomene Kocher for her diligence in preparing the manuscript for publication, and Valerie Angus for her secretarial services. Also, we would like to acknowledge the expert guidance and support that we received from C. Terry Hendrix, Jim Nageotte, Nancy Hale, and Vicki Baker at Sage Publications. It has been a pleasure working with them. While preparing this volume, David Wolfe was on the faculty of the University of Western Ontario, Bob McMahon was on the faculty of the University of Washington, and Ray Peters was on the faculty of Queen's University. The assistance and support of these institutions is gratefully acknowledged.

*We are especially grateful to the Children's Mental Health Unit of Health Canada for their support and contributions to the 1994 and 1995 conferences.

—David A. Wolfe

—Robert J. McMahon

—Ray DeV. Peters

PART I

Prevention and
Treatment of
Child Physical Abuse

1

Marital Conflict, Abuse, and Adversity in the Family and Child Adjustment

A DEVELOPMENTAL PSYCHOPATHOLOGY PERSPECTIVE

E. MARK CUMMINGS

Multiple and co-occurring forms of child adversity and maltreatment occur within the context of marital conflict. Marital conflict is likely to enhance the adversity of abuse, for example, by increasing the child's general arousal or tension level. Effects of interspousal abuse have been reported to be similar to those linked with physical child abuse (Jaffe, Wolfe, Wilson, & Zak, 1986). Interspousal abuse is psychologically and emotionally highly distressing for children to witness. But marital conflict is not unitary and can take positive, neutral, negative, or highly negative forms of expression from the perspective of the child (Cummings & Davies, 1994). The arena of marital conflict provides a sort of microcosm in which to consider co-occurring forms of adversity, but also familial sources of resiliency and the operation of protective factors.

Until recently, familial sources of adversity and abuse were often considered only in terms of parent-child interaction. The effects of broader family systems, including the marital system, were not examined. Accordingly, on the basis of their assessment of the literature, Jaffe, Wolfe, and Wilson (1990) noted in their volume *Children of Battered Women* that "it was not until the past decade that family discord and spousal violence reached center stage as possible predeterminants of developmental psychopathology" (p. 33).

Although the parent-child system is likely the single most powerful family system in its impact on children's development, a sole focus on this system fosters a limited and oversimplified view of pathways of influence within the family. For example, the behavior of both parents and children in parent-child interaction is influenced by marital conflict and the overall quality of the marital relationship, as well as by other family events and relationships outside the parent-child system. Simply the day-to-day exposure to the operation of the marital system and other family systems has significant direct effects on children's functioning and development (Cummings & Davies, 1994). It is important for models of the impact of abuse on children to begin to incorporate the effects of the marital system on children's functioning and the functioning of the family. Incorporating marital factors is likely to increase the prediction of child outcomes and, at a conceptual level, provide a more sophisticated view of the familial causes and consequences of abuse for children.

This chapter considers themes pertinent to marital conflict as a familial process related to abuse and proposes new directions for the conceptualization and study of the impact of marital conflict and related family events on children. The chapter begins with an overview of evidence that (a) marital conflict is a significant source of adversity and risk for adjustment problems in children and (b) marital conflict and other forms of adversity in the family may be interrelated.

Next, the developmental psychopathology perspective and related approaches are examined as important directions toward greater understanding of the processes that mediate the impact of marital conflict on children. Research on stress and adversity has neglected positive processes and events, but these are also significant to understanding development in adverse family circumstances. The concepts of resiliency and protective factors, in particular, are promising directions for an advanced understanding of the role of positive processes in children's functioning in adverse family circumstances.

The literature on children's stress and coping with marital conflict is then reviewed as (a) an area of substantive concern related to familial adversity and abuse meriting focused study and (b) a specific application of a developmental psychopathology perspective. Although research during the past several decades has charted basic relations between family and child variables, productively outlining the scope of the problem, there is a need for a second generation of research that focuses on process, including the direction of effects, causal relations, and the differentiation of relations between well-defined family and child variables (Cummings, 1995).

The developmental psychopathology perspective is examined as a useful way to conceptualize process, and its application to the study of marital conflict effects on children is considered, including the identification of stress, resilience, and compensatory and protective factors. In particular, evidence suggests that some forms of marital conflict are highly destructive, increasing children's risk for the development of psychopathology, whereas other forms of marital conflict buffer or even help children, thereby reducing risk for psychopathology.

Finally, the chapter turns to questions about how we can think about these effects at a conceptual level. A significant gap is the relative absence of theory, particularly with regard to the identification of specific psychopathological processes mediating relations between marital conflict and child outcomes. An emotional security theory is proposed to account for some important aspects of the impact of marital conflict and other family adversity on children's adjustment. The chapter closes with suggestions toward a broader family-wide view of vulnerability and protective factors based on the emotional security theory and the broader developmental psychopathology literature.

COMORBIDITY AMONG MARITAL CONFLICT, ADVERSITY, AND ABUSE WITHIN THE FAMILY

Marital relations are central to the functioning of the family, and there may be a comorbidity among marital conflict, adversity, and abuse. Given space limitations and the recency of extensive reviews on this subject (e.g., Cummings & Davies, 1994, 1995; Davies & Cummings, 1994; Grych & Fincham, 1990), the treatment below provides only a brief overview of the evidence, focusing on outlining key points.

Marital Conflict as Adversity

From the children's perspective, exposure to extreme marital conflict is abusive, if not emotionally abusing. Although one may question the use of the word *abuse* for children's experiences with marital conflict, depending on one's definition of terms, exposure to highly negative expressions of marital conflict, at the least, is a significant source of adversity that contributes to children's risk for the development of psychopathology.

Marital discord and children's psychological problems have long been known to be associated (Grych & Fincham, 1990). Although these relations are significant, albeit modest, in nonclinic samples, effects can be quite robust in clinic samples (Fincham & Osborne, 1993), particularly when there is marital violence (Wolfe, Jaffe, Wilson, & Zak, 1985). The more negative outcomes associated with marital conflict in children from dysfunctional families are likely to be a result, in part, of the far more intense expressions of marital conflict in these families than in harmonious families.

Furthermore, marital conflict factors in children's adjustment in homes characterized as disturbed for other reasons. For example, the level and characteristics of marital conflict are among the strongest predictors of the impact of divorce and custody arrangements on children's mental health (Amato & Keith, 1991). Marital conflict and parental depression are positively correlated, and marital conflict predicts psychological problems in children from families with parental depression (Downey & Coyne, 1990).

Marital Conflict Co-Occurs With Dysfunction in Other Family Systems

Marital conflict is correlated with difficulties in parent-child discipline and child-rearing practices, coercive family interactions, insecure parent-child attachment, and negative sibling relations. Problems in family functioning interact with children's dispositions in influencing the likelihood that children develop dysfunctional coping responses, processes, and styles. Dysfunctional behavioral styles, in turn, are linked with the development of psychopathology (see Figure 1.1).

Evidence also suggests associations between marital conflict and abuse. Interspousal aggression and child physical abuse have been linked (e.g., Jouriles, Barling, & O'Leary, 1987). Marital conflict has also been associated with child sexual abuse (e.g., Browne & Finkelhor, 1986).

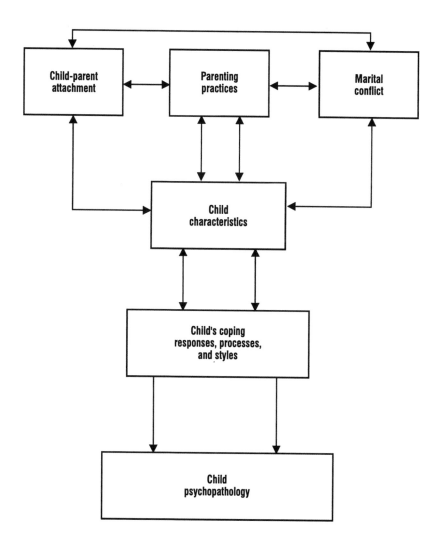

Figure 1.1. Multiple family systems, child characteristics, coping responses, processes, and styles, and child psychopathology. (From Cummings & Davies, 1994)

The evidence thus fosters a view of close interrelations between marital conflict and the functioning of other family systems that also affect children's risk for the development of psychopathology. Accordingly, on the basis of a review of this evidence, Cummings and Davies (1994) concluded:

> Children's mental health problems do not develop out of parallel and independent disturbances within the family. Rather, disturbances in each family subsystem affect the other subsystems, and broad problems in family functioning are likely to be associated with negative child outcomes. (p. 106)

Marital Conflict and Negative Emotional and Behavioral Processes in Families: The Cumulative Impact of Family Stress

Exposure to high marital conflict is associated with children's emotional and behavioral dysregulation, attempts to control or regulate the dysfunctional interactions between the mother and the father, and representations of the self and family members' relationships that are negative and pessimistic about the future. These negative processes bear similarities to those linked with the impact of dysfunction in other family systems, such as coercive parent-child relations and insecure parent-child attachment (e.g., Cummings & Davies, 1994; Davies & Cummings, 1994). For example, children who are witnesses of spousal abuse exhibit adjustment problems similar to those of children who are victims of parental violence (Jaffe et al., 1986). Thus, children's functioning in the face of adverse family circumstances may be a product of the cumulative impact on similar response processes of multiple family stressors (see Figure 1.1).

On the basis of a review of this evidence, Cummings and Davies (1994) also concluded that "family subsystems may affect children's development through their action on common processes and mechanisms. Consequently, ". . . joint effects may occur, which could be additive, interactive, or multiplicative" (p. 108). Similarly, with regard to the physical, emotional, and sexual abuse of children, Jaffe et al. (1990) stated, "It is widely acknowledged that . . . different forms of maltreatment also give rise to many of the same developmental adjustment problems, suggesting that very similar psychological processes may be commonly responsible for the children's reactions to trauma" (p. 68).

In summary, an emerging literature supports the notion that marital relations are central to an understanding of family processes and events, including the negative impact of extremely negative family events, such as abuse. Marital relations may serve as a foundation for emotional processes and their regulation within the family and thus have a role in modulating or exaggerating the risk associated with abuse in the parent-child system.

FROM CORRELATIONAL RESEARCH TO THE STUDY OF DYNAMIC PROCESS RELATIONS: CONTRIBUTIONS OF A DEVELOPMENTAL PSYCHOPATHOLOGY PERSPECTIVE

There is increasing consensus that simply mapping correlations between global marker variables has reached a point of diminishing returns in research on family functioning and child psychopathology (Cummings, 1995). The developmental psychopathology approach provides avenues for moving beyond static models to the study of dynamic process interactions of intra- and extraorganismic factors that underlie children's development (Cicchetti & Garmezy, 1993).

For example, marital conflict is inevitable in marriages and can be constructive and positive for both marriages and families. Observing marital conflict may help children learn to handle their own problems. But intense forms of marital conflict and abuse increase children's risk for psychopathology. The small to moderate correlations reported between global assessments of marital conflict and child adjustment in community samples present a misleading picture of the benign, and even constructive, effects of some types of conflict, whereas the destructive impact of other forms of conflict is underestimated.

The study of process requires the study of multiple response processes (e.g., emotional, cognitive, social) at various levels of responding (e.g., specific responses, styles across multiple responses), differentiation of the effects of specific contexts, and the inclusion of normal, at-risk, and deviant populations (e.g., see Figure 1.2). Furthermore, the study of normal development and deviant development can be seen as mutually informative, more effectively mapping the universe of process relations between family functioning and child outcomes. High-risk children who do not develop problems are as interesting as high-risk children who do (Cicchetti & Garmezy, 1993). For example, many children from high-conflict homes do not develop clinically significant problems despite such adversity.

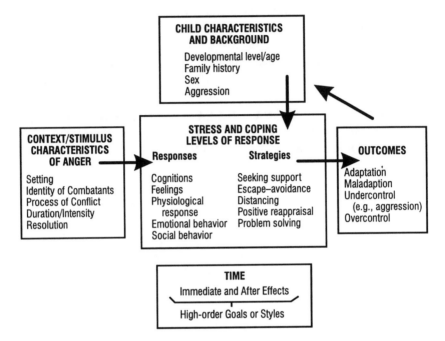

Figure 1.2. A framework for the study of the processes mediating relations between family anger and child outcomes. (From Cummings and Cummings, 1988)

A particular contribution of the developmental psychopathology approach is recognition that most children develop adaptively and competently. Some children are resilient even in the face of extreme adversity. But there is probably no such thing as an "invulnerable" child (Cicchetti & Garmezy, 1993). *Resilience* is a relative term, and it is important to specify the risk and protective mechanisms that account for positive outcomes (Egeland, Carlson, & Sroufe, 1993). Thus, attention is called to the importance of identifying compensatory and protective factors, as well as of adversity and vulnerability factors.

However, there is still considerable definitional diversity, even disagreement, about how to define these terms. For example, with regard to resilience, Cicchetti and Garmezy (1993) stated:

> At present, various researchers employ different definitions of resilience that can range from the absence of psychopathology in the child of a mentally ill parent to the recovery of functioning in a brain injured patient. . . . It still may be premature to agree on the definition of resilience. (p. 499)

Nonetheless, there appear to be some areas of agreement (Conrad & Hammen, 1993; Gest, Neemann, Hubbard, Masten, & Tellegen, 1993; Werner, 1993). On the one hand, *risk or adversity* and *resource or compensatory* variables contribute to negative versus positive outcomes, respectively, regardless of a child's risk status. In other words, these are "main effects," operating comparably at high and low levels of exposure to adversity. On the other hand, *vulnerability* and *protective* factors decrease or increase, respectively, functioning for children under adversity and may have little or no effect, or even opposite effects, for children with low levels of adversity exposure. In other words, these are interaction effects, affecting primarily children under adversity. Finally, *resilience* refers to children's development of competence even under conditions of pervasive or severe adversity (Egeland et al., 1993). The discussion below reflects these definitions of terms.

CHILDREN'S STRESS AND COPING WITH MARITAL CONFLICT: A DEVELOPMENTAL PSYCHOPATHOLOGY PERSPECTIVE

At this point, I review what is known about children's stress and coping with marital conflict. After a brief overview of key findings, I consider how the current literature can be formulated from a developmental psychopathology perspective, including consideration of adversity, compensatory, vulnerability, and protective factors that may foster children's resilience.

Marital Conflict as a Stressor

Marital and interadult conflicts are stressful for children to observe. Findings from analog, observational, and field research converge to demonstrate this point and to show that conflict is stressful for children to observe throughout childhood, from infancy through late adolescence (Cummings & Davies, 1994). Furthermore, negative emotional arousal is evident in children's self-reports, facial expressions, motoric behavior (e.g., hands over the ears), and even their physiological functioning (e.g., increased blood pressure). Some supportive studies are listed in Table 1.1.

Interadult conflict also increases children's aggressiveness. Clinical field studies have long reported positive correlations between marital conflict and

TABLE 1.1. Studies of Links between Interadult Anger and Children Emotional Arousal

Study	Sample	Comparison	Response
Studies of behavioral emotional responding			
Cummings, Zahn-Waxler, and Radke-Yarrow (1981)	24 children between 10 and 20 months of age; behavior in the home reported over a period of 9 months	Naturally occurring anger > naturally occurring affection	Distress, no attention and response
Cummings, Iannotti, and Zahn-Waxler (1985)	90 2-year-old children	Adults' anger > adults' positive emotions	Distress
Cummings (1987)	85 5-year-old children	Adults' anger > adults' positive emotions	Negative emotions, positive emotions, preoccupation
El-Sheikh, Cummings, and Goetsch (1989)	34 4- to 5-year-old children	Adults' anger > adults' positive emotions	Freezing, facial distress, verbal concern, anger, smiling, preoccupation
Klaczynski and Cummings (1989)	40 first- to third-grade boys	Adults' anger > adults' positive emotions	Facial distress, postural distress, freezing
Studies of self-reported emotions			
Cummings, Vogel, Cummings, and El-Sheikh (1989)	121 4- to 9-year-old children	Hostile, verbal, and nonverbal anger all > friendly interactions	Negative emotional responses (anger, fear, sadness)
Ballard and Cummings (1990)	35 6- to 10-year-old children	Verbal, indirect nonverbal, distructiveness, and aggressive anger all > friendly interactions	Anger, distress
Cummings, Ballard, El-Sheikh, and Lake (1991)	98 5- to 19-year-olds	Unresolved anger > partially resolved anger > friendly interactions	Anger, sadness, fear
Cummings, Ballard, and El-Sheikh, (1991)	60 9- to 19-year-olds	Hostile, verbal and nonverbal anger all > friendly interactions	Negative emotional responses (anger, fear, sadness)

From Cummings and Zahn-Waxler (1992). Copyright 1992 by Springer-Verlag. Adapted by permission.

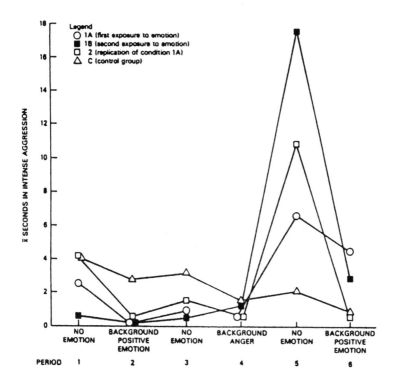

Figure 1.3. Children's aggression before, during, and after background conditions of anger or positive emotion between adults: An experimental demonstration. (From Cummings, Iannotti, and Zahn-Waxler, 1985)

children's externalizing behavioral problems (e.g., aggressiveness). More recent experimental studies, by examining this relation in controlled laboratory settings, document a causal relation between interadult conflict and children's aggressiveness. For example, Cummings, Iannotti, and Zahn-Waxler (1985) examined changes in aggressiveness between 2-year-old friends as a function of changes in the emotionality of interadult interactions. As Figure 1.3 shows, aggressiveness increased in Period 5 for each of the groups exposed to interadult anger in Period 4 (1A, 1B, and 2), but no change occurred in aggressiveness in Period 5 for a control group (C) exposed to a friendly interaction in Period 4.

Other studies demonstrate that marital conflict is a stressor that activates behavioral coping responses in children. For example, by preschool age, attempts by children to ameliorate marital conflict situations through direct intervention (mediating, comforting, taking sides) are not uncommon. Children's distress responding and intervention behaviors are positively correlated with family history of intense marital conflict (e.g., Cummings, Zahn-Waxler, & Radke-Yarrow, 1981).

A central theme of a developmental psychopathology perspective and other process-oriented approaches, however, is that responding depends on specific person environmental transactions and that these must be carefully defined and differentiated in order to understand dynamic process relations. In fact, a child's reactions to adults' conflicts are highly dependent on both the personality of the child and the specific characteristics of conflict expression, as well as their interaction (Cummings & Davies, 1994). Below, I examine the impact of immediate and historical contexts of marital conflict expression on children's responding from this perspective. The discussion explores (a) immediate contexts of exposure to adults' conflict as conditions of adversity or compensation and (b) protective or vulnerability factors for children with histories of exposure to intense marital conflict. The role of the personality and temperament of the child in responding is also important, and although less well investigated, there are some promising directions in this regard (see Cummings & Davies, 1994, for more information). In addition, evidence suggests differential effects on boys versus girls and on children of particular ages, but the findings are complex and not amenable to easy interpretation (see Cummings & Davies, 1994). Children of both sexes and all ages are clearly vulnerable to exposure to interadult discord, but certain interpretation of the precise nature of age and sex differences awaits further investigation and is beyond the scope of this chapter.

Immediate Contexts of Marital Conflict: Adversity and Compensatory Factors

Children's reactions to adults' conflicts are not simply a function of the expression of negative emotion or conflict, but are highly influenced by the specific manner in which conflict is expressed. The findings underline that reactions reflect a dynamic process of interaction of intra- (e.g., children's appraisal of the meaning of conflict) and extraorganismic (e.g., the form of expression and resolution of conflict) factors, with specific elements of conflict situations and conflict history critical to whether conflict affects children as adversity.

Conditions of Adversity: Contexts That Increase Negative Responding

Several types of conflict contexts increase children's experience of adversity when faced with adults' conflicts. Children perceive interspousal aggression as highly negative and report considerable emotional distress in reaction (e.g., Cummings et al., 1981). Exposure to interspousal violence is also one of the strongest predictors of psychopathology in children (see Cummings & Davies, 1994). Children react to high-intensity conflicts and marital conflicts over child-related themes with greater negative emotional responding and more negative self-attributions (e.g., self-blame, shame) than to low-intensity conflicts and marital conflicts over non-child-related themes, respectively (e.g., Grych & Fincham, 1993). Finally, children are sensitive to nonverbal anger: Their responses to nonverbal anger may be as negative as for verbal conflicts (e.g., Cummings, Vogel, Cummings, & El-Sheikh, 1989).

Compensatory Factors: Contexts That Reduce Negative Responding

The resolution of conflict and various forms of communication of information about resolution substantially reduce the negative impact of conflict and thus may be regarded as compensatory factors. Children respond to the same expression of conflict between adults very differently if the conflict is resolved. For example, Cummings et al. (1989) found that whereas certain conflict scenarios left unresolved elicited moderate to high distress, the same conflict scenarios followed by brief resolutions resulted in little or no distress responding. The degree of resolution matters, with any progress toward resolution ameliorating the negative impact of conflict (Cummings, Ballard, El-Shiekh, & Lake, 1991). Children are able to infer when conflicts are resolved "behind closed doors," and such inferences significantly reduce their negative reactions. Their distress is reduced when adults only explain a conflict resolution even when the children never actually observe the resolution (Cummings, Simpson, & Wilson, 1993).

Historical Contexts of Marital Conflict and Abuse: Vulnerability and Protective Factors

By definition, vulnerability factors increase children's problems in functioning under adversity, whereas protective factors decrease children's difficulties under adversity. As family histories of high marital conflict or abuse constitute adversity, any conditions that increase or decrease difficulties for children from high-conflict or abusing homes relative to other children can be viewed as vulnerability or protective factors, respectively.

Vulnerability Factors

Children from high-conflict family backgrounds evidence more emotional distress, behavioral dysregulation (e.g., aggressiveness), and effortful coping (e.g., mediation in the parents' dispute) in response to unresolved conflicts than other children (Cummings & Davies, 1994); that is, children from high-conflict families are disproportionately more vulnerable or sensitized to unresolved conflicts than other children. Thus, exposure to unresolved conflicts between adults functions as a vulnerability factor for children from high-conflict family environments. One implication is that family histories of unresolved, intense conflict may create cycles of vulnerability that leave children increasingly susceptible to the impact of marital and family conflict with increased exposure.

Children with a history of physical abuse also appear to be more vulnerable to the impact of unresolved parental conflicts. Cummings, Hennessy, Rabideau, and Cicchetti (1994) conducted observationally based assessments of the responses of physically abused and nonabused boys to interadult anger involving their mothers. Notably, the two groups did not differ significantly in socioeconomic status or any dimension of marital conflict history. Nonetheless, physically abused boys were more behaviorally reactive to interadult anger than comparison subjects, evidencing more problem-focused coping behavior and greater aggressiveness following exposure. Physically abused boys also reported greater fear than nonabused boys in response to all forms of unresolved anger (Hennessy, Rabideau, Cicchetti, & Cummings, 1994).

Consistent with the model outlined above (Jaffe et al., 1990; Jaffe et al., 1989), marital conflict and child physical abuse thus may have some similar effects on children through certain common psychological processes and mechanisms. Emerging evidence suggests that greater anger and aggression across multiple family subsystems (e.g., parent-child, interparental) may have cumulative effects on arousal and other response processes (Cummings & Davies, 1994), although much more study of this issue is required before firm conclusions can be reached.

Protective Factors

Although the resolution of conflict reduces stress reactions for children in general, it may hold greater benefit for children from particularly adverse family circumstances than for others. Thus, conflict resolution might be both a compensatory factor (generally help all children cope with marital conflict) and a protective factor (hold particular benefits for subgroups of children from especially adverse backgrounds of intense marital and family conflict).

Evidence for conflict resolution as a protective factor was recently reported in a study that compared the responses of physically abused and nonabused boys to videotaped segments of adults in angry and friendly interactions (Hennessy et al., 1994). Boys were presented with segments of interadult anger that varied on a variety of elements of how anger was expressed, including whether anger was resolved. Analyses for degree of anger resolution revealed a significant Condition X Abuse History interaction. Physically abused boys were particularly sensitive to whether anger between adults was resolved; that is, they reported greater fear than nonabused boys to unresolved anger but not to resolved anger. Thus, complete resolution of conflict appeared to protect physically abused boys from the particularly negative effects that interadult conflict has on them in comparison with other children (Cummings et al., 1994; Hennessy et al., 1994).

What Factors Foster Resilience in Children's Coping With Marital Conflict?

Resilience thus may be fostered by children's experiential history with marital conflict; that is, although exposure to marital and interadult conflict is likely to be stressful for children in general during exposure, children's capacities for coping appear to be fostered by the communication to the children of information about the resolution of conflict immediately after the conflict has ended or some time later. The resilience of children may also derive from their historical exposure to conflict. Children without histories of exposure to intense, unresolved marital conflict or physical abuse appear to be better able to regulate their functioning in the face of interadult conflict. Furthermore, children with family histories of intense marital conflict fare better than those exposed to both physical abuse and intense marital conflict. For children with family histories of very intense conflict, the resolution of conflict may be particularly significant to their relative vulnerability versus resilience.

A CONCEPTUAL MODEL FOR DYNAMIC PROCESSES UNDERLYING THE IMPACT OF MARITAL CONFLICT AND ABUSE: AN EMOTIONAL SECURITY HYPOTHESIS

A final topic is the consideration of theory. The complexity introduced by the focus of developmental psychopathology on the study of dynamic process relations (e.g., multiple responses; multiple and highly differentiated contexts; multiple normal, at-risk, and deviant populations), as opposed simply to correlations between global marker variables, makes theory especially important. Theory is needed to integrate and organize the findings, point directions for research, and conceptualize the nature of the effects that have emerged. With regard to marital conflict and children, many empirical studies have been published in the past decade, but few attempts at theory have been made. Thus, theory is urgently needed and may even be vital for continued advances to occur in this area.

Several requirements for an adequate theory are evident. First, theory should be consistent with the core findings. The data make it clear that marital conflict is a personal and emotional event for children, as opposed to abstract and unemotional. Theory should acknowledge that children appraise conflict for its personal *meaning* to them and their families, and not simply just the occurrence of conflict as an abstract event. Observational studies indicate that the most immediate and salient responses are children's emotional reactions (e.g., Cummings, 1987; Cummings et al., 1981). Theory should also take into account that children's reactions are emotionally based, perhaps even primarily emotional, as well as cognitive and behavioral.

Second, theory should be consistent with a family-wide model of the impact of conflict and abuse on children. As we have seen, marital conflict, physical and sexual abuse, and other adversities are interrelated in their occurrence in families and may have effects through similar or common mechanisms. Theory should foster an integrative model with regard to multiple sources of adversity and victimization in families, as opposed to treating forms of adversity as if they occurred in isolation, with entirely independent effects on developmental processes.

Third, the continuum or range of effects associated with marital conflict should be accounted for, not simply the psychopathological outcomes associated with intense family conflict or the normal outcomes linked with everyday, relatively constructive conflict. The assumption that effects identified under normal and adverse family circumstances are mutually informative with regard to underlying developmental processes is at the heart of a developmental psychopathology approach (Cicchetti & Garmezy, 1993). Relatedly, theory should attempt to identify how similar or common mechanisms along a continuum may foster either negative outcomes, on the one hand, or positive results, on the other—in other words, a general model of how variations in a key phenomenon can cause systematic variations in outcomes.

Definition of an Emotional Security Theory

Patrick Davies and I recently advanced the theory that children's emotional security is affected by intense marital conflict and abuse, with implications for both their immediate functioning and long-term development (Cummings & Davies, 1995; Davies & Cummings, 1994). Specifically, we proposed that children's sense of emotional security plays a role in organizing and directing the children's responses to marital conflict and, over time, mediates relations between family backgrounds of marital conflict and abuse, on the one hand, and children's adjustment, on the other. Thus, in Davies and Cummings (1994), we stated:

> Children's concerns about emotional security play a role in their regulation of emotional arousal and organization and motivation to respond in the face of marital conflict. Over time these response processes have implications for children's long-term adjustment. Emotional security is seen as a product of past experience with marital conflict and a primary influence on future responding. (p. 387)

In a more recent paper (Cummings & Davies, in press), we further developed the conceptual and empirical foundation for a theory of emotional security as a regulatory system. We proposed:

> Emotional security is a latent construct that can be inferred from the overall organization and meaning of children's emotions, behaviors, thoughts, and physiological responses, and serves as a set goal by which children regulate their own functioning in social contexts, thereby directing social, emotional, cognitive, and physiological reactions.

Below, I show how an emotional security hypothesis satisfies the certain general requirements for a theory that I have outlined. In addition, I consider how an emotional security hypothesis can account for two additional major findings that are also somewhat perplexing: (a) the very substantial impact of conflict resolution on children's reactions to adults' conflicts and (b) the sensitization to conflict evident in children's behavioral and emotional reactions that is linked with high or intense historical exposure to conflict and abuse in the family.

An Emotional Security Theory as a General Model

The emotional security theory specifies the emotional and personal concerns that might motivate children's reactions to marital conflict. Children have realistic reasons for their sense of emotional security to be based, in part, on the course of marital and family conflict. Day-to-day, intense marital conflict causes family life to be unpleasant. Marital conflict is also threatening to children, perhaps even physically threatening as suggested by associations between interparental and parent-child physical abuse. Furthermore, marital conflict is linked with breakdowns in discipline and reduced sensitivity and responsivity by parents to children's needs (Cummings & Davies, 1994). For the long term, intense marital conflict has negative implications for the future intactness of the family and the child's general emotional, social, physical, and financial security, safety, and well-being. In summary, the emotional security theory specifies the *particular* meaning against which children appraise the implications of marital and family conflict for themselves and their families, suggests how that meaning is personal, and indicates why children may respond emotionally.

The emotional security theory is also consistent with other familial models of dynamic processes that mediate normal and deviant development in children. Thus, attachment theory and research indicate that emotional security concerns derived from the quality of parent-child emotional interactions influence children's development (Bretherton, 1985). It makes intuitive sense that children's sense of emotional security would derive not only from the quality of parent-child relationships but also from the quality of other emotional relationships in the family that children care about (especially the quality of the interparental relationship) and, furthermore, that children's emotional security would be affected by other deviant family occurrences, such as physical or sexual abuse, or parental depression. Thus, the emotional security hypothesis indicates processes that are consistent with the broader developmental literature and are established as important, particularly in the attachment theory tradition. Moreover, recent studies indicate links between marital conflict and security of attachment (see Davies & Cummings, 1994).

Finally, the construct of emotional security is pertinent to development in normal, at-risk, and deviant populations. Variations in emotional security have been systematically linked with variations in the qualities of children's experiential histories in the home (Bretherton, 1985). Thus, positive experiences with interparental relations might be expected to foster emotional security, which may serve as a compensatory or protective factor in children from adverse family backgrounds, increasing children's resilience in the face of other adversity. Emotional insecurity that results from negative experiences with intense family conflict and abuse, however, may be a risk or vulnerability factor, decreasing children's capacity for resilience when faced with adversity.

An Emotional Security Theory as an
Explanation for Two Major Findings

A challenge for any theoretical model is to account for major empirical findings and to do so more cogently than alternative models. Below, I consider the adequacy of the emotional security theory for two major findings that have been replicated repeatedly (Cummings, 1994; Davies & Cummings, 1994). It is important to note that these findings make sense in terms of an emotional security theory but are not readily explained by some other models.

Resolution of Conflict Greatly Reduces or Eliminates Distress in Response to Adults' Conflicts. If exposure to conflict simply affected children through emotional contagion, then the resolution of conflict should make relatively little difference to children's reactions; that is, children's distress reactions should reflect the intensity, duration, or other characteristics of the degree and extent of conflict expression.

The fact that the resolution of conflict greatly reduces children's distress reactions supports the notion that children evaluate the meaning, not simply the occurrence, of conflict between adults. The meaning of anger expression between adults appears to be very different for children if conflicts are resolved. Several specific findings particularly emphasize this point: (a) Conflict resolution reduces distress reactions even when actors, scripts, degree, and manner of anger expression are controlled (Cummings et al.,

1989); (b) conflict resolution reduces distress reactions even when the resolution segment is brief in duration in relation to the longer duration of anger expression (Cummings, Ballard, El-Sheikh, & Lake, 1991); and (c) conflict resolution reduces distress reactions even when conflict intensity is high (verbal-physical conflict) (Cummings et al., 1993). By contrast, various forms of unresolved conflicts appear to have somewhat similar, negative implications for children, although conflict involving physical aggression has more negative implications than other forms of conflict expression (Cummings & Davies, 1994).

Why are negative reactions so dramatically ameliorated by the resolution of conflict, and why are children so sensitive to resolution? An emotional security theory makes better sense of these data than does an emotional contagion hypothesis. Children do not seem to react so much to the fact that the adults are fighting as to the implications of the adults' fights to relationships. Resolution is one type of information that relationships are positive at the end of conflictual interactions, although undoubtedly there are many other important sources of information in actual family conflicts (e.g., a consistently constructive interactional quality even in the midst of disagreement; see Easterbrooks, Cummings, & Emde, 1994), and there are also likely to be limits to the effectiveness of resolution (e.g., abusive anger may not be resolvable).

Children With Negative Histories of Family Conflict and Abuse Appear "Sensitized" to Conflict. Why do children from high-conflict homes evidence more emotional and behavioral dysregulation in reaction to conflict than other children? If information processing was the key process, then repeated exposure should lead to *reduced* reactivity; that is, children from high-conflict homes should habituate to conflict and show less reaction than other children. Instead, children with histories of high marital conflict and abuse appear sensitized to conflict in their behavioral and emotional responding.

Although these data may not make sense from an information processing perspective, they do make sense in terms of an emotional security theory. Repeated, intense conflicts between the parents have increasingly negative implications for the parents' relationship and, consequently, the children's appraisal of their personal well-being within the family. Thus, children are apt to feel increasingly insecure about parental conflicts as conflicts intensify; and this reduced sense of security would be expected to reduce the children's ability to regulate their emotions and behavior, particularly when faced with conflict situations. For example, an extensive literature within the attachment theory tradition indicates reduced regulatory capacities associated with reduced security (Davies & Cummings, 1994).

This theory can also explain why children intervene more in parents' fights when the historical level of fighting in the home is high. Children from high-conflict families experience more distress than other children during marital conflict (Cummings & Davies, 1994), and their involvement in marital conflict may be more risky than for other children, given positive correlations between spousal and child physical abuse (Cummings & Davies, 1994). Thus, one might expect that children's involvement would diminish as marital conflict became more serious and significant.

However, if one assumes that children's sense of emotional security is a paramount concern and derives from the perceived quality of marital relations, it makes sense that children from high-conflict homes would be more likely to intervene and would actually be motivated to do so by their greater feelings of distress (Emery, 1989). In other words, regulating the parents' conflicts is a vital concern for children when parents are having difficulty, and children from high-conflict homes are thus less likely to ignore or otherwise stay out of parental conflicts than children from harmonious homes. Furthermore, these concerns may outweigh the immediate threat of parental conflicts.

TOWARD A FAMILY-WIDE PERSPECTIVE ON MARITAL CONFLICT, ABUSE, AND ADVERSITY

A family-wide perspective on marital conflict, abuse, and adversity is an important goal for future research. Increasing evidence suggests multiple sources of adversity and their interrelations within the family. There may be a continuum of family discord and abuse, with impact on children a function of multiple family systems (e.g., marital, parent-child). Furthermore, there is no necessarily single ordering of adversity by intensity of expression. Qualitative aspects also matter. For example, with regard to marital conflict, children's reactions depend on the extent to which (a) conflicts are resolved versus unresolved; (b) conflict themes have negative versus positive meaning for family relationships (e.g., suggest marital dissolution, hold the threat of physical harm, or indicate increased understanding of interpersonal problems); and (c) children feel responsibility or are blamed for family discord.

From a developmental psychopathology perspective, views of compensatory, adversity, vulnerability, protective, and resilience factors also should benefit from a broader family-wide view of interrelations between systems. *Theoretical* development, however, is needed to achieve a better integrated model of children's functioning in the family around adversity. An emotional security theory provides an explanation that fosters such a broader integration. For example, a broad array of familial or extrafamilial factors that increase children's sense of security may be regarded as compensatory factors, or possibly protective factors in the case of high-risk groups, adding to their resilience when faced with circumstances of marital conflict. It follows, on the one hand, that positive influences in coping with marital conflict could include an emotionally secure attachment with at least one parent; other aspects of positive family functioning and emotionally secure relationships with others besides the parents; and resolved conflict patterns or other constructive conflict styles as appraised by the child. On the other hand, vulnerability or adversity factors could include other family-wide sources of emotional insecurity (e.g., problems in parent-child discipline practices, insecure parent-child attachment, insecure or conflictual relations with siblings, parental depression, parent-child physical or sexual abuse), interspousal *abuse* (not just anger), behavioral patterns of holding-in anger (the silent treatment), and child-related marital conflict.

In closing, marital conflict should be included as part of a family-wide model for the impact of adversity and abuse on children. An emotional security theory provides a conceptualization for organizing a multiplicity of effects within the family that may have implications for children's affect regulation, representational systems, and interpersonal functioning within the family (Davies & Cummings, 1994). Furthermore, an emotional security theory provides one avenue, consistent with a developmental psychopathology perspective, for conceptualizing mediating processes in developmental outcomes because of marital conflict and associated adversity and abuse, including the identification of resilience and protective factors. These directions for study have just begun, however, and much more research and theory are clearly necessary.

REFERENCES

Amato, P. R., & Keith, B. (1991). Parental divorce and the well-being of children: A meta-analysis. *Psychological Bulletin, 110,* 26-46.

Ballard, M., & Cummings, E. M. (1990). Response to adults' angry behavior in children of alcoholic and nonalcoholic parents. *Journal of Genetic Psychology, 151,* 195-210.

Bretherton, I. (1985). Attachment theory: Retrospect and prospect. In I. Bretherton & E. Waters (Eds.), Growing points of attachment theory and research. *Monographs of the Society for Research in Child Development, 50*(12D2, Serial No. 209), 167-193.

Browne, A., & Finkelhor, D. (1986). Impact of sexual abuse: A review of the research. *Psychological Bulletin, 99,* 66-77.

Cicchetti, D., & Garmezy, N. (1993). Prospects and promises in the study of resilience. *Development and Psychopathology, 5,* 497-502.

Conrad, M., & Hammen, C. (1993). Protective and resource factors in high- and low-risk children: A comparison of children with unipolar, bipolar, medically ill, and normal mothers. *Development and Psychopathology, 5,* 593-608.

Cummings, E. M. (1987). Coping with background anger in early childhood. *Child Development, 58,* 976-984.

Cummings, E. M. (1994). Marital conflict and children's functioning. *Social Development, 3,* 16-36.

Cummings, E. M. (1995). The usefulness of experiments for the study of the family. *Journal of Family Psychology, 9,* 175-185.

Cummings, E. M., Ballard, M., & El-Sheikh, M. (1991). Responses of children and adolescents to interadult anger as a function of gender, age, and mode of expression. *Merrill-Palmer Quarterly, 37,* 543-560.

Cummings, E. M., Ballard, M., El-Sheikh, M., & Lake, M. (1991). Resolution and children's responses to interadult anger. *Developmental Psychology, 27,* 462-470.

Cummings, E. M., & Cummings, J. S. (1988). A process-oriented approach to children's coping with adults' angry behavior. *Developmental Review, 3,* 296-321.

Cummings, E. M., & Davies, P. T. (1994). *Children and marital conflict: The impact of family dispute and resolution.* New York: Guilford.

Cummings, E. M., & Davies, P. T. (1995). The impact of parents on their children: An emotional security hypothesis. *Annals of Child Development, 10,* 167-208.

Cummings, E. M., & Davies, P. T. (in press). Emotional security as a regulatory process in normal development and the development of psychopathology. *Development and Psychopathology.*

Cummings, E. M., Hennessy, K., Rabideau, G., & Cicchetti, D. (1994). Responses of physically abused boys to interadult anger involving their mothers. *Development and Psychopathology, 6,* 31-41.

Cummings, E. M., Iannotti, R. J., & Zahn-Waxler, C. (1985). The influence of conflict between adults on the emotions and aggression of young children. *Developmental Psychology, 21,* 495-507. Reprinted in Parke, R. D., & Hetherington, M. (1987). *Contemporary readings in child psychology* (3rd ed.). New York: McGraw-Hill.

Cummings, E. M., Simpson, K. S., & Wilson, A. (1993). Children's responses to interadult anger as a function of information about resolution. *Developmental Psychology, 29,* 978-985.

Cummings, E. M., Vogel, D., Cummings, J. S., & El-Sheikh, M. (1989). Children's responses to different forms of expression of anger between adults. *Child Development, 60,* 1392-1404.

Cummings, E. M., & Zahn-Waxler, C. (1992). Emotions and the socialization of aggression: Adults' angry behavior and children's arousal and aggression. In A. Fraczek & H. Zumkley (Eds.), *Socialization and aggression* (pp. 61-84). New York: Springer-Verlag.

Cummings, E. M., Zahn-Waxler, C., & Radke-Yarrow, M. (1981). Young children's responses to expressions of anger and affection by others in the family. *Child Development, 52,* 1274-1282.

Davies, P. T., & Cummings, E. M. (1994). Marital conflict and child adjustment: An emotional security hypothesis. *Psychological Bulletin, 116,* 387-411.

Downey, G., & Coyne, J. C. (1990). Children of depressed parents: An integrative review. *Psychological Bulletin, 108,* 50-76.

Easterbrooks, M. A., Cummings, E. M., & Emde, R. N. (1994). Young children's responses to constructive marital disputes. *Journal of Family Psychology, 8,* 160-169.

Egeland, B., Carlson, E., & Sroufe, L. A. (1993). Resilience as process. *Development and Psychopathology, 5,* 517-528.

El-Sheikh, M., Cummings, E. M., & Goetsch, V. (1989). Coping with adults' angry behavior: Behavioral, physiological, and self-reported responding in preschoolers. *Developmental Psychology, 25,* 490-498.

Emery, R. E. (1989). Family violence. *American Psychologist, 44,* 321-328.

Fincham, F. D., & Osborne, L. N. (1993). Marital conflict and children: Retrospect and prospect. *Journal of Clinical Child Psychology, 13,* 75-88.

Gest, S. D., Neemann, J., Hubbard, J. J., Masten, A. S., & Tellegen, A. (1993). Parenting quality, adversity, and conduct problems in adolescence: Testing process-oriented models of resilience. *Development and Psychopathology, 5,* 663-682.

Grych, J. H., & Fincham, F. D. (1990). Marital conflict and children's adjustment: A cognitive-contextual framework. *Psychological Bulletin, 108,* 267-290.

Grych, J. H., & Fincham, F. D. (1993). Children's appraisals of marital conflict: Initial investigations of the cognitive-contextual framework. *Child Development, 64,* 215-230.

Hennessy, K. D., Rabideau, G. J., Cicchetti, D., & Cummings, E. M. (1994). Responses of physically abused children to different forms of interadult anger. *Child Development, 65,* 815-828.

Jaffe, P. G., Wolfe, D. A., & Wilson, S. K. (1990). *Children of battered women.* Newbury Park, CA: Sage.

Jaffe, P. G., Wolfe, D. A., Wilson, S. K., & Zak, L. (1986). Family violence and child adjustment: A comparative analysis of girls' and boys' behavioral symptoms. *American Journal of Psychiatry, 143,* 74-77.

Jouriles, E. N., Barling, J., & O'Leary, K. D. (1987). Predicting child behavior problems in maritally violent families. *Journal of Abnormal Child Psychology, 15,* 165-173.

Klaczynski, P. A., & Cummings, E. M. (1989). Responding to anger in aggressive and nonaggressive boys. *Journal of Child Psychology and Psychiatry, 30,* 309-314.

Werner, E. E. (1993). Risk, resilience, and recovery: Perspectives from the Kauai Longitudinal Study. *Development and Psychopathology, 5,* 503-516.

Wolfe, D. A., Jaffe, P., Wilson, S. K., & Zak, L. (1985). Children of battered women: The relation of child behavior to family violence and maternal stress. *Journal of Consulting and Clinical Psychology, 53,* 657-665.

2

Child Physical Abuse

REVIEW OF OFFENDER
CHARACTERISTICS

JOEL S. MILNER

CYNTHIA DOPKE

This chapter provides an overview of child physical abuse offender characteristics as described in controlled studies published in the literature.
Although not reviewed here, evidence suggests that factors beyond the
individual are associated with child physical abuse. Therefore, to be properly
understood, the description of offender characteristics should be considered one
part of a broader perspective that includes familial and societal factors. For
example, a classic organizational model of child abuse described by Belsky
(1980, 1993) suggests that factors from four ecological levels contribute to
child physical abuse: ontogenic level (individual factors), microsystem level

AUTHORS' NOTE: Preparation of this chapter was supported, in part, by National Institute
of Mental Health Grant MH34252 to Joel S. Milner. Correspondence concerning this chapter
should be addressed to Joel S. Milner, Family Violence and Sexual Assault Research Program,
Department of Psychology, Northern Illinois University, DeKalb, Illinois 60115-2892.

(family factors), exosystem level (community factors), and macrosystem level (cultural factors). Offender characteristics, which represent factors at the ontogenic level, are thought to interact with factors from the other ecological levels.

Another useful organizational model, described by Cicchetti and Rizley (1981), focuses on the types of characteristics that may exist at each ecological level. Cicchetti and Rizley classify factors along two dimensions: type of influence (potentiating or compensatory) and temporal influence (transient or enduring). Thus, factors at each of the four ecological levels described by Belsky (1980, 1993) can be evaluated as potentiating or compensatory factors of a short- or long-term nature that may influence the likelihood of child physical abuse. Together, these organizational models define the complete range of domains and factor characteristics that may contribute to child physical abuse.

Although our review is not guided by any particular etiological model, the offender characteristics described in the various sections of our review can be viewed as supporting different theoretical perspectives within the framework of the organizational models described above. Consequently, the initial part of each section contains a brief description of the models, theoretical perspectives, and/or general hypotheses that guided the associated research.

BIOLOGICAL FACTORS

Two types of biological risk factors for child physical abuse are mentioned in the literature: offender-related psychophysiological and neuropsychological characteristics. As described below, data from controlled studies provide varying degrees of support for the role of biological factors in child physical abuse.

Psychophysiological Factors

As part of the conceptual basis for research on psychophysiological factors in child physical abuse, Disbrow, Doerr, and Caulfield (1977) suggested that increased psychophysiological reactivity may reflect the difficulty that abusive parents have in tolerating stress. Similarly, Knutson (1978) proposed that physically abusive parents possess a hyperreactive trait that manifests as a generalized hyperreactivity to stress, and Bauer and Twentyman (1985) suggested that abusers may be hyperresponsive to child-related and non-child-related stimuli. More specifically, Wolfe, Fairbank, Kelly, and Bradlyn (1983) suggested that emotional arousal may mediate the expression of child physical abuse. Drawing on extant theories of aggression (e.g., Bandura, 1973; Berkowitz, 1974), Wolfe et al. (1983) suggested that "an aversive child behavior . . . can function as a cue capable of eliciting aggressive parental actions if the parent's emotional arousal is sufficiently high" (p. 364).

Although study results are often mixed and, in some cases, difficult to interpret (see McCanne & Milner, 1991, for a detailed review and critique), investigators have uniformly concluded that child physical abusers are more physiologically reactive to child-related stimuli (Disbrow et al., 1977; Friedrich, Tyler, & Clark, 1985; Frodi & Lamb, 1980; Wolfe et al., 1983). In the study with the most clear-cut results, Frodi and Lamb (1980) presented physically abusive and demographically matched comparison mothers with videotapes of a crying infant, a quiescent but alert infant, and a smiling infant. Although the crying infant elicited increases in heart rate, diastolic blood pressure, and skin conductance in both groups, the abusive mothers displayed greater increases in heart rate and reported higher levels of aversion. In response to the smiling infant, the comparison mothers showed no increase in reactivity, whereas the abusive mothers responded to the smiling infant in the same way they responded to the crying infant. Partial support for the Frodi and Lamb findings are provided in a study by Friedrich et al. (1985) that used audiotapes of a crying child. The researchers found that abusive and comparison mothers differed on skin resistance measures, but expected group differences on cardiovascular measures were not found.

In addition to the studies that used child stimuli, two studies used parent-child interaction stimuli that varied the level of conflict (Disbrow et al., 1977; Wolfe et al., 1983). Disbrow et al. (1977) reported data that indicated an abuser-neglecter group, relative to a comparison group, entered the experiment with higher resting levels of physiological activity and responded across all stimuli with higher levels of physiological reactivity (heart rate and skin resistance). Wolfe et al. (1983) reported that abusive mothers, compared with nonabusive mothers, showed greater skin conductance changes in response to stressful scenes. In addition, abusive mothers had higher respiration rates across both stressful and nonstressful scenes. Heart rate differences were not found. Across the studies that used abusive and nonabusive participants, the most consistent finding appears to be that abusive mothers show greater changes on skin conductance measures during presentations of stimuli that include children.

Supporting the findings that physically abusive parents are more reactive to child-related stimuli, two studies of high-risk individuals (nonparents) reported that high-risk subjects, compared with low-risk subjects, tended to display more physiological reactivity to child-related stimuli (e.g., crying child) (Crowe & Zeskind, 1992; Pruitt & Erickson, 1985). As is the case with the studies that used abusive parents, however, expected differences in reactivity in the high-risk and low-risk participants were not found on all measures. In addition, one study of at-risk and low-risk male college students failed to find differences in physiological reactivity (Stasiewicz & Lisman, 1989). Because of equipment malfunction in this study, however, only one psychophysiological measure (diastolic blood pressure) was evaluated. Further, the lack of consistent findings may be a result of the use of different at-risk criteria. In the two studies in which reactivity differences were reported (Crowe & Zeskind, 1992; Pruitt & Erickson, 1985), the Child Abuse Potential Inventory (Milner, 1986, 1994) was used to determine risk status. In the study in which differences were not observed (Stasiewicz & Lisman, 1989), the Adult/Adolescent Parenting Inventory (Bavolek, 1989) was used to screen for risk status. The findings that some nonparent high-risk groups show more reactivity to child-related stimuli are important because these data suggest that some individuals enter the parenting role with increased child-related reactivity and that the reactivity is not necessarily the result of negative parent-child interactions with one's own child, as initially suggested by Frodi and Lamb (1980). Finally, available data suggest that abusive mothers, compared with nonabusive mothers (Friedrich et al., 1985), and high-risk mothers, compared with low-risk mothers (Casanova, Domanic, McCanne, & Milner, 1992), are more physiologically reactive to stressful non-child-related stimuli (e.g., a cold pressor and a film depicting industrial accidents).

Although studies tend to support the view that physically abusive and high-risk individuals are more reactive to a variety of stimuli, the way increased physiological reactivity contributes to child physical abuse is unknown. Wolfe et al.'s (1983) suggestion that negative child behavior may serve as a cue that elicits aggressive parental actions if arousal is sufficiently high remains to be investigated. It should be noted, however, that our review provides some support for the notion that abusive parents show increased reactivity to both positive and negative child behavior. Finally, the possibility that stress-related autonomic reactivity may disrupt social information processing and response implementation by the parent (e.g., Milner, 1993) has not been explored in controlled experiments.

Neuropsychological Factors

With respect to neuropsychological factors, Elliott (1988) concluded from case data that disorders associated with neuropsychological deficits, such as episodic dyscontrol, minimal brain dysfunction, and antisocial personality, are associated with child abuse. More specifically, Elliott suggested that cognitive deficits, such as verbal processing problems and an inability to perceive cues in others, reduce the parent's ability to deal with family problems, increasing the likelihood of abuse. The suggestion that cognitive deficits contribute to child physical abuse is discussed in detail in social information processing models (e.g., Milner, 1993) and is congruent with studies (e.g., Hansen, Pallotta, Tishelman, Conaway, & MacMillan, 1989) that suggest a lack of cognitive abilities (e.g., flexibility in understanding children's behavior, ability to generate appropriate child management strategies) is associated with child physical abuse. Finally, the role of neuropsychological deficits in child abuse has been of interest because the experience of childhood physical assault may produce head injury and related neuropsychological problems that, in some cases, may contribute to the intergenerational transmission of child physical abuse (Milner & McCanne, 1991).

Our literature review, however, failed to find any controlled studies that directly assessed neuropsychological characteristics of child physical abusers and demographically matched comparison subjects by using standard neuropsychological measures. An unpublished controlled study has been completed in the senior author's laboratory and will be described only because no published controlled studies were found. This study, by Nayak and Milner (1995), provides support for some of Elliott's (1988) hypotheses described above. Nayak and Milner administered a selected group of standard neuropsychological measures to demographically matched groups of high- and low-risk mothers. They reported that high-risk, compared with low-risk, mothers showed differences (inferior performance) on neuropsychological measures that assessed conceptual ability, cognitive flexibility, and problem-solving ability. Several of the neuropsychological differences were also found in analyses that included IQ as a covariate, supporting Elliott's view that cognitive differences exist apart from overall differences in intelligence. It is important to note, however, that expected differences were not found between high- and low-risk mothers on neuropsychological measures of attention, distractibility, and verbal fluency. Because this is the only known study in the child physical abuse area that has investigated putative neuropsychological differences in a controlled design, additional research is needed before any conclusions can be drawn about neuropsychological limitations in physically abusive parents.

COGNITIVE/AFFECTIVE FACTORS

Cognitive-behavioral models of child physical abuse and most contemporary models of aggression posit a role for cognitive and affective factors as mediators of physical assault. Examples of different theoretical perspectives on the putative roles of various cognitive and affective factors in child physical abuse and the supporting literature are discussed in the following sections.

Self-Esteem/Ego-Strength

At the conceptual level, low self-esteem is thought to be an important risk factor or moderator variable for child maltreatment because it is associated with other parent-related characteristics commonly viewed as important in models of child physical abuse. For example, individuals with low self-esteem are reported to have more negative perceptions of children (e.g., Mash, Johnston, & Kovitz, 1983) and less ability to deal with family stress (e.g., McCubbin, Cauble, & Patterson, 1982). With the exception of one study that failed to find differences in perpetrator self-esteem (Perry, Wells, & Doran, 1983) and another study that reported differences in personal worth but not in self-esteem (Shorkey, 1980), the literature supports the view that physically abusive mothers, relative to demographically matched comparison mothers, have lower levels of self-esteem, ego-strength, and feelings of personal worth (Culp, Culp, Soulis, & Letts, 1989; Evans, 1980; Melnick & Hurley, 1969; Oates & Forrest, 1985; Rosen, 1978; Shorkey & Armendariz, 1985). In addition to the cross-sectional evidence, two longitudinal studies have reported links, albeit modest, between maternal self-esteem and later child maltreatment (Altemeier, O'Connor, Vietze, Sandler, & Sherrod, 1982; Christensen et al., 1994).

A major limitation of this area of research is that ego-strength and self-esteem are multifaceted constructs and that many models and measures have been used to define and assess these constructs. Thus, the reader must carefully determine exactly which individual characteristics are being defined when such terms as *self-esteem, ego-strength,* and *personal worth* are being discussed. For example, it would be valuable to know whether definitions of self-esteem and ego-strength that are related to interpersonal relationships (e.g., "an individual's evaluation of his or her ability and success in social relationships and of his or her ability to maintain emotional stability and feelings of worth as they relate to social relationships," Milner, 1988, p. 152) contribute most to the association between self-esteem and child abuse risk, as opposed to definitions that focus on academic and physical self-components.

Perceptions of Child Behavior

With respect to perceptions of children's behavior, it has been speculated that parents who physically abuse their children are less aware of their children's behavior, which leads to an incorrect understanding of their children and inappropriate parenting behaviors (e.g., Milner, 1993; Newberger & Cook, 1983). The lack of awareness is thought to be manifested in a variety of ways, such as abusive parents, relative to nonabusive parents, viewing their children's behavior as more problematic and having less ability to perceive their children's emotional state.

As expected, abusive parents, relative to comparison parents, report more negative behaviors when rating children's behavior (Mash et al., 1983; Reid, Kavanagh, & Baldwin, 1987; Wood-Shuman & Cone, 1986). Similar results have been found in a controlled study that used a mixed group of abusive and neglectful parents (Oates, Forrest, & Peacock, 1985). It is important to note, however, that in two studies that used independent raters/observers (Mash et al., 1983; Reid et al., 1987), the higher levels of child behavior problems reported by abusive parents were not confirmed by the observers, which supports the view that abusive parents' reports of their children's behavior problems may be biased. These findings are qualified by the fact that the independent observers used different measures to assess child behavior than those used by the parents.

In addition, differences between abusers' and nonabusers' reports of child behavior have not been found in all contexts. For example, Wood-Shuman and Cone (1986) found that abusive mothers, compared with nonabusive mothers, gave higher ratings of negative child behaviors when asked to rate normal living, child unattended, and mildly aversive situations; but abusive mothers did not give higher ratings when they were asked to evaluate clearly noncompliant situations. Perhaps overlapping with the perception that one has a child who exhibits frequent problem behaviors, especially in normal living and mildly aversive situations, high-risk mothers, compared with matched low-risk mothers, evaluate minor child transgressions as more wrong, whereas no group differences were found in high- and low-risk mothers' evaluations of serious transgressions (Chilamkurti & Milner, 1993). These findings in abusive and at-risk mothers indicate that the greatest differences in the child behavior ratings may be found in marginal situations where factors such as the abusive parent's preexisting beliefs about children and their behaviors may affect the parent's evaluations.

Other studies have investigated the ability of physically abusive parents to correctly perceive affective states in children. The ability to distinguish emotions in children is believed to be important because the differentiation of a child's emotional signals is necessary for the parent to respond appropriately to the child's needs. The speculation is that parents who are unaware of or who lack the ability to read a child's emotional states are more likely to respond inappropriately. It is believed that failure to meet the child's needs contributes to the child becoming an aversive stimulus, which increases the risk of parental aggression toward the child (Kropp & Haynes, 1987).

Although an initial study reported that abusive mothers, relative to matched comparison mothers, demonstrated less skill in the recognition of children's emotional expressions (Kropp & Haynes, 1987), subsequent studies failed to find differences in the abusive mother's ability to recognize emotional expressions in children (Camras et al., 1988; During & McMahon, 1991) and in adults (During & McMahon, 1991). It should be noted that methodological differences may account for the different study results. For example, whereas Kropp and Haynes (1987) used facial expressions that were presented at different angles to participants, Camras et al. (1988) and During and McMahon (1991) used the same set of full-frontal facial expressions, which During and McMahon suggested may have been more obvious. To test this possibility, During and McMahon recommended that a stimulus fading procedure be used in a subsequent study to test the possibility that physically abusive parents have more difficulty identifying children's emotional states when the stimulus is relatively ambiguous.

In summary, there is support for the view that physically abusive parents, relative to nonabusive parents, view their children's behavior as more problematic and negative in normal living situations and in situations where their children engage in minor transgressions. At present, however, the extent to which the abusive and nonabusive parents' views are the result of differences in the parents' perception and awareness of their children's behavior, as opposed to differences in other cognitive activities such as attributions and evaluations of their children's behavior, is not clear.

Attributions

As part of cognitive-behavioral models of child abuse, Twentyman and his associates (Larrance & Twentyman, 1983; Twentyman, Rohrbeck, & Amish, 1984) and others (Azar, 1986, 1989; Milner, 1993; Wolfe, 1987) have suggested that certain types of parental attributional styles set the stage for child physical abuse. Initial support for the view that abusive parents have different attributional styles came from a report by Larrance and Twentyman (1983) that abusive mothers make internal and stable attributions for children's negative behaviors and external and unstable attributions for children's positive behaviors, whereas nonabusive mothers display the opposite attributional style. Supporting this finding, a study by Bradley and Peters (1991) found that abusive parents were less likely to hold themselves responsible for unsuccessful parent-child interactions and were less likely to give their child credit for successful parent-child interactions. Somewhat confusing, however, is the fact that the latter difference appeared between abusive and matched comparison mothers but no differences were found between the abusive mothers and a comparison group of middle-class nonabusive mothers. Further, other studies failed to find the pattern of attributional differences described by Larrance and Twentyman in child physical abusers, relative to nonabusive parents, (Rosenberg & Reppucci, 1983) and in at-risk, compared to low-risk, individuals (Milner & Foody, 1994).

Although evidence for the existence of an overall pattern of attributional differences is mixed, there is some support for selected attributional differences. For example, abusive and nonabusive parents differ in the degree of hostile intent attributed to children's behavior (Bauer & Twentyman, 1985). High-risk individuals make fewer attributions of child competence (Diaz, Neal, & Vachio, 1991) and make fewer changes in their attributions after receiving mitigating information about a child's behavior (Milner & Foody, 1994). In the latter instance, although group differences in attributions were not found, low-risk individuals changed their attributions toward unstable and unintentional for children's behavior following the receipt of mitigating information, whereas high-risk individuals did not change their attributions toward unstable and unintentional. Collectively, these data suggest that child physical abusers attribute responsibility for events to their children and are less likely to modify their child-related attributions in response to moderating contextual factors.

Expectations of Child Behavior

Another cognitive variable that has been proposed in cognitive-behavioral models as a factor that leads to child physical abuse is inappropriate parental expectations related to child development and behavior (e.g., Azar, 1986, 1989; Larrance & Twentyman, 1983; Milner, 1993; Twentyman et al., 1984). The literature is unclear, however, as to exactly what offender expectation differences exist. Several investigations failed to find child-related expectation differences in abusive parents, relative to comparison parents (Gaines, Sandgrund, Green, & Power, 1978; Kravitz & Driscoll, 1983; Starr, 1982). In contrast, other studies have reported that physically abusive parents, relative to matched comparison parents, have lower child-related expectations (Perry et al., 1983; Twentyman & Plotkin, 1982; Williamson, Borduin, & Howe, 1991), whereas still other studies have indicated that abusive parents have higher child-related expectations (Oates et al., 1985; Spinetta, 1978).

It is interesting to note that whereas a study by Azar, Robinson, Hekimian, and Twentyman (1984) failed to find expectation differences when subjects were asked about developmental milestones, differences between abusive and matched comparison mothers were found when mothers were asked about complex child behaviors, a finding that was later replicated (Azar & Rohrbeck, 1986). This finding led Azar et al. to suggest that the way parental expectations are operationalized and measured may account for differences in study results. Additional support for this speculation is provided in a study of high- and low-risk mothers (Chilamkurti & Milner, 1993), which found that expectation differences varied with the situation (type of transgression). High-risk mothers, compared with low-risk mothers, had lower expectations of child compliance following discipline for serious transgressions and higher expectations of child compliance following minor transgressions.

The high-risk mothers' expectations that their children would be less likely to comply following discipline for serious transgressions may be related to abusive parents' negative perceptions of their children, which were previously discussed. Further, the high-risk mothers' higher expectations of child compliance following minor transgressions may be unrealistic, given that their own children indicated their compliance was less likely following minor transgressions (Chilamkurti & Milner, 1993) and may result in high-risk parents perceiving discipline failure when their children repeat the behavior. This outcome may also result in high-risk parents viewing their children as oppositional, and this interpretation may be used to justify the use of more aversive disciplinary techniques. This possibility is supported by Dietrich, Berkowitz, Kadushin, and McGloin (1990), who reported that child defiance was significantly related to the extent to which physical abusers felt justification for their maltreating behavior. Collectively, the findings suggest that unrealistic parental expectations of child compliance, which increase the likelihood of perceived child defiance when noncompliance occurs, is an important cognitive component of physically abusive behavior and warrants attention during assessment and intervention.

Stress/Distress

Perhaps the most commonly accepted view across different models of child physical abuse is that the experience of high levels of stress increases the likelihood of child physical abuse. Extant models suggest a variety of mechanisms through which stress may act, which include changes in information processing events and in the selection and implementation of parenting behaviors (e.g., Hillson & Kupier, 1994; Milner, 1993).

With respect to total life stress, Starr (1982) failed to find life stress differences between child physical abusers and nonabusers. However, many studies have found that physical abusers report more life stress (Chan, 1994; Conger, Burgess, & Barrett 1979; Gaines et al., 1978; Perry et al., 1983) as well as personal distress (Lahey, Conger, Atkeson, & Treiber, 1984; Mash et al., 1983; Milner & Wimberley, 1979, 1980; Rosenberg & Reppucci, 1983). In addition, abusive mothers, compared with nonabusive mothers (Frodi & Lamb, 1980), and high-risk mothers, relative to low-risk mothers (Milner, Halsey, & Fultz, 1995), report more distress when they are presented with a videotape of a crying child. Further, in longitudinal studies, stress has been predictive of later inadequate child care and maltreatment (Altemeier et al., 1979; Egeland, Breitenbucher, & Rosenberg, 1980).

It is unclear, however, whether abusive parents experience more life stress or simply identify more events as stressful or experience life events as more distressing. Further, given the central role frequently assigned to the stress/distress construct, it is surprising that there is a paucity of controlled studies that manipulate stress levels to investigate the impact of different stressors on cognitive and behavioral factors thought to be related to abuse, such as child-related perceptions, attributions, expectations, evaluations, and disciplinary choice.

Available data from the controlled studies are mixed. Disbrow et al. (1977) failed to find differences between abusers and nonabusers in the use of verbal and physical directives in response to stressful scenes (parent-child interactions). Lawson and Hays (1989), who studied abusive and matched nonabusive couples, did not find an expected interaction effect between participants' self-esteem and life stress and abuse. In contrast, Bauer and Twentyman (1985) found mixed results in response to a mild stressor (crying male child). Although physically abusive mothers, compared with non-abusive mothers, did not react (with annoyance) more quickly in response to a mild stressor, they did respond with more intensity. Passman and Mulhern (1977) conducted a study on the impact of mild non-child-related and child-related stress on maternal punitiveness. The study was designed as an analogue study of the effects of stress on child abuse. Passman and Mulhern found that heightened non-child-related situational stress increased the mother's punitiveness toward her child. However, only trends toward increases in the mother's punitiveness were found for child-related stress. Finally, Mash et al. (1983) reported that, in response to stress, physically abusive mothers, compared with nonabusive mothers, were more controlling of their children but only for stressful task situations in which increased demands for performance were placed on both mother and child. Given the few studies that have been conducted, the modest study results, and the important role posited for stress in the child abuse literature, the surprising conclusion is that additional stress research is needed before research-based statements can be made about the role of stress as a moderator or mediator of child physical abuse.

Psychopathology/Emotional Problems

Early views of child physical abuse suggested that abuse was caused by parent psychopathology (e.g., Blumberg, 1974; Kempe, Silverman, Steele, Droegemueller, & Silver, 1962; Steele & Pollock, 1974). Although it is now clear that most offenders are not mentally ill (estimates are that only 5% to 10% are mentally ill; Kelly, 1983), it is still apparent that parents who suffer from some forms of psychopathology can be at increased risk for parenting problems. Further, case data suggest that serious psychopathology may be associated with very severe forms of child assault (e.g., murder). Although severe psychopathology may not be associated with most cases of child physical abuse, the literature, with one exception (Starr, 1982), provides support for an association between parental emotional problems (e.g., high levels of frustration, negative feelings) and child physical abuse (Conger et al., 1979; Melnick & Hurley, 1969; Oates et al., 1985; Wright, 1976). Further, in a longitudinal study, the lack of parental emotional stability was the best predictor of subsequent child maltreatment (Pianta, Egeland, & Erickson, 1989).

Negative Affectivity

Conceptually, the presence of negative affectivity, especially depression, is believed to be an important risk factor for child physical abuse because negative feelings are thought to interfere with adequate parent-child interactions by affecting parenting abilities, such as child-monitoring skills (e.g., Dumas, Gibson, & Albin, 1989). The view that depression may contribute to child abuse is supported by research that indicates depressed mothers are more distant, irritable, and punitive toward their children, resulting in a lower threshold for perceived child misbehavior and more punitive reactions to the behavior (Lahey et al., 1984).

Supporting the reports that child physical abusers have more emotional problems (mentioned in the previous section), studies uniformly report that child physical abusers, relative to comparison subjects, display a variety of negative emotions that appear to represent general negative affectivity (Milner et al., 1995). On a variety of measures in different contexts, child physical abuse offenders, relative to comparison subjects, reported more anxiety (Lahey et al., 1984) and more depression/unhappiness/sadness (Culp et al., 1989; Evans, 1980; Famularo, Stone, Barnum, & Wharton, 1986; Friedrich et al., 1985; Frodi & Lamb, 1980; Kelleher, Chaffin, Hollenberg, & Fischer, 1994; Lahey et al., 1984; Milner & Robertson, 1990; Milner & Wimberley, 1979, 1980). With the exception of one study that reported mixed findings (Melnick & Hurley, 1969), studies also have uniformly reported that child physical abusers, in a variety of situations, report more feelings of annoyance, anger, hostility, and aggression (Bauer & Twentyman, 1985; Evans, 1980; Frodi & Lamb, 1980; Lyons-Ruth, Connell, Zoll, & Stahl, 1987;

Rosenberg & Reppucci, 1983; Spinetta, 1978; Susman, Trickett, Iannotti, Hollenbeck, & Zahn-Waxler, 1985; Trickett & Kuczynski, 1986; Trickett & Susman, 1988). Although the way negative affect influences (i.e., mediates and moderates) parenting behavior remains to be fully delineated, the data indicate that negative emotional states, such as feelings of depression and hostility, are associated with child physical abuse and warrant consideration in child abuse assessment and intervention protocols.

Empathy

Lack of parental empathy is considered a possible risk factor in child physical abuse because general models of aggression have proposed that a lack of empathy increases the likelihood of aggressive behavior (e.g., Feshbach & Feshbach, 1982; Parke & Slaby, 1983). Empathy is thought to inhibit aggression because it facilitates actions, such as helping behavior, that are incompatible with aggression (Feshbach, 1964). Separate from the child abuse literature, studies generally support the view that empathy inhibits aggression (Miller & Eisenberg, 1988).

Controlled studies in the child abuse literature are uniform in reporting empathy differences between abusive and matched comparison groups on a variety of empathy measures under different experimental conditions (Frodi & Lamb, 1980; Letourneau, 1981; Melnick & Hurley, 1969; Wiehe, 1987). With respect to high-risk individuals, a recent study failed to find the expected dispositional empathy differences between high- and low-risk mothers (Milner et al., 1995). However, predicted situational differences in empathy were observed. Milner et al. (1995) found that low-risk mothers reported a significant increase in empathy (compared with baseline) in response to a crying infant, whereas the high-risk mothers did not show a significant change. The high-risk mothers, nevertheless, reported increases in sadness, distress, and hostility in response to the crying child, which low-risk mothers did not report. The Milner et al. study indicates that context (e.g., measuring empathy in response to selected stimuli, such as a crying child) may be an important consideration in the assessment of empathy in high-risk individuals. Although prosocial behavior (e.g., helping behavior) was not measured, the association between the lack of an increase in empathy and the reported increase in hostility is congruent with the view that the level of parental empathy may play a role in the expression of aggression.

BEHAVIORAL FACTORS

Social interaction models and social skills models of child abuse emphasize the role that problems in relationships and deficits in parenting skills play in child physical abuse. As the literature review indicates, a substantial amount of data supports the perspective that parenting-related social skill deficits are associated with the occurrence of child physical abuse.

Isolation and Loneliness

Early descriptive studies indicated that child physical abusers were not involved in community activities (Young, 1964) and experienced less family and peer support (Gil, 1970). Subsequent sociological and social interactional models (Tzeng, Jackson, & Karlson, 1991) frequently described a role for parental isolation in the etiology of child abuse. Isolation and loneliness are thought to be related to a lack of social support, which is viewed as important because social support is thought to be a buffering variable in models of stress, aggression, and problematic parenting behaviors. Although one study reported only a trend toward abusive mothers, compared with nonabusive mothers, reporting more social alienation (Shorkey, 1980), studies indicate that child physical abusers, relative to comparison subjects, report more isolation and feel more loneliness (Chan, 1994; Evans, 1980; Kelleher et al., 1994; Milner & Wimberley, 1979, 1980; Shorkey & Armendariz, 1985; Spinetta, 1978; Starr, 1982; Trickett & Susman, 1988). It should also be noted, however, that in some studies, such as the study conducted by Starr (1982), differences were not found on every measure of social isolation. For example, Starr did not find differences on the rates of verbal (telephone) and written (letters) communication, whereas Starr did find differences in the number of people visited each week and the number of weekly meetings with relatives. Finally, abusive parents appear to be less likely to use resources when they are available. For example, evidence suggests that individuals at the greatest risk for abuse are more likely to drop out of treatment programs (Wolfe, Edwards, Manion, & Koverola, 1988). In summary, although research provides substantial support for the view that child physical abusers have fewer social contacts, perceive less social support, and feel more isolated than matched nonabusive parents, it also appears that the abusive parent may actively seek social isolation while perceiving that support is not forthcoming from others.

Problematic Parent-Child Interactions

Parent-child interactions have been a key area of interest in child abuse research because many social interactional models suggest that child physical abuse results from problems in parents' attempts to discipline their children. For example, in one early social interactional model, Reid, Taplin, and Lorber (1981) suggested that two important contributors to child physical abuse are a "lack of parental skill in effectively handling day-to-day discipline confrontations, and high rates of aversive behaviors by both parents and children" (p. 84). Guided by this and similar models that suggest that parenting skill deficits contribute to child physical abuse, a substantial amount of controlled research has been conducted on parents' interactions with their children.

Compared with nonabusive parents, abusive parents engage in fewer interactions and communicate less with their children (e.g., Bousha & Twentyman, 1984; Browne & Saqi, 1988; Burgess & Conger, 1978; Disbrow et al., 1977; Frodi & Lamb, 1980; Schmidt & Eldridge, 1986). When abusive parents do interact, the literature generally supports the view that abusive parents exhibit increased rates of negative parenting behaviors. Child physical abusers use more aversive behaviors (Reid et al., 1981), more commands (Oldershaw, Walters, & Hall, 1986), more verbal aggression (Bousha & Twentyman, 1984), more negative physical behaviors (Bousha & Twentyman, 1984; Lahey et al., 1984; Oldershaw et al., 1986; Susman et al., 1985), more anxiety and guilt in conjunction with authoritarian methods (Susman et al., 1985), more punitive behaviors (Disbrow et al., 1977; Trickett & Kuczynski, 1986), and more intrusive and interfering behaviors (Crittenden, 1981; Lyons-Ruth et al., 1987; Oldershaw et al., 1986).

In general, physically abusive parents have poor problem-solving ability in child-related situations (Azar et al., 1984) and are inconsistent in their responding to children (Lyons-Ruth et al., 1987; Oldershaw et al., 1986; Susman et al., 1985). Further, compared with matched low-risk mothers, high-risk mothers use more harsh disciplinary strategies, including verbal and physical assault (Chilamkurti & Milner, 1993). In contrast, several authors failed to find expected differences in abusive parents' rates of some negative parenting attitudes and behaviors (e.g., Burgess & Conger, 1978; Evans, 1980; Starr, 1982). Given the diversity of samples, designs, and measures used in the studies reviewed, it is difficult to determine the basis for the mixed findings with respect to the rates at which abusive parents use negative parenting behaviors.

In contrast, studies consistently indicate that child physical abusers display fewer positive parenting behaviors, relative to matched comparison groups. Child physical abusers engage in or provide less facilitation (Disbrow et al., 1977), less mutual engagement (Dietrich, Starr, & Weisfeld, 1983), fewer vocalizations and visual behaviors directed toward children (Browne & Saqi, 1988), less play behavior (Bousha & Twentyman, 1984), less reasoning and simple commands (Trickett & Kuczynski, 1986), less verbal and nonverbal instruction and affection (Bousha & Twentyman, 1984; Susman et al., 1985), fewer positive responses (Burgess & Conger, 1978; Lahey et al., 1984), and less contingent praise for appropriate behavior (Schmidt & Eldridge, 1986). Although the literature is uniform in reporting that physically abusive parents use fewer positive parenting behaviors, it should be noted that one study reported no difference between abusers' and nonabusers' attitudes about the use of rewards (Evans, 1980).

In summary, the data on parent-child interactions indicate that abusive and nonabusive parents can be differentiated on the following variables: level of parent-child interaction, level of intrusiveness, degree of consistent responding, level of attentiveness, level of affection, use of simple instructions and reasoning disciplinary techniques, and use of negative verbal and physical parenting behaviors. Although the data support the view that abusive parents display parenting skill deficits, the literature does not clearly demonstrate whether the observed parenting behavior differences are a result of the lack of parenting skills or different cognitive processing of child-related information, which can lead to the use of more negative parenting behaviors.

Coping Skills

Some authors have suggested that, in addition to parenting skill deficits, child physical abusers have general coping skill deficits, which increase frustration and risk of aggression (e.g., Kelly, 1983). In addition, general coping deficits may decrease a parent's ability to deal with stress and to maintain social relationships that might reduce the likelihood of abuse. Although extensive data are available on abusive parents' parenting skills, however, only one controlled study was found on abusive parents' level of general coping skills. Hansen et al. (1989) studied abusive, neglectful, and two control groups of parents and found that child physical abusers displayed more deficits in problem-solving skills. At present, additional data are needed to determine the degree to which child physical abusers, relative to demographically matched groups of nonabusers, have more deficits in general coping skills.

Attachment

Extensive speculation about the relationship between child maltreatment and parent-infant attachment problems has appeared in the literature. On the basis of attachment theory, early abusive parental behavior is thought to lead to an *insecure attachment* between the infant and the abusive parent. More specifically, theory suggests that *secure attachment* is associated with sensitive/responsive parenting, *anxious avoidant attachment* is associated with intrusive parenting, and *anxious ambivalent attachment* is associated with inconsistent parenting (Ainsworth, Blehar, Waters, & Wall, 1978). As expected, studies of mixed maltreating parent groups (which include parents who are abusive, neglectful, both abusive and neglectful, and/or target children who may or may not be the maltreated children), relative to nonmaltreating parents, indicate that maltreating mothers more frequently have infants with insecure mother-infant attachments (e.g., Aber & Allen, 1987; Carlson, Cicchetti, Barnett, & Braunwald, 1989; Cicchetti & Barnett, 1992; Crittenden, 1985, 1988; Crittenden, Partridge, & Claussen, 1991; Egeland & Sroufe, 1981a, 1981b; Lamb, Gaensbauer, Malkin, & Schultz, 1985; Lyons-Ruth et al., 1987; Schneider-Rosen, Baunwald, Carlson, & Cicchetti, 1985; Schneider-Rosen & Cicchetti, 1984). However, surprisingly little controlled research has focused on investigating attachment problems in groups consisting of only child physical abusers and demographically matched comparison parents.

In an analysis of different types of maltreating parents, Egeland and Sroufe (1981a) found that, in a group of four physical abusers, two of the abusers' children had insecure attachments. Although comparison data suggested that the physical abusers' children had a significantly higher rate of insecure attachment, the rate for a demographically matched comparison group was not provided. Cicchetti and Barnett (1992) also reported subgroup analyses by type of maltreatment, which appeared to include a group of physical abusers. Cicchetti and Barnett, however, found that although some differences were found between types, most maltreatment types did not differ in the degree of insecure attachment. They did not report which maltreatment types yielded significant and nonsignificant differences, and the maltreating participants were not matched on several demographic variables; furthermore, some individuals in the maltreatment groups may have been members of maltreating families but not the identified perpetrator.

Only one study (Browne & Saqi, 1988) contained a clearly defined group of child physical abusers and demographically matched comparison parents. The study, which was conducted in England, examined 23 abusing mother-infant pairs and 23 nonabusing mother-infant pairs that were matched "as far as possible." In addition, physical injury was not required. Mothers were placed in the physical abuse group because they had produced physical injury or because they had engaged in "severely rough handling." As expected, the abused infants had higher rates of insecure attachments (44% avoidant and 26% ambivalent attachments) than the nonabused infants (13% avoidant and 13% ambivalent attachments).

In conclusion, although most of the existing studies can be criticized for the lack of clear distinctions and/or definitions of maltreatment types, as well as the lack of individually matched comparison groups, the relatively high rates of insecure attachments found in the mixed groups of maltreating parents and in the study of physically abusive parents suggest that additional attachment studies using groups of child physical abusers are warranted and are likely to yield high rates of insecure infant attachments. In addition, investigations of the types of parent-child attachments observed across time (at different developmental levels) in children of physically abusive parents are needed.

Alcohol and Drug Use

Historically, suggestions have been made that child physical abuse and substance abuse are related (Leonard & Jacob, 1988). Many investigators have noted, however, the lack of controlled studies to support the suspected relationship. For example, the quality of the studies reporting an association between child abuse and drug use has been questioned on a variety of methodological grounds (e.g., Kelleher et al., 1994; Leonard & Jacob, 1988). However, using a probability sample from a community population (NIMH Epidemiological Catchment Area Study) with demographically matched comparison subjects and statistical control of potential confounding vari-ables, Kelleher et al. (1994) reported the expected association between child physical abuse and alcohol and drug disorders. Forty percent of adults who reported physically abusive behaviors met criteria for alcohol or drug disorders during their lifetime, and the rate was even higher for child neglect. Further,

Kelleher et al. noted that "the contribution of substance abuse disorders to predicting physical abuse or neglect remained significant after controlling for depression, household size, antisocial personality disorder, and social support" (p. 1589). Although the study lacks details related to the abuse incident and leaves unanswered questions about the causal role of alcohol and drug disorders in child physical abuse, the Kelleher et al. study provides the clearest evidence to date that a substantial association exists between a person's history of substance abuse and child physical abuse.

SUMMARY

Based on the foregoing review, evidence supports the following conclusions. Physically abusive mothers, relative to comparison mothers, are hyperreactive to both child-related and non-child-related stimuli. Abusive mothers have low self-esteem and negative views of their children. Abusers report more problematic behavior in their children, which is most evident in specific contexts (everyday living situations, ambiguous situations, and mildly aversive situations). Also, in some contexts, abusive mothers make different attributions for children's behavior, most often attributing more blame and hostile intent to a child when judging the child's negative behaviors. Although the literature is mixed on whether child physical abusers have higher or lower expectations with respect to developmental milestones, abusers are likely to have inappropriate expectations regarding their children's abilities in situations that involve complex child behaviors.

Many studies indicate that physically abusive parents have high levels of life stress and personal distress; however, controlled research is generally lacking on how stress affects other parental characteristics thought to contribute to child physical abuse. Although offenders generally do not exhibit severe psychopathology, abusive parents are more likely than comparison parents to report emotional problems and negative affectivity, especially depression and hostility. Although experiencing higher levels of hostility in response to a distressed child, abusers also have less empathy for their children, which may increase their likelihood of child assault. Abusive parents have more social isolation and feelings of loneliness, factors associated with reduced levels of social support, a potential buffering factor for child abuse.

In terms of parent-child interactions, physically abusive parents, relative to nonabusive parents, engage in fewer interactions and communicate less with their children. When interactions occur, abusive parents are more intrusive and inconsistent. Abusive parents, relative to nonabusive parents, use more harsh disciplinary techniques and fewer positive parenting behaviors to manage their children's behavior. Although these data suggest that physically abusive parents may have parenting skill deficits, the extent to which the frequent use of punitive parenting behaviors is a result of skill deficits or of different perceptions, evaluations, and attributions made by the parent that lead to the more frequent use of negative parenting behaviors remains to be determined.

Although controlled research has broadened our knowledge of physically abusive parents, the database continues to be plagued by gaps in knowledge about abusive parents' characteristics. As indicated in the foregoing review, many putative risk factors need additional investigation. Further, attention to possible gender and ethnic differences has been lacking. For example, the overwhelming majority of controlled studies reviewed in this chapter were conducted on abusive mothers. Abusive samples are often small and non-representative, including only mothers from lower socioeconomic status who have been involved with a social service agency. Inadequate attention is often given to the definition of the study groups and to the complete demographic matching of abusive and comparison parents. In the majority of studies, no attention is paid to the possible interaction of parental factors that may increase the likelihood of child physical abuse and to how contextual factors may interact with parental characteristics to produce abuse. Most important, we continue to lack an understanding of which offender characteristics are marker variables and which are causal factors in abusive behavior. Additional discussions of research limitations in the child physical abuse field are available elsewhere (e.g., see Mash & Wolfe, 1991). Although previously noted by other authors, it is worth repeating that we need to increase our understanding of offender characteristics through rigorous research designs to further our efforts to successfully assess, treat, and ultimately prevent child physical abuse.

REFERENCES

Aber, J. L., & Allen, J. P. (1987). Effects of maltreatment on young children's socioemotional development: An attachment theory perspective. *Developmental Psychology, 23,* 406-414.

Ainsworth, M. D. S., Blehar, M., Waters, E., & Wall, S. (1978). *Patterns of attachment.* Hillsdale, NJ: Lawrence Erlbaum.

Altemeier, W. A., O'Connor, S., Vietze, P. M., Sandler, H. M., & Sherrod, K. B. (1982). Antecedents of child abuse. *Journal of Pediatrics, 100,* 823-829.

Altemeier, W. A., Vietze, P. M., Sherrod, K. B., Sandler, H. M., Falsey, S., & O'Connor, S. (1979). Prediction of child maltreatment during pregnancy. *Journal of the American Academy of Child Psychiatry, 18,* 205-218.

Azar, S. T. (1986). A framework for understanding child maltreatment: An integration of cognitive behavioral and developmental perspectives. *Canadian Journal of Behavioral Science, 18,* 340-355.

Azar, S. T. (1989). Training parents of abused children. In C. E. Schaefer & J. M. Briesmeister (Eds.), *Handbook of parent training* (pp. 414-441). New York: John Wiley.

Azar, S. T., Robinson, D. R., Hekimian, E., & Twentyman, C. T. (1984). Unrealistic expectations and problem-solving ability in maltreating and comparison mothers. *Journal of Consulting and Clinical Psychology, 52,* 687-691.

Azar, S. T., & Rohrbeck, C. A. (1986). Child abuse and unrealistic expectations: Further validation of the Parent Opinion Questionnaire. *Journal of Consulting and Clinical Psychology, 54,* 867-868.

Bandura, A. (1973). *Aggression: A social learning analysis.* Upper Saddle River, NJ: Prentice Hall.

Bauer, W. D., & Twentyman, C. T. (1985). Abusing, neglectful, and comparison mothers' responses to child-related and non-child-related stressors. *Journal of Consulting and Clinical Psychology, 53,* 335-343.

Bavolek, S. J. (1989). Assessing and treating high-risk parenting attitudes. In J. T. Pardeck (Ed.), *Child abuse and neglect: Theory, research, and practice* (pp. 97-110). New York: Gordon & Breach.

Belsky, J. (1980). Child maltreatment: An ecological integration. *American Psychologist, 35,* 320-335.

Belsky, J. (1993). Etiology of child maltreatment: A developmental-ecological analysis. *Psychological Bulletin, 114,* 413-434.

Berkowitz, L. (1974). Some determinants of impulsive aggression: Role of mediated associations with reinforcement for aggression. *Psychological Review, 81,* 165-176.

Blumberg, M. (1974). Psychopathology of the abusing parent. *American Journal of Psychotherapy, 28,* 21-29.

Bousha, D. M., & Twentyman, C. T. (1984). Mother-child interactional style in abuse, neglect, and control groups: Naturalistic observations in the home. *Journal of Abnormal Psychology, 93,* 106-114.

Bradley, E. J., & Peters, R. D. (1991). Physically abusive and nonabusive mothers' perceptions of parenting and child behavior. *American Journal of Orthopsychiatry, 61,* 455-460.

Browne, K., & Saqi, S. (1988). Mother-infant interaction and attachment in physically abusing families. *Journal of Reproductive and Infant Psychology, 6,* 163-182.

Burgess, R. L., & Conger, R. D. (1978). Family interaction in abusive, neglectful, and normal families. *Child Development, 49,* 1163-1173.

Camras, L. A., Ribordy, S., Hill, J., Martino, S., Spaccarelli, S., & Stefani, R. (1988). Recognition and posing of emotional expressions by abused children and their mothers. *Developmental Psychology, 24,* 776-781.

Carlson, V., Cicchetti, D., Barnett, D., & Braunwald, K. (1989). Disorganized/disoriented attachment relationships in maltreated infants. *Developmental Psychology, 25,* 525-531.

Casanova, G. M., Domanic, J., McCanne, T. R., & Milner, J. S. (1992). Physiological responses to non-child-related stressors in mothers at risk for child abuse. *Child Abuse & Neglect, 16,* 31-44.

Chan, Y. C. (1994). Parenting stress and social support of mothers who physically abuse their children in Hong Kong. *Child Abuse & Neglect, 18,* 261-269.

Chilamkurti, C., & Milner, J. S. (1993). Perceptions and evaluations of child transgressions and disciplinary techniques in high- and low-risk mothers and their children. *Child Development, 64,* 1801-1814.

Christensen, M. J., Brayden, R. M., Dietrich, M. S., McLaughlin, F. J., Sherrod, K. B., & Altemeier, W. A. (1994). The prospective assessment of self-concept in neglectful and physically abusive low income mothers. *Child Abuse & Neglect, 18,* 225-232.

Cicchetti, D., & Barnett, D. (1992). Attachment organization in maltreated preschools. *Development and Psychopathology, 3,* 397-411.

Cicchetti, D., & Rizley, R. (1981). Developmental perspectives on the etiology, intergenerational transmission, and sequelae of child maltreatment. In R. Rizley & D. Cicchetti (Eds.), *Developmental perspectives on child maltreatment* (pp. 31-55). San Francisco: Jossey-Bass.

Conger, R. D., Burgess, R. L., & Barrett, C. (1979). Child abuse related to life change and perceptions of illness: Some preliminary findings. *Family Coordinator, 28,* 73-78.

Crittenden, P. M. (1981). Abusing, neglecting, problematic, and adequate dyads: Differentiating by patterns of interaction. *Merrill-Palmer Quarterly, 27,* 201-218.

Crittenden, P. M. (1985). Maltreated infants: Vulnerability and resilience. *Journal of Child Psychology and Psychiatry, 26,* 85-96.

Crittenden, P. M. (1988). Distorted patterns of relationship in maltreating families: The role of internal representation models. *Journal of Reproductive and Infant Psychology, 6,* 183-199.

Crittenden, P. M., Partridge, M. F., & Claussen, A. H. (1991). Family patterns of relationships in normative and dysfunctional families. *Development and Psychopathology, 3,* 491-512.

Crowe, H. P., & Zeskind, P. S. (1992). Psychophysiological and perceptual responses to infant cries varying in pitch: Comparison of adults with low and high scores on the Child Abuse Potential Inventory. *Child Abuse & Neglect, 16,* 19-29.

Culp, R. E., Culp, A. M., Soulis, J., & Letts, D. (1989). Self-esteem and depression in abusive, neglecting, and nonmaltreating mothers. *Infant Mental Health Journal, 10,* 243-251.

Diaz, R. M., Neal, C. J., & Vachio, A. (1991). Maternal teaching in the zone of proximal development: A comparison of low- and high-risk dyads. *Merrill-Palmer Quarterly, 37,* 83-107.

Dietrich, D., Berkowitz, L., Kadushin, A., & McGloin, J. (1990). Some factors influencing abusers' justification of their child abuse. *Child Abuse & Neglect, 14,* 337-345.

Dietrich, K. N., Starr, R. H., Jr., & Weisfeld, G. E. (1983). Infant maltreatment: Caretaker-infant interaction and developmental consequences at different levels of parenting failure. *Pediatrics, 72,* 532-540.

Disbrow, M. A., Doerr, H., & Caulfield, C. (1977). Measuring the components of parents' potential for child abuse and neglect. *Child Abuse & Neglect, 1,* 279-296.

Dumas, J. E., Gibson, J. A., & Albin, J. B. (1989). Behavioral correlates of maternal depressive symptomatology in conduct-disordered children. *Journal of Consulting and Clinical Psychology, 57,* 1-6.

During, S. M., & McMahon, R. J. (1991). Recognition of emotional facial expressions by abusive mothers and their children. *Journal of Clinical Child Psychology, 20,* 132-139.

Egeland, B., Breitenbucher, M., & Rosenberg, D. (1980). Prospective study of the significance of life stress in the etiology of child abuse. *Journal of Consulting and Clinical Psychology, 48,* 195-205.

Egeland, B., & Sroufe, L. A. (1981a). Attachment and early maltreatment. *Child Development, 52,* 44-52.

Egeland, B., & Sroufe, L. A. (1981b). Developmental sequela of maltreatment in infancy. *New Directions for Child Development, 11,* 77-92.

Elliott, F. A. (1988). Neurological factors. In V. B. Van Hasselt, R. L. Morrison, A. S. Bellack, & M. Hersen (Eds.), *Handbook of family violence* (pp. 359-382). New York: Plenum.

Evans, A. L. (1980). Personality characteristics and disciplinary attitudes of child-abusing mothers. *Child Abuse & Neglect, 4,* 179-187.

Famularo, R., Stone, K., Barnum, R., & Wharton, R. (1986). Alcoholism and severe child maltreatment. *American Journal of Orthopsychiatry, 56,* 481-485.

Feshbach, N., & Feshbach, S. (1982). Empathy training and the regulation of aggression: Potentialities and limitations. *Academic Psychology Bulletin, 4,* 399-413.

Feshbach, S. (1964). The function of aggression and the regulation of aggressive drive. *Psychological Review, 71,* 257-272.

Friedrich, W. N., Tyler, J. D., & Clark, J. A. (1985). Personality and psychophysiological variables in abusive, neglectful, and low-income control mothers. *Journal of Nervous and Mental Disease, 173,* 449-460.

Frodi, A. M., & Lamb, M. E. (1980). Child abusers' responses to infant smiles and cries. *Child Development, 51,* 238-241.

Gaines, R., Sandgrund, A., Green, A. H., & Power, E. (1978). Etiological factors in child maltreatment: A multivariate study of abusing, neglecting, and normal mothers. *Journal of Abnormal Psychology, 87,* 531-540.

Gil, D. G. (1970). *Violence against children.* Cambridge, MA: Harvard University Press.

Hansen, D. J., Pallotta, G. M., Tishelman, A. C., Conaway, L. P., & MacMillan, V. M. (1989). Parental problem-solving skills and child behavior problems: A comparison of physically abusive, neglectful, clinic, and community families. *Journal of Family Violence, 4,* 353-368.

Hillson, J. M. C., & Kupier, N. A. (1994). A stress and coping model of child maltreatment. *Clinical Psychology Review, 14,* 261-285.

Kelleher, K., Chaffin, M., Hollenberg, J., & Fischer, E. (1994). Alcohol and drug disorders among physically abusive and neglectful parents in a community-based sample. *American Journal of Public Health, 84,* 1586-1590.

Kelly, J. A. (1983). *Treating child-abusive families: Intervention based on skills-training principles.* New York: Plenum.

Kempe, C. H., Silverman, F. N., Steele, B. F., Droegemueller, W., & Silver, H. K. (1962). The battered child syndrome. *Journal of the American Medical Association, 181,* 105-112.

Knutson, J. F. (1978). Child abuse as an area of aggression research. *Journal of Pediatric Psychology, 3,* 20-27.

Kravitz, R. I., & Driscoll, J. M. (1983). Expectations for childhood development among child-abusing and nonabusing parents. *American Journal of Orthopsychiatry, 53,* 336-344.

Kropp, J. P., & Haynes, O. M. (1987). Abusive and nonabusive mothers' ability to identify general and specific emotion signals of infants. *Child Development, 58,* 187-190.

Lahey, B. B., Conger, R. D., Atkeson, B. M., & Treiber, F. A. (1984). Parenting behavior and emotional status of physically abusive mothers. *Journal of Consulting and Clinical Psychology, 52,* 1062-1071.

Lamb, M. E., Gaensbauer, T. J., Malkin, C. M., & Schultz, L. A. (1985). The effects of child maltreatment on security of infant-adult attachment. *Infant Behavior and Development, 8,* 35-45.

Larrance, D. T., & Twentyman, C. T. (1983). Maternal attributions and child abuse. *Journal of Abnormal Psychology, 92,* 449-457.

Lawson, K. A., & Hays, J. R. (1989). Self-esteem and stress as factors in abuse of children. *Psychological Reports, 65,* 1259-1265.

Leonard, K. E., & Jacob, T. (1988). Alcohol, alcoholism, and family violence. In V. B. Van Hasselt, R. L. Morrison, A. S. Bellack, & M. Hersen (Eds.), *Handbook of family violence* (pp. 383-406). New York: Plenum.

Letourneau, C. (1981). Empathy and stress: How they affect parental aggression. *Social Work, 26,* 383-389.

Lyons-Ruth, K., Connell, D. B., Zoll, D., & Stahl, J. (1987). Infants at social risk: Relations among infant maltreatment, maternal behavior, and infant attachment behavior. *Developmental Psychology, 23,* 223-232.

Mash, E. J., Johnston, C., & Kovitz, K. (1983). A comparison of the mother-child interactions of physically abused and non-abused children during play and task situations. *Journal of Clinical Child Psychology, 12,* 337-346.

Mash, E. J., & Wolfe, D. A. (1991). Methodological issues in research on physical child abuse. *Criminal Justice and Behavior, 18,* 8-29.

McCanne, T. R., & Milner, J. S. (1991). Physiological reactivity of physically abusive and at-risk subjects to child-related stimuli. In J. S. Milner (Ed.), *Neuropsychology of aggression* (pp. 147-166). Boston: Kluwer Academic.

McCubbin, H. I., Cauble, A. E., & Patterson, J. M. (1982). *Family stress, coping, and social support.* Springfield, IL: Charles C. Thomas.

Melnick, B., & Hurley, J. R. (1969). Distinctive personality attributes of child-abusing mothers. *Journal of Consulting and Clinical Psychology, 33,* 746-749.

Miller, P. A., & Eisenberg, N. (1988). The relation of empathy to aggressive and externalizing/antisocial behavior. *Psychological Bulletin, 103,* 324-344.

Milner, J. S. (1986). *The Child Abuse Potential Inventory: Manual* (2nd ed.). Webster, NC: Psytec.

Milner, J. S. (1988). An ego-strength scale for the Child Abuse Potential Inventory. *Journal of Family Violence, 3,* 151-162.

Milner, J. S. (1993). Social information processing and physical child abuse. *Clinical Psychology Review, 13,* 275-294.

Milner, J. S. (1994). Assessing physical child abuse risk: The Child Abuse Potential Inventory. *Clinical Psychology Review, 14,* 547-583.

Milner, J. S., & Foody, R. (1994). The impact of mitigating information on attributions for positive and negative child behavior by adults at low- and high-risk for child-abusive behavior. *Journal of Social and Clinical Psychology, 13,* 335-351.

Milner, J. S., Halsey, L. B., & Fultz, J. (1995). Empathic responsiveness and affective reactivity to infant stimuli in high- and low-risk for physical child abuse mothers. *Child Abuse & Neglect, 19,* 767-780.

Milner, J. S., & McCanne, T. R. (1991). Neuropsychological correlates of physical child abuse. In J. S. Milner (Ed.), *Neuropsychology of aggression* (pp. 131-145). Boston: Kluwer Academic.

Milner, J. S., & Robertson, K. R. (1990). Comparison of physical child abusers, intrafamilial sexual child abusers, and child neglecters. *Journal of Interpersonal Violence, 5,* 37-48.

Milner, J. S., & Wimberley, R. C. (1979). An inventory for the identification of child abusers. *Journal of Clinical Psychology, 35,* 95-100.

Milner, J. S., & Wimberley, R. C. (1980). Prediction and explanation of child abuse. *Journal of Clinical Psychology, 36,* 875-884.

Nayak, M., & Milner, J. S. (1995). *Neuropsychological correlates of physical child abuse.* Unpublished manuscript.

Newberger, C. M., & Cook, S. J. (1983). Parental awareness and child abuse and neglect: A cognitive developmental analysis of urban and rural samples. *American Journal of Orthopsychiatry, 53,* 512-524.

Oates, R. K., & Forrest, D. (1985). Self-esteem and early background of abusive mothers. *Child Abuse & Neglect, 9,* 89-93.

Oates, R. K., Forrest, D., & Peacock, A. (1985). Mothers of abused children: A comparison study. *Clinical Pediatrics, 24,* 9-13.

Oldershaw, L., Walters, G. C., & Hall, D. K. (1986). Control strategies and noncompliance in abusive mother-child dyads: An observational study. *Child Development, 57,* 722-732.

Parke, R. D., & Slaby, R. G. (1983). The development of aggression. In E. M. Hetherington (Ed.), *Manual of child psychology: Vol. 4. Socialization, personality, and social development* (pp. 549-641). New York: John Wiley.

Passman, R. H., & Mulhern, R. K. (1977). Maternal punitiveness as affected by situational stress: An experimental analogue of child abuse. *Journal of Abnormal Psychology, 86,* 565-569.

Perry, M. A., Wells, E. A., & Doran, L. D. (1983). Parent characteristics in abusing and nonabusing families. *Journal of Clinical Child Psychology, 12,* 329-336.

Pianta, R., Egeland, B., & Erickson, M. F. (1989). The antecedents of maltreatment: Results of the Mother-Child Interaction Research Project. In D. Cicchetti & V. Carlson (Eds.), *Child maltreatment: Theory and research on the causes and consequences of child abuse and neglect* (pp. 203-253). New York: Cambridge University Press.

Pruitt, D. L., & Erickson, M. T. (1985). The Child Abuse Potential Inventory: A study of concurrent validity. *Journal of Clinical Psychology, 41,* 104-111.

Reid, J. B., Kavanagh, K., & Baldwin, D. V. (1987). Abusive parents' perceptions of child problem behaviors: An example of parental bias. *Journal of Abnormal Child Psychology, 15,* 457-466.

Reid, J. B., Taplin, P. S., & Lorber, R. (1981). A social interactional approach to the treatment of abusive families. In R. B. Stewart (Ed.), *Violent behavior: Social learning approaches to prediction, management, and treatment* (pp. 83-101). New York: Brunner/Mazel.

Rosen, B. (1978). Self-concept disturbance among mothers who abuse their children. *Psychological Reports, 43,* 323-326.

Rosenberg, M. S., & Reppucci, N. D. (1983). Abusive mothers: Perceptions of their own and their children's behavior. *Journal of Consulting and Clinical Psychology, 51,* 674-682.

Schmidt, E., & Eldridge, A. (1986). The attachment relationship and child maltreatment. *Infant Mental Health Journal, 7,* 264-273.

Schneider-Rosen, K., Braunwald, K. G., Carlson, V., & Cicchetti, D. (1985). Current perspectives in attachment theory: Illustration from the study of maltreated infants. In I. Bretherton & E. Waters (Eds.), Growing points in attachment theory and research. *Monographs of the Society for Research in Child Development, 50*(1-2, Serial No. 209), 194-210.

Schneider-Rosen, K., & Cicchetti, D. (1984). The relationship between affect and cognition in maltreated infants: Quality of attachment and the development of visual self-recognition. *Child Development, 55,* 648-658.

Shorkey, C. T. (1980). Sense of personal worth, self-esteem, and anomia of child-abusing mothers and controls. *Journal of Clinical Psychology, 36,* 817-820.

Shorkey, C. T., & Armendariz, J. (1985). Personal worth, self-esteem, anomia, hostility, and irrational thinking of abusing mothers: A multivariate approach. *Journal of Clinical Psychology, 41,* 414-421.

Spinetta, J. J. (1978). Parental personality factors in child abuse. *Journal of Consulting and Clinical Psychology, 46,* 1409-1414.

Starr, R. H., Jr. (1982). A research-based approach to the prediction of child abuse. In R. H. Starr, Jr. (Ed.), *Child abuse prediction: Policy implications* (pp. 105-134). Cambridge, MA: Ballinger.

Stasiewicz, P. R., & Lisman, S. A. (1989). Effects of infant cries on alcohol consumption in college males at risk for child abuse. *Child Abuse & Neglect, 13,* 463-470.

Steele, B. F., & Pollock, C. B. (1974). A psychiatric study of parents who abuse infants and small children. In R. E. Helfer & C. H. Kempe (Eds.), *The battered child* (2nd ed., pp. 103-147). Chicago: University of Chicago Press.

Susman, E. J., Trickett, P. K., Iannotti, R. J., Hollenbeck, B. E., & Zahn-Waxler, C. (1985). Child-rearing patterns in depressed, abusive, and normal mothers. *American Journal of Orthopsychiatry, 55,* 237-251.

Trickett, P. K., & Kuczynski, L. (1986). Children's misbehaviors and parental discipline strategies in abusive and nonabusive families. *Developmental Psychology, 22,* 115-123.

Trickett, P. K., & Susman, E. J. (1988). Parental perceptions of child-rearing practices in physically abusive and nonabusive families. *Developmental Psychology, 24,* 270-276.

Twentyman, C. T., & Plotkin, R. C. (1982). Unrealistic expectations of parents who maltreat their children: An educational deficit that pertains to child maltreatment. *Journal of Clinical Psychology, 38,* 497-503.

Twentyman, C. T., Rohrbeck, C. A., & Amish, P. L. (1984). A cognitive-behavioral model of child abuse. In S. Saunders, A. M. Anderson, C. A. Hart, & G. M. Rubenstein (Eds.), *Violent individuals and families: A handbook for practitioners* (pp. 87-111). Springfield, IL: Charles C. Thomas.

Tzeng, O. C. S., Jackson, J. W., & Karlson, H. C. (1991). *Theories of child abuse and neglect: Differential perspectives, summaries, and evaluations.* New York: Praeger.

Wiehe, V. R. (1987). Empathy and locus of control in child abusers. *Journal of Social Service Research, 9,* 17-30.

Williamson, J., Borduin, C., & Howe, B. (1991). The ecology of adolescent maltreatment: A multilevel examination of adolescent physical abuse, sexual abuse, and neglect. *Journal of Consulting and Clinical Psychology, 59,* 449-457.

Wolfe, D. A. (1987). *Child abuse: Implications for child development and psychopathology.* Newbury Park, CA: Sage.

Wolfe, D. A., Edwards, B., Manion, I., & Koverola, C. (1988). Early intervention for parents at risk of child abuse and neglect: A preliminary investigation. *Journal of Consulting and Clinical Psychology, 56,* 40-47.

Wolfe, D. A., Fairbank, J. A., Kelly, J. A., & Bradlyn, A. S. (1983). Child abusive parents' physiological responses to stressful and non-stressful behavior in children. *Behavioral Assessment, 5,* 363-371.

Wood-Shuman, S., & Cone, J. D. (1986). Differences in abusive, at-risk for abuse, and control
        mothers' descriptions of normal child behavior. *Child Abuse & Neglect, 10,* 397-405.
Wright, L. (1976). The "sick but slick" syndrome as a personality component of parents of
        battered children. *Journal of Clinical Psychology, 32,* 41-45.
Young, L. (1964). *Wednesday's children: A study of child abuse and neglect.* New York:
        McGraw-Hill.

3

Children and Youth Who Witness Violence

NEW DIRECTIONS IN INTERVENTION AND PREVENTION

MARLIES SUDERMANN

PETER JAFFE

Children and youth who witness wife assault/domestic violence are a neglected high-risk group. They are at greatly elevated risk of becoming involved in violent relationships, both with peers and in adult relationships. In addition, they are at significantly elevated risk for a wide spectrum of serious emotional and behavioral problems, and their school achievement is often compromised. Yet their needs remain poorly recognized and understood. The needs and risks of children who witness violence in the home are not sufficiently recognized by mental health and child protection professionals, law enforcement personnel, school teachers or administrators, health care providers, or social science researchers. The myth that there are no substantial consequences for children as long as the children themselves are not physically harmed in incidents of domestic violence/wife assault remains prevalent in the beliefs and protocols of the above-mentioned groups.

In large part, this myth is a consequence of society's slowness in acknowledging the widespread nature and seriousness of wife assault and people's unwillingness to take action to stop it. The American Medical Association has indicated that U.S. women are four times more likely to suffer physical injury at the hands of their own male partners than from motor vehicle accidents (American Medical Association, 1992). Murray Straus, in the first large-scale U.S. survey, estimated that 1.8 million women experience at least one act of violence by their husband or common-law partner *each year* and that 500,000 women experience a severe beating *each year* (Straus, 1978). Straus also indicated that these numbers are underestimates because of the stigma of reporting such incidents in a survey. A well-conducted random telephone survey found that *one in four* women has experienced violence at the hands of a current or past marital partner and that of those women who reported violence in a current marriage, 34% have at some point thought their lives were in danger (Statistics Canada, 1993). Moreover, severe repeated violence is estimated to take place in 1 out of 14 families (Dutton, 1988). Yet up until the present, many if not most police interventions, mental health services, family and emergency physicians, and school programs had no provision for meeting the needs of children in these circumstances. Child protection legislation in many jurisdictions makes little reference to children who witness violence as a group in need of protection. Primary prevention of violence in relationships, domestic violence, or wife assault has been very slow to get started.

This chapter provides an overview of the evidence that children who witness violence are harmed in terms of their emotional health and behavioral adjustment. Evidence relating witnessing violence to becoming involved in violent behavior and relationships is presented, and group programs for children who witness wife assault are described. Finally, a description and evaluation of an innovative school-based primary-prevention program for violence in relationships is presented.

EFFECTS ON CHILDREN WHO WITNESS VIOLENCE

Children who witness violence are affected by it in a serious and broad-ranging manner. Deleterious effects may occur in the emotional, behavioral, and school areas. These children may experience depression, anxiety, somatic (bodily) complaints of no physical cause, peer conflicts, social isolation and preoccupation, and noncompliance with adults and conflict with the law, as well as a host of other behavioral problems. Many children experience full-blown post-traumatic stress disorder. The effects on a particular child or youth are mediated by many factors, including age, strengths and coping style, gender, severity and frequency of violence witnessed, whether the violence has stopped or may resume, and severity of attendant stressors, especially the effects on the mother's parenting availability because of her own trauma. The availability of legal and social protection for the mother and children has an important effect in ameliorating or exacerbating the effects on children. Children who witness violence at home are children who are living in a war zone, but the aggressor is their own father, or father figure in many cases. These children often have no safe place in which to escape the violence, and most often there are strong familial and social pressures not to tell about the violence when it is occurring. We examine this area of research in more detail in the following sections.

Children in Shelters

Much of the first research on the effects of witnessing domestic violence was done by shelter workers who noted the difficulties of children who accompanied their mothers to shelters. Prior to the availability of shelters, very little was noted or observed about these children because the problem was so hidden. For example, Layzer, Goodson, and deLange (1985) reported on their observations from six shelter-based projects. They noted that these children typically (over 70%) showed mood-related problems such as anxiousness, excessive crying, and sadness. Sleep disturbance was also common, and in addition, about 40% of the children had difficulties interacting with adults. Hughes (1982) noted a similar picture, calling these children "emotionally needy." In addition, she noted that boys in her sample were more likely to be defiant and destructive, acting out their anger and confusion. Young girls, in contrast, were noted to be more clingy and dependent. Hughes noted that many of the latency-age boys (ages 6-11) identified strongly with their fathers and expressed more ambivalence with regard to their mothers than other children. These boys also seemed to be conflicted in their feelings toward their fathers, on the one hand missing them greatly, but on the other hand believing that reuniting with them was not desirable. Sopp-Gilson (1980) also noted the ambivalence of children, especially boys, about being at the shelter. She also noted a 24-hour crisis period after admission, but thereafter the children were more settled in their behavior. After settling in, however, many children, especially young boys, began mimicking the aggressive behavior they had witnessed by being aggressive toward females, including girls, female staff, and their mothers. Sopp-Gilson also described the girls' behavior as being very withdrawn, as if they were trying hard not to be noticed. Other problems noted by shelter workers include sleep, appetite, and weight-gain disturbances in infants; wetting and soiling problems; and facial tics (Hughes, 1982). Many children are angry and upset about having to leave their homes, neighborhoods, and schools, but at the same time some children find the shelter environment a relief after the violent and often socially isolated family life they have been used to (Sopp-Gilson, 1980).

How Many Children Witness the Violence?

Often, parents believe they have shielded their children from much of the violence. However, children have often seen or overheard much more than the parents, both mothers and fathers, realize or are willing to admit. Estimates of the amount of domestic violence in which children are present ranges from 40% to 80% (Jaffe, Wolfe, & Wilson, 1990). Even in those instances where the children do not witness the physical violence, they may overhear the incident and witness the aftermath, such as injuries to their mother and damage to the home. It is important to recognize that a violent marital relationship has many aspects other than the physical violence itself; almost all physical violence is accompanied by verbal abuse and attempts by the abuser to belittle, dominate, and control the person who is abused. Therefore, even if the children do not witness all the acute episodes, they still experience a very hostile/fearful and unhealthy environment between their parents. Often, the violence does not end with separation. The period of separation may be the most dangerous for the abused woman and her children, and many courts may even ignore this fact while ordering inappropriate custody or visitation arrangements (Jaffe, 1995).

Post-Traumatic Stress Disorder

Post-traumatic stress disorder (PTSD) is a reaction or syndrome increasingly recognized in children who have witnessed violent episodes. The criteria for PTSD (American Psychiatric Association, 1994) include (a) exposure to an event involving threat of death or serious injury to self or others, and a reaction of fear and helplessness (or, in children, agitation or disorganized behavior); (b) reexperiencing of the traumatic event, in the form of recurrent and intrusive distressing recollections of the event (or, in young children, expression of the same through play), or recurrent and distressing dreams about the event, or reactivity to the event that resembles or symbolizes the event; (c) persistent avoidance of stimuli associated with the trauma and numbing of general responsiveness; and (d) persistent symptoms of increased arousal, including some or all of difficulty falling or staying asleep, irritability or outbursts of anger, difficulty concentrating, hypervigilance, and exaggerated startle response. Avoidance symptoms can sometimes manifest themselves as general unresponsiveness to others and feelings of detachment, as well as a restricted range of feelings. Duration of the symptoms must be more than 1 month, and the disturbance causes clinically significant distress or lowering of functioning in social and occupational (or school) areas. This syndrome was first described in conjunction with Vietnam veterans to capture the serious and continuing effects that many of these persons experienced. Because exposure to violence, unpredictability, and lack of control over the situation was similar for children who lived with domestic violence, it would be natural for researchers to explore this syndrome with respect to these children.

Pioneering work in the area of post-traumatic stress in children focused on children who witness extremes of woman abuse, such as children who witness their mother's murder (Black & Kaplan, 1988), or looked at the symptoms of children who have witnessed murder, rape, or severe assault of their mother (e.g., Pynoos & Eth, 1984, 1985). These studies found that PTSD is present in virtually all these children. Studies of PTSD in children who witness woman abuse of a less catastrophic severity toward their mother by their father have just begun to be reported. One study that noted the presence of PTSD symptoms in children who had witnessed family violence had actually intended to study the traumatic effects of community violence on children (Osofsky, Wewers, Hann, & Fick, 1993).

Lehmann (1995) conducted a well-controlled study of PTSD in more than 80 children who had witnessed wife assault/domestic violence, most of whom were residing in a shelter for battered women. Some children were also recruited from second-stage housing, programs for women who have been in a shelter but who desire help in getting established in the community once they separate from their partners. Some children were from community-based treatment groups for children who have witnessed violence. Lehmann's results indicated that fully 57% of his sample met criteria for full-blown PTSD and that most of the other children had some of the symptoms. This study shows the seriousness of the aftereffects of witnessing domestic violence/wife assault.

Magnitude and Nature of Symptoms

The level of severity of symptoms for children who have witnessed violence has been explored in a number of studies. A series of studies by Jaffe, Wolfe, and colleagues indicated that the magnitude and breadth of effects on children is serious and considerable. For example, Jaffe, Wolfe, Wilson, and Zak (1986) found that boys who witnessed violence had similar levels of emotional and behavioral problems as boys from matched socio-demographic groups who had themselves been physically abused. Both groups were much more disturbed in their emotions and behavior than nonabused, nonwitnessing children. A number of studies have found that both boys and girls who have witnessed violence tend to have elevated scores on the Achenbach Child Behavior Checklist (CBCL; Jaffe et al., 1986; Moore & Pepler, 1989; Sternberg et al., 1993). Sternberg et al. (1993) also found that children who had witnessed violence had higher scores on the Children's Depression Inventory than comparison children. The level of the depression scores was considered similar to that of children referred to children's mental health centers. In the Sternberg et al. study, the percentage of children whose CBCL scores were in the clinical intervention range ($t = 63$) and above was similar across groups of children who had witnessed spousal abuse and those who were both witnesses and victims of physical abuse. Both groups of children who had witnesssed violence were significantly more disturbed than the comparison group.

Hughes (1988) found that children who had witnessed violence had lower scores on measures of self-concept than comparison children. Other noted symptoms include less sense of control and self-efficacy, lowered levels of social competence (Wolfe, Zak, Wilson, & Jaffe, 1986), and poorer school achievement and social problem solving (Pepler, Moore, Mae, & Kates, 1989). Hughes found lowered self-esteem in children who had witnessed violence. In short, a wide range of children's functioning appears compromised in children who have witnessed domestic violence.

Many of the symptoms that children experience as a result of witnessing violence interfere with normal development in the emotional and social areas, as well as in the behavioral area. Children who have witnessed violence are often using their energies to avoid being reminded of the abuse or are preoccupied with various forms of reexperiencing, such as nightmares and flashbacks. They are, at latency and adolescent ages, often very concerned with such matters as the safety of their mother, incidents of harassment by the abuser, and how their father is doing after the separation, and with adjusting to the life changes that occur as a result of the violence, such as separating from and possibly reuniting with father or mother's partner. Thus, they are often not paying attention to school or peers or normal activities to the same extent as children who have not witnessed violence.

Gender Differences

Findings with regard to gender differences in reaction to witnessing violence have been mixed. As mentioned earlier, observations from shelters have tended to find that boys react with more overt violence and conduct problems, whereas girls tend to become clingy, inhibited, and timid in the immediate aftermath of violence. This pattern was found in a number of studies (Hughes & Barad, 1983; Rosenbaum & O'Leary, 1981; Wolfe, Jaffe, Wilson, & Zak, 1985). Rosenberg (1984), however, found an interaction between level of violence witnessed and the child's coping methods. Specifically, where a lower level of violence was observed, boys tended to have aggression problems and girls tended to be too passive and to have internalizing problems. Where a higher level of violence was observed, this pattern tended to be reversed, with girls becoming more aggressive and boys more passive. Also, Sternberg et al. (1993) found that girls had more internalizing and externalizing (aggression) problems than boys when a sample of children who witnessed violence and a group who both witnessed violence and were themselves abused were combined. In the Sternberg et al. study, girls who witnessed violence but were not themselves physically abused had markedly higher levels of internalizing problems than boys but were at comparable levels to boys in externalizing problems. Whatever the group tendencies, in clinical practice and in the shelter setting, one is likely to encounter both boys and girls with internalizing and externalizing problems.

Age Differences

One myth that practitioners in legal, police, mental health, and other areas sometimes believe is that very young children will not be significantly affected by witnessing violence in their families. In fact, even infants have been noted to have severe problems, including disruption of eating and sleeping patterns, excessive crying (Jaffe et al., 1990), poor weight gain, and slowing of development. The research of Cummings and Davies (1994) has shown that even very young children react negatively and become very distressed when they overhear or witness verbal conflict between their adult caretakers and others. In general, fear, anxiety, and development of aggressive, noncompliant patterns tend to express themselves in the main developmental tasks of each age-group. Very young children have difficulties in their eating, sleeping, and mood; preschool and latency-age children show disruption in social skills and compliance with adults; school-age children show problems in school achievement; and adolescents may run away, be truant from school, become involved with substance abuse, or come in conflict with the law (Jaffe et al., 1990).

Areas for Further Study

Clearly, the study of children who witness violence is in the early stages. Factors such as the severity and frequency of violence witnessed, the age of onset and cessation of witnessing violence, and the relative effects of witnessing the violence itself versus mediation of the effects on children through the effects on the mother's stress, coping, and availability, and the disruption to home settings need to be addressed. The concurrent effects of child physical and sexual abuse in combination with witnessing violence is another area to address, especially because the co-occurrence of child and spousal abuse has been estimated to be around 30% to 40% (Jaffe at al., 1990; Straus, Gelles, & Steinmetz, 1980). Methodological issues also need to be addressed in further studies, including the appropriate use of control groups and the difficulty in obtaining reliable measures of the frequency and severity of violence witnessed.

Links With Adult Problem Behavior and Violence

Although few or no longitudinal studies have been done to follow up children who have witnessed violence, there are increasing indicators that witnessing violence as a child or youth in the home predisposes a person toward involvement in violent relationships. For example, the large-scale Statistics Canada survey of 1993 found that women who reported having a violent father-in-law were at three times higher risk than women with nonviolent fathers-in-law. Straus et al. (1980), in their large U.S. national survey, found that males who had observed their parents attack each other were three times more likely to have assaulted their wives within the past year than were men who had not witnessed family violence. Thirty-five percent of men who had witnessed domestic violence had hit their wives in the preceding year, compared with 10.7% of men who had not witnessed domestic violence. Head (1988), in a study of dating violence in high school students, found that males who said the adults in their home sometimes used violence on each other were four times more likely (30% vs. 7.2% for all males) to report using physical force with a dating partner. The convergence of the findings in these studies is very close and adds to the confidence in the finding that witnessing violence in the family of origin has a profound influence on violence in the next generation.

GROUPS FOR CHILDREN WHO
HAVE WITNESSED VIOLENCE

The severity and frequency of symptoms among children who have witnessed woman abuse/domestic violence indicate the need for intervention with these children. *Structured group treatment* (Jaffe et al., 1990; Peled & Edleson, 1995) is a common intervention preference for these children. The groups are usually 6 to 10 sessions in length and have a strong educative component. Jaffe et al. (1990) reported implementing groups for 8- to 10-year-olds, and 11- to 13-year-olds, with 10 sessions of about 90 minutes each. The issues addressed include labeling feelings, dealing with anger, safety skills, social support, social competence and self-concept, responsibility for parent/violence, understanding family violence, and wishes about family. Evaluation of this method indicated that, after the intervention, children showed significant improvement in safety skills; and their perception of each parent improved, possibly as a result of increased understanding of the impact of the violence on their mothers, increased separation of their feelings of love toward their fathers, and their rejection of the fathers' violent behavior. Whereas mothers reported improved behavior on the part of their children after the group, these perceptions were not discernable on the CBCL. In conclusion, these authors noted that group intervention may be best suited to children who have mild to moderate behavioral problems. The group process is less successful for children who have been exposed to repeated acts of severe violence over many years.

Peled and Edleson (1995) noted four goals for the groups run in association with the Minneapolis Domestic Program: (a) breaking the secret, (b) learning to protect oneself, (c) having a positive experience, and (d) strengthening self-esteem. Their qualitative evaluation of these groups indicates that these goals can be met in the context of children's groups.

Recently, a new questionnaire for evaluating children's responses to groups for children who have witnessed violence has been developed (Sudermann, Marshall, Miller, & Miller-Hewitt, 1995) and is being used to evaluate a series of children's groups. Preliminary findings indicate positive results in all the areas addressed, including improving safety skills, assigning appropriate responsibility for violence, dispelling myths about wife assault, and learning a wider range of nonviolent responses to conflict. Each of these evaluations of children's group interventions was relatively informal in nature and did not include design features such as control groups of children who did not participate in the intervention. Therefore, caution must be exercised in drawing conclusions from these two studies. A study of children including a wait-list control group, as well as a follow-up evaluation, would be desirable.

PRIMARY PREVENTION OF
RELATIONSHIP VIOLENCE

Given the serious nature of the problems that face children who have witnessed wife assault/domestic violence, as well as the links between witnessing violence and engaging in violence later on, it makes sense to develop primary prevention programs that address the problems of violence in relationships. As we have argued elsewhere (Sudermann & Jaffe, 1995), high school is a prime opportunity for offering primary prevention programs aimed at violence in relationships. Youth are just becoming involved in dating relationships and consolidating their values and identity separate from their parents during this period. In broad-based school programs, one can also affect the knowledge and attitudes of youth who will not themselves become involved in physical violence in relationships, but who may become the future health, social service and legal professionals, front-line workers, and community residents. Also, violence begins early in dating relationships and is widespread. O'Leary, Malone, and Tyree (1994) conducted a longitudinal study of more than 300 couples who were first recruited while they were dating, just prior to their marriage. They found that "it became evident that we would have had to interview many of these young adults almost as soon as they began dating to assess the first instance of physical aggression in the relationship" (p. 594). Also, more than half the couples reported some form of physical aggression when they were interviewed prior to the marriage. Early intervention on a broad scale is preferable to treating only the worst cases of relationship violence after the problems become pronounced.

Although interest in school-based violence prevention programs is strong in many areas, with numerous programs being published (Sudermann, Jaffe, & Hastings, 1993), very few programs have been evaluated as to outcome. Jones (1987) employed a brief assessment measure to evaluate changes after an intervention focusing on family and dating violence. It was found that although knowledge increased, attitudes were not affected. Hilton, Harris, and Rice (1994) conducted an intervention that was modeled, in part, after the approach of the London Family Court Clinic (London, Ontario), with 2,168 high school students at nine high schools. They employed speakers in large group sessions, as well as classroom sessions, for a total of 2 hours of intervention. This intervention focused mostly on improving knowledge about violence in dating relationships, but in a departure from the approach we use, attitude change was not a focus. The evaluation employed a 7-item questionnaire, administered before, immediately after, and about 6 weeks following the intervention. Modest increases were found in the students' willingness to help a friend and knowing where to get help, and these changes were still present, but not as strong, at follow-up. Girls changed more than boys. There was no impact on attitudes about date rape, which is not surprising, given that attitude change was not targeted for intervention. Because changes in the boys' responses were less marked than expected, the researchers suggested that future interventions focus less on relationship violence and more on topics such as anger control and "fair fighting." However, not targeting the issues of relationship violence specifically might lead to even less change in this area.

Macgowan (1995) studied a sample of 440 students in Grades 6 to 9 who received a 5-hour intervention with regard to relationship violence. The design included pre- and posttest measures of knowledge, attitudes, and methods of dealing with relationship violence, and an untreated control group was employed. The results indicated positive gains in the treatment group, compared with the control group, in the areas of knowledge and attitudes about nonphysical violence. No changes were seen in attitudes about physical violence or in methods of dealing with relationship violence. There was an interaction between gender and academic level, with male advanced students making more gains than males in the general academic level.

We previously evaluated a large-scale intervention program for high school students that focused on family violence, its effects on children and youth, and dating violence (Jaffe, Sudermann, Reitzel, & Killip, 1992). The intervention was part of a larger effort that included training for teachers and administrators and curriculum integration. The focus of the evaluation, however, was the student special event. Each school had a school-based committee that organized a large-group auditorium presentation, followed by classroom-based discussion. The special event was either a full- or half-day special session for students that involved speakers from community groups, videos, a theater presentation, and classroom discussion facilitated by teachers and a community representative in each classroom. The community representatives were from social agencies and were knowledgeable about issues of family violence, wife assault, and dating violence. This study used the London Family Court Clinic Questionnaire on Violence in Relationships with 737 students. The subjects were a stratified (by grade and academic program level) random sample from four high schools. The questionnaire was administered immediately prior to, about 1 week after, and about 6 weeks after a 1-day intervention on violence in relationships. Students received both the intervention and the questionnaire, and no control group was used.

The results were very interesting in several respects. Significant changes were found from pre- to postintervention, and the majority of these changes were maintained at the delayed posttest or follow-up. Significant positive changes were found in students' knowledge about violence in relationships, in their beliefs and attitudes about violence in relationships, and in their behavioral intentions with regard to intervening in dating violence. Again, however, more positive changes occurred for girls than for boys. A few changes in the undesired direction also occurred at posttest, for males only. Other interesting aspects of the study were the extent of gender differences in knowledge and attitudes at the pretest level, with females having significantly more positive beliefs and attitudes than males on 13 of 16 items measuring attitudes and beliefs. Similarly, differences were found in behavioral intentions with regard to intervening in dating violence among peers, with girls being more likely to intervene, both at pre- and posttest. We concluded that the program was effective over all and that students were highly supportive of interventions such as this. Although a 1-day program is not sufficient to address the issue of preventing dating violence and violence in the family, it does have a positive, measurable impact.

Questions remaining include ways to reduce the negative changes in attitudes that some boys in this study experienced at posttest. Some possible explanations of this effect are that some boys may already have been engaged in dating violence and they found that this program produced cognitive dissonance or guilt (to which they reacted by reporting worse attitudes after the intervention). Even males who were not involved in abusive relationships may have perceived the intervention as being directed against values of male toughness or against male preeminence in relationships, values their families or society have led them to hold. The program may have conflicted with these values and may have seemed anti-male to some students. This was expressed in the classroom discussions in more than one instance, directly and indirectly. For example, one male indicated that he did not believe that equal power sharing in marital relationships was going to happen for young people from his neighborhood, that someone had to be in charge, preferably the male. A more common, but less direct, response was for male students (and even teachers) to challenge statistics on violence that were presented. A challenge for further programs is to overcome this resistance while still addressing issues of relationship violence.

Since the evaluation mentioned above, programs for violence prevention in our local school systems have developed and evolved. More curriculum integration of violence prevention objectives is occurring at all grade levels. Teachers are more informed and involved, and both the schools and the administration are focusing on reducing all forms of violence in the school environment. We now turn to a description of A.S.A.P., an antiviolence program for schools.

A.S.A.P.: A SCHOOL-BASED
ANTIVIOLENCE PROGRAM

To disseminate our violence prevention approach, we wrote *A.S.A.P.: A School-Based Antiviolence Program* (Sudermann, Jaffe, & Hastings, 1993), a 234-page manual that describes a model of preventing violence with school-based programs that have the support of community agencies and members. Although A.S.A.P. deals with a broad range of violence issues, such as bullying and violence in the media and in literature, its special focus is on violence in relationships and violence against women. A.S.A.P. outlines how to encourage involvement from all sectors of a school system, including students, administrators, teachers, and support staff, for violence prevention. Techniques for involving community agencies and survivors of violence are also included. How to organize professional development for educators and support staff, information events for parents, and special events for students are outlined. Special awareness techniques that have been proven successful include theatrical productions (by students or professional companies), videos, speakers who are older students and survivors of violence, and community speakers. Other issues are described, such as dealing with disclosures and developing protocols for children who are residing in shelters with their mothers.

Curriculum integration of violence prevention is described, and recommendations are made for developing a violence-free school climate. School climate issues are addressed by development of school mission statements and codes of conduct with explicit references to violence, sexual harassment, and racial and ethnic-based harassment. The role of prompt, firm, and consistent handling of violent incidents on the schoolyard and in the school is stressed, as is the need for a warm and accepting school environment. The importance of changing school traditions with a violent component, including school sports and sports team names, is stressed. School award programs that reward prosocial, nonviolent social skills are described. Also, the importance of fostering gender equity and racial/ethnic equity in the school, including staff and student leadership positions, is stressed as an important substrate of a nonviolent school climate. An extensive resource section is provided so that teachers and administrators can make an easy and informed choice of resource materials, such as videos and curricular resource materials, to support their violence prevention efforts. Finally, a section on ways to overcome resistance and roadblocks is included.

A focus on preventing violence in relationships often entails a type of cultural change in a school and is best seen as a process, rather than as a limited, one-time event or effort (although a well-planned special event can be an excellent starting point for moving to a nonviolent school environment). Many factors, characteristics, and behaviors differentiate schools that have successfully implemented violence prevention from those that have not. Some of the differences that we see as important are shown in Table 3.1.

TABLE 3.1   Violent Versus Nonviolent School Climate

Nonimplementation/Violent	*Successful Implementation/Nonviolent*
Violent school symbols (e.g., team names)	Nonviolent school symbols (e.g., team names)
No mention of sexual or ethnic/racial harassment or sexual assault in school code of conduct	School code of conduct explicitly recognizes and provides sanctions for different forms of violence, including sexual and racial harassment and sexual assault
Gender imbalance in school sports funding	Gender balance in school sports funding
Violent school sports encouraged and glorified	Nonviolent wide-participation sports emphasized
Gender imbalance in student leadership positions	No sexism and racism in school administrative structure and there is appropriate gender balance in student government
Teachers unaware of prevalence and symptoms of children who witness violence	Teachers well versed in prevalence and symptoms of children who are witnessing violence at home, are being abused, or are experiencing dating violence
Social skills and conflict resolution not included in the curriculum	Peer mediation and conflict resolution taught and practiced
No outreach to parents on the issue of violence and sexual and racial/ethnic violence	School disclosure protocol for different forms of violence, which includes liaison with community agencies and police
No specific curriculum content addressing dating or family violence, and violence is included without scrutiny	Effective, consistent school policies for dealing with violent incidents, including bullying and harassment
No school disclosure policy for children who live with violence	
Discipline policy for violent incidents is vague and/or inconsistently enforced and does not include harassment	Violence eliminated from school curriculum or, where it is included, appropriate critical discussion is employed to address the issue/policies of violent incidents
Violence condoned in school curriculum	Teachers practice effective, nonviolent classroom management and do not use put-downs and belittling as a control technique
Teachers use verbal put-downs and belittle students	Special violence awareness events implemented from time to time

TABLE 3.1 *continued*

Nonimplementation/Violent	Successful Implementation/Nonviolent
	Outreach to parents on the nonviolence philosophy of the school
	Social skills and prosocial behaviors are explicitly taught and are recognized in the school's awards program

We find that the vast majority of students are supportive of violence prevention at school because they believe that violence is a pressing and real concern for them. They also indicate that they want these programs at their school. For example, in a previous large-scale evaluation of a violence prevention program based on the A.S.A.P. approach, 81% of a sample from five high schools either agreed or strongly agreed with the statement "Schools should have a role in increasing awareness of the effects of violence and how to prevent it" prior to the intervention (Jaffe et al., 1992). A.S.A.P. is unusual with regard to school-based violence prevention programs in that we have been able to evaluate the program on a fairly large scale, as described previously (Jaffe et al., 1992).

A NEW EVALUATION OF A LARGE-SCALE
PRIMARY PREVENTION PROGRAM

Recently, we had the opportunity to evaluate another high school violence prevention program, which took place in two area high schools (Sudermann & Jaffe, 1993). Planning of the violence prevention program was initiated by vice principals in two high schools. Working together with a student group in their respective schools and the Violence Prevention staff of the London Family Court Clinic, a joint school initiative was designed to increase student awareness about violence in relationships. A new feature of this violence prevention program was the involvement of students in a planning capacity. A student planning committee was formed, in addition to the adult planning committee. The role of the students' planning committee was to help students feel ownership of the intervention and to involve them in "marketing" and promoting the program in a way that would appeal to other students. Students decided on the theme of preventing dating violence and took part in inviting speakers, previewing videos, and publicizing the event. Students also produced a press release and conducted their own survey (added to the adult evaluators' survey) of what their fellow students liked and did not like about the event. A half-day was set aside for a special event at each school, and the student committee selected the special focus of dating violence for the theme. It was decided that because the Grades 11, 12, and 13 students had already had exposure to a special awareness event about violence in relationships in previous years, whereas the Grades 9 and 10 students had not, there would be distinct programs for the junior and senior students.

The Junior Assembly Program (for Grades 9 and 10) had several components. A dramatic presentation about dating violence and healthy dating relationships was written and performed by a young people amateur theater group. A video, *Right from the Start* (Victoria Women's Transition House, 1992), which shows early warning signs of violent dating relationships and the dynamics of possible outcomes of these relationships, was shown. Classroom discussion with facilitators from community agencies and the school system followed to allow students to process the content of the play and video and for the community facilitators to answer questions about community resources and other matters. Written material, in the form of a brochure about family violence and effects on children, with community resources listed, was made available. This program was similar to the previously evaluated program, except for the larger student planning and sponsorship component.

The Senior Workshop Program was designed to allow students in Grades 11, 12, and 13 to select from a number of workshops presented by community resource persons. The 22 different workshops were on such topics as date rape, male issues in relationships, anger control, self-defense for women, assertiveness, communication in relationships, and violence in intimate relationships. All workshop presenters related their topics to the overall theme of preventing dating violence.

At both schools, a presentation was made to teachers at a staff meeting prior to the intervention to educate them on the material that would be presented, and tips were given on handling classroom discussion and student disclosures. Special arrangements were put in place for the day of the presentation for counselors to be present in the school so that any student wishing immediate counseling could receive it. Several students either took advantage of this opportunity or commented on the feedback sheets that the topics did bring back disturbing memories for them. This is an important factor to consider in planning student programs.

We evaluated the responses of 1,547 students from the two high schools. Only those students who attended the program and answered both sets of questionnaires were retained in the sample, for a total of 1,112 complete sets of data from 594 females (53.4%) and 518 males (46.6%). Included in the sample were 488 Grades 9 and 10 students and 624 Grades 11, 12, and 13 students. The evaluation instrument was a slightly revised version of the London Family Court Clinic Questionnaire on Violence in Relationships. Questions about experiences of dating violence were added in this version, and some items from the previous version of the questionnaire were dropped to reduce the length of administration. A qualitative questionnaire was added, including some of the student committee's evaluation questions. Here, students could comment on the different components of the intervention. The questionnaire had items related to knowledge about violence in intimate relationships, attitudes and beliefs about violence in intimate relationships, attitudes about forced intercourse in dating relationships, behavioral intentions with regard to intervening in dating violence, and the role of schools in violence prevention. In addition, several questions concerned experiences of dating violence.

Significant positive changes on all knowledge items were found following the intervention, and many significant attitude changes were made in the desired direction. Positive attitude changes were highest among females in Grades 9 and 10, but changes in the desired direction were found in all groups studied. On one item related to violence in adult relationships ("Poverty causes family violence"), a change occurred in the undesired direction, with more students believing this after the intervention than before. This finding may be a reflection of the greater focus on dating violence in this intervention, with less time spent on violence in adult relationships, compared with other programs with which we have been involved. Items on which positive, significant attitude/belief changes occurred include "Assaulted women could just leave their partner if they really wanted to"; "Alcohol causes family violence"; "When a man abuses a woman, he tries to control her"; and "If someone swears at or intimidates another person, this is abuse."

The questionnaire also involved questions on the acceptability of forced intercourse, adapted from Giarusso, Johnson, Goodchilds, and Zellman's (1979) work. These take the following form: "Is it all right if a male holds a female down and forces her to engage in sexual intercourse if . . . He spends a lot of money on her? He is stoned or drunk? They have dated a long time? She gets him sexually excited and she has led him on?" With these items, in each case changes occurred in the desired direction after the intervention, although these did not reach statistical significance. Also of interest was the fact that the initial percentage of students agreeing with any of these items was lower than in the preceding evaluation; that is, the students seemed to know more, which may indicate some effect of the cumulative dating violence intervention efforts in the school system over the years, or it might be because of the particular schools involved.

With regard to changes in behavioral intentions about intervening in dating violence, statistically significant changes occurred in the desired direction on four of the five questions asked. For example, in response to the scenario "If you were at a party and you saw a guy grab the arm of his girlfriend because he did not want her to leave the party, would you . . . Say something then and there?" prior to the intervention, 33.8% of the students responded yes, whereas after the intervention, 40.7% indicated they would do so.

With regard to the students' experiences of dating violence overall, at pretest 38.5% of female students and 24.9% of male students indicated they had experienced verbal or emotional abuse in dating relationships; 13.2% of females and 2.8% of males had experienced physical abuse in dating relationships; and 13.3% of females and 3.2% of males had experienced sexual abuse in dating relationships. Of students who reported currently dating, 52.5% of females and 30.0% of males reported experiencing verbal or emotional abuse; 20.5% of females and 5.6% of males reported experiencing physical abuse in a dating relationship; and 22.6% of females and 6.3% of males reported experiencing sexual abuse in a dating relationship. At posttest, each of these figures changed somewhat. For example, at posttest, 23.3% of females and 3.3% of males who were currently dating reported experiencing sexual abuse in a dating relationship. The figures were slightly higher again for students in steady dating relationships.

These results indicate the scope of the problem of dating violence. In future studies, we intend to change the questions about dating violence to make them specific as to being a victim or perpetrator of dating violence and also as to categories of behavior. With regard to the item "Schools should have a role in increasing awareness of and preventing violence," we are seeing an increase in endorsement to 88.9% of students (from 84%). This increase may reflect a systemic change as a result of continuing violence prevention efforts in the school system over the years since the last evaluation, or it may again reflect the specific schools chosen or societal increases in concern about violence prevention. The schools chosen in this study were, however, very representative schools for our city, as were the schools in the previous intervention.

In comparing the changes among male and female groups and junior (Grades 9 and 10) and senior grades (Grades 11 to 13), it was apparent that the most positive changes occurred in the Grades 9 and 10 girls, and the least in the Grades 11 to 13 boys. It was not considered advisable to compare the changes in the junior and senior groups statistically, as the groups had different pretest levels on many of the responses. (Future studies could employ a covariance procedure with regard to pretest scores.) It was also our impression that pretest levels of responses were, in some cases, better than at the previous intervention, but this data set contained too many demographic variables that we did not or could not measure directly to allow a meaningful comparison as to trends within the student body over time. It is encouraging to note, however, that changes appear to be moving in a positive direction over time, even if causality cannot be definitively established. In the intervening period, the school systems in our area have placed considerable emphasis on preventing violence in relationships, preventing all kinds of violence and harassment at school, and dealing more effectively with any incidents of harassment and violence.

Finally, student comments on the qualitative portion of the evaluation indicated an overwhelmingly positive response to the intervention. Students suggested changes such as more programming, repeating the program for younger students, and repeating the program on an annual basis.

SUMMARY AND DIRECTIONS
FOR THE FUTURE

Children who witness domestic violence suffer serious consequences to their emotional and behavioral adjustment and are at increased risk of becoming or staying involved in violent relationships with peers and teen and adult partners in intimate relationships. Society, including legal and social services, has been slow to come to grips with this problem because of the general silence about family violence. The first need of children who are witnessing violence is for personal safety and for the violence to stop. To this end, the well-being of children is closely related to protection, support, and intervention programs for women and children who are experiencing violence, including legal and social supports and improved public attitudes.

Improvement in such areas as quick, centrally registered and easily accessible protection orders; provisions for quick access to possession of the matrimonial home, where the abuser has been charged but the wife and children have had to leave; availability of shelter services for women and children; increased sensitivity to the impact of wife assault on children in the context of child protection and child custody and access proceedings; sensitive counseling for women and children that takes into account such issues as the dynamics of abuse, the impact on children, PTSD, and related issues; and increased education and sensitivity of all social and legal agencies and professionals are all pressing matters that should be addressed in every community and jurisdiction.

Group treatment to help process the experience, dispel myths about family violence, clarify responsibility for the violence, and focus on nonviolent conflict resolution can be most helpful for children. For children exposed to severe or repeated violence in the home, treatment needs will be more in-depth and long-term. Research in the area of children who witness domestic violence, as well as in the area of school-based prevention of violence in relationships, is still in a pioneering phase. Many of the studies discussed in this chapter reflect the relatively recent nature of the research in this area, and further research, methodological refinement, and replication are certainly required.

Directions for future research in the area of effects of witnessing violence could include assessing the positive impact on children of stronger legal remedies and protection for battered women and their children; such remedies would include access to orders for police protection with a central registry easily accessible to police and quick possession of the family home for the mother and children (where the father is charged with assault). The impact of stronger, more easily available supports for women who are experiencing abuse and on the women's ability to protect and nurture their children would also be worth addressing. In the area of effects on child symptoms and adjustment, one of the greatest needs is a study with a longitudinal research design, addressing the long-term consequences of witnessing violence. Issues such as PTSD and its unique manifestations among this child and youth group would be of benefit. For example, what are the special effects, within PTSD, of having the perpetrator of the violence also being a family member and an attachment figure? Interventions that thwart the tendency of children exposed to violence to grow up to be more involved in adult abusive relationships should be developed and evaluated carefully. Methodological issues such as differentiating witnesses and victim/witnesses, delineating the amount and type of violence witnessed, and seeking out child witnesses in both shelter and nonshelter settings will be important. Prospective longitudinal studies of child witnesses and follow-up studies on effects of children's groups would both be valuable additions to cross-sectional group designs.

With regard to prevention, large-scale school-based programs hold considerable promise for changing societal attitudes and beliefs about domestic violence. Replications and extensions of the type of school-based violence prevention program described here are needed, together with accompanying evaluation. Methods to overcome some male students' and teachers' resistance to this type of prevention program need to be further addressed. Although the evaluations of the programs to date have focused on relatively short-term effects of discrete special violence awareness events, the full A.S.A.P. program, including the emphasis on proactive, equality-based climate and integration of violence prevention into the curriculum in all subjects and grade levels, has yet to be examined in a formal evaluation. Long-term follow-up as to the stability of the changes achieved in such programs is needed. The impact of school-based awareness and prevention programs may need to be coupled with communitywide prevention and intervention programs so that changes can be maintained. It is our hope and belief that, with the involvement of youth in changing societal attitudes about the acceptability of violence in any kind of interpersonal relationships, a revolution in societal standards and actions can occur to greatly reduce violence in all its forms. As one student commented on her evaluation questionnaire, "We can't give up. We have to change the world—stop violence."

REFERENCES

American Medical Association. (1992). Violence against women. *Journal of the American Medical Association, 267*(23), 107-112.
American Psychiatric Association. (1994). *Diagnostic and statistical manual of mental disorders* (4th ed.). Washington, DC: Author.
Black, D., & Kaplan, T. (1988). Father kills mother. *British Journal of Psychiatry, 153,* 624-630.
Cummings, E. M., & Davies, P. T. (1994). *Children and marital conflict.* New York: Guilford.
Dutton, D. G. (1988). *The domestic assault of women: Psychological and criminal justice perspectives.* Needham Heights, MA: Allyn & Bacon.
Giarusso, R., Johnson, P., Goodchilds, J., & Zellman, G. (1979). Adolescents' cues and signals: Sex and assault. In P. Johnson (Chair), *Acquaintance rape and adolescent*

sexuality. Symposium conducted at the meeting of the Western Psychological Association, San Diego, CA.

Head, S. (1988). *A study of attitudes and behavior in dating relationships with special reference to the use of force.* Unpublished report, Board of Education for the City of Scarborough, Scarborough, Ontario.

Hilton, Z., Harris, G. T., & Rice, M. (1994). Evaluation of an educational intervention on aggression in high school students' relationships: Change without backlash. *Research Reports, XI*(6). Penetanguishene, Ontario: Mental Health Center.

Hughes, H. M. (1982). Brief interventions with children in a battered women's shelter: A model preventive program. *Family Relations, 31,* 495-502.

Hughes, H. M. (1988). Psychological and behavioral correlates of family violence in child witnesses and victims. *American Journal of Orthopsychiatry, 58*(1), 77-90.

Hughes, H. M., & Barad, S. J. (1983). Psychological functioning of children in a battered women's clinic. *American Journal of Orthopsychiatry, 53,* 525-531.

Jaffe, P.G. (1995). Children of domestic violence: Special challenges in custody and visitation resolution. In Lemon, N.K.D., Carter, J., Hart, B., & Heisler, C. (Eds.) *Domestic Violence & Children: Resolving Custody and Visitation Disputes. A National Judicial Curriculum.* Family Violence Prevention Fund and Judicial College, Supreme Court of Ohio.

Jaffe, P., Sudermann, M., Reitzel, D., & Killip, S. M. (1992). An evaluation of a secondary school primary prevention program on violence in relationships. *Violence and Victims, 7,* 129-146.

Jaffe, P., Wolfe, D., & Wilson, S. K. (1990). *Children of battered women.* Newbury Park, CA: Sage.

Jaffe, P., Wolfe, D. A., Wilson, S., & Zak, L. (1986). Emotional and physical health problems of battered women. *Canadian Journal of Psychiatry, 31,* 625-629.

Jones, L.E. (1987). *Dating violence among Minnesota teenagers: A summary of survey results.* St. Paul, MN: Minnesota Coalition for Battered Women.

Layzer, J. I., Goodson, B. D., & deLange, C. (1985). Children in shelters. Response, 9(2), 2-5.

Lehmann, P. (1995, June) *Posttraumatic stress disorder in children who have witnessed their mothers being assaulted.* Presentation at the Children's Aid Society of London and Middlesex, London, Ontario. Based on an unpublished Ph.D. dissertation at Wilfrid Laurier University, Waterloo, Ontario, Canada.

Macgowan, M. (1995). *An experimental evaluation of a dating violence prevention program for middle school students.* Manuscript submitted for publication.

Moore, T. E., & Pepler, D. (1989, August). *Domestic violence and children's psychosocial development: Exploring the linkage.* Paper presented at the American Psychological Association Annual Meeting, New Orleans.

Moore, T.E., Pepler, D., Mae, R., Katos, M. (1989). Effects of family violence on children: New directions for research and intervention. In B. Pressman, G. Cameron and M. Rothery (Eds.) *Intervening with assaulted women: Current theory, research and practice,* 75-91.

O'Leary, K. D., Malone, J., & Tyree, A. (1994). Physical aggression in early marriage: Prerelationship and relationship effects. *Journal of Consulting and Clinical Psychology, 62*(3), 594-602.

Osofsky, J. D., Wewers, S., Hann, D. M., & Fick, A. C. (1993). Chronic community violence: What is happening to our children? *Psychiatry, 56,* 36-45.

Peled, E., & Edleson, J. L. (1995). Process and outcome in small groups for children of battered women. In E. Peled, P. G. Jaffe, & J. L. Edleson (Eds.), *Ending the cycle of violence: Community responses to children of battered women* (Chap. 5). Thousand Oaks, CA: Sage.

Pynoos, R. S., & Eth, S. (1984). The child as witness to homicide. *Journal of Social Issues, 40*(2), 87-108.

Pynoos, R. S., & Eth, S. (1985). Children traumatized by witnessing acts of personal violence: Homicide, rape, or suicide behavior. In S. Eth & R. Pynoos (Eds.), *Post-traumatic stress disorder in children* (pp. 17-44). Washington, DC: American Psychiatric Press.

Rosenbaum, A., & O'Leary, K. D. (1981). Children: The unintended victims of marital violence. *American Journal of Orthopsychiatry, 51,* 692-699.

Rosenberg, M. S. (1984, August). *Intergenerational family violence: A critique and implications for witnessing children.* Paper presented at the 92nd Annual Convention of the American Psychological Association, Toronto.

Sopp-Gilson, S. (1980). Children from violent homes. *Journal of Ontario Children's Aid Societies, 23*(10), 1-5.

Statistics Canada. (1993, November 18). The Violence Against Women Survey. *The Daily: Statistics Canada.* Ottawa, Ontario: Author.

Sternberg, K. L., Lamb, M. E., Greenbaum, C., Cicchetti, D., Dawud, S., Cortes, R. M., Krispin, O., & Lorey, F. (1993). Effects of domestic violence on children's behavior problems and depression. *Developmental Psychology, 29*(1), 44-52.

Straus, M. A. (1978). Wife beating: How common and why? *Victimology: An International Journal, 2*(3-4), 443-458.

Straus, M. A., Gelles, R. J., & Steinmetz, S. (1980). *Behind closed doors: Violence in the American family.* Garden City, NY: Doubleday.

Sudermann, M., & Jaffe, P. G. (1993, August). *Violence in teen dating relationships: Evaluation of a large-scale primary prevention program.* Paper presented at the Annual Meeting of the American Psychological Association, Toronto.

Sudermann, M., Jaffe, P. G., & Hastings, E. (1993). *A.S.A.P.: A school-based antiviolence program.* (Available from London Family Court Clinic, 254 Pall Mall St., London Ontario, Canada, N6A 5P6)

Sudermann, M., Jaffe, P. G., & Hastings, E. (1995). Prevention programs in secondary schools. In E. Peled, P. Jaffe, & J. Edelson (Eds.), *Ending the cycle of violence: Community responses to children of battered women* (pp. 232-254). Thousand Oaks, CA: Sage.

Sudermann, M., Marshall, L., Miller, N., & Miller-Hewitt, S. (1995). *Children's questionnaire for groups for children who have witnessed violence.* Unpublished document, London Family Court Clinic.

Victoria Women's Transition House. (1992). *Right from the start* [Video]. (Available from Kinetic, Inc., 408 Dundas St. E., Toronto, Canada, M5A 2A5; and 255 Delaware Ave., Suite 340, Buffalo, NY, U.S.A. 14202)

Wolfe, D. A., Jaffe, P., Wilson, S., & Zak, L. (1985). Children of battered women: The relation of child behavior to family violence and maternal stress. *Journal of Consulting and Clinical Psychology, 53,* 657-665.

Wolfe, D. A., Zak, L., Wilson, S., & Jaffe, P. (1986). Child witnesses to violence between parents: Critical issues in behavioral and social adjustment. *Journal of Abnormal Child Psychology, 14*(1), 95-104.

4

A Cognitive Behavioral Approach to Understanding and Treating Parents Who Physically Abuse Their Children

SANDRA T. AZAR

Until the last decade, the prevailing etiological theories of child abuse were psychodynamic ones and focused on personality disturbances in parents. Such models have not received empirical support and have not proved fruitful for developing effective intervention strategies. More recent behavioral models have taken a different strategy, focusing on narrow-band aversive parental behaviors (e.g., Friedman, Sandler, Hernandez, & Wolfe, 1981; Wolfe, Kaufman, Aragona, & Sandler, 1981). These newer approaches, using standard behavioral child management training, have been successful in reducing the negative aspects of family interactions. However, the equally important introduction of refined positive responses into parents' repertoires has been more difficult to accomplish (e.g., responsive and socioemotional growth-producing transactions). In other words, parents may become better at managing child behavior at a gross level (e.g., lower use of coercive responses), but still may not display the kind of spontaneous and sensitive caregiving that has been associated with optimal child social, cognitive, and emotional development.

Skills to prevent abuse are one thing; skills that "right" the family environment for the child's overall social and emotional development are another. Competent parenting is more than managing children's behavior. It involves a myriad of fine-tuned responses that contribute to a broad range of children's cognitive, social, and emotional outcomes. A lack of attentive, nurturant, and caring behaviors may continue to characterize many abusive homes. For example, abusive parents may not provide the kind of secure base from which children can explore the world (e.g., spontaneously offering comfort when their child is fearful, anticipating and modifying situations that might harm their child before they happen); they may not engage in behaviors that act as scaffolding for cognitive development; or they may not provide an atmosphere of unconditional positive regard crucial for perceptions of competence and self-efficacy. From this perspective, the presence of abuse can be seen as the "tip of an iceberg" of parenting difficulties, and its elimination may not, in fact, make the home "safe" for children's overall development.

In addition, although extreme forms of aggression may no longer be present, there may still be subtle forms of rejection and disengagement. These more psychological aspects of child abuse may be just as stressful and damaging to children's development (McGee & Wolfe, 1991). Instead of bruises to annotate a parent's cruelty, children may be left with more indirect cues by which the parent's dissatisfaction with them is communicated (e.g., lack of spontaneous positive interaction and support, lack of supervision, neglect of their emotional needs). Children are less sophisticated participants in social interaction, and their identities are still being formed. Although overt physical abuse is harmful both physically and emotionally in childhood, the behaviors involved are at such a gross level that children can label them as aberrant. With such clarity, as children grow up, an external attribution can develop whereby the parent can be seen as disturbed and at fault. With the more subtle psychological maltreatment, it may be more difficult to make such an external attribution. Children may blame themselves for their parents' reactions to them or overgeneralize from this one negative relationship to an expectancy of this type of treatment from all their relationships. Children may come to develop schemas regarding the self, others, and the world that are laced with these negative elements and that ultimately undermine the very foundation of their emotional well-being and social adjustment.

Because of such concerns, the call within the field is for more comprehensive frameworks that might account for both the underlying deficits in the relational transactions between parent and child, as well as the negative outcomes seen in abused children (Azar, 1986; Cicchetti & Rizley, 1981; Farber & Egeland, 1987). It has been suggested that such frameworks should be based in children's developing needs. For example, attachment theory has been invoked in attempts to widen views on maltreatment. Insecure attachment between parent and child has been used to explain both the disturbances seen in the parent-child relationship and the development of negative or disorganized "internal working models" in children (Ainsworth, 1980; Crittenden & Ainsworth, 1989; Klaus & Kennell, 1982). Yet, like psychodynamic theories, attachment models have not proved themselves useful in forming the basis for constructing interventions (e.g., attempts to increase early bonding; Klaus & Kennell, 1982). Classic attachment theory emphasized critical periods for the development of secure attachments, and one would assume that intervention after a certain age would be useless. Even more recent reformulations that emphasize the formation of "internal working models" with early caretakers argue that change requires sustained and marked changes in relational experiences (Rogosch, Cicchetti, Shields, & Toth, 1995) but have not specified the nature of such experiences in operational terms. The implications for intervention, therefore, remain vague. A more flexible model with an expanded view of development and the potential for specifiable targets for intervention is required for effective interventions to be devised.

One such framework that incorporates some elements of cognitive reformulations of attachment theory (the idea that people form relational schema that guide behavior), as well as behavioral skill views (skills are required to manage and respond to child behavior) is a cognitive-behavioral theory (Azar, 1986, 1989a; Azar & Twentyman, 1986). This model holds promise as a base for the development of interventions that would address the full spectrum of responses required for competent parenting. The idea of *relational schema* is central to this model. Such schema are seen as guiding a myriad of responses and are also thought to be malleable (Fiske & Taylor, 1991). In contrast with attachment formulations, this model does not carry with it the baggage of the primacy of early relational history and does not focus exclusively on abusive parents' aggressive behavior. Rather, it focuses on a set of underlying cognitive processes that may drive the full range of parents' repertoires of responses.

This framework builds upon earlier clinical theorizing by cognitive behaviorists such as Lazarus and Folkman (1984) in stress coping; Spivack,

Platt, and Shure (1976) and D'Zurilla and Goldfried (1971) in problem solving; Novaco (1975) in anger control; and Patterson and Reid (1970) in behavioral parenting work. It is also consistent with cognitive views regarding disturbances in parents of behaviorally disordered children (Johnston, 1996). In addition, however, it also uses elements of Vygotsky's developmental theory (see Rogoff & Wertsch, 1984) and cognitive-behavioral family systems theory (Epstein, Schlesinger, & Dryden, 1988) in its theoretical formulation for understanding the damaging aspects of abusive homes. That is, there is a clear recognition that parenting requires sensitivity to children's present level of capabilities in order to respond in a way that fosters new skills (Rogoff & Wertsch, 1984). It also emphasizes the role that context (e.g., social support, stress, parental mood state) directly plays in determining the nature of the quality of parents' interpretive and behavioral responses to children, as well as the indirect role that parents' modeling of social behaviors (e.g., problem solving, emotion regulation, stress management, social skills) plays in children's own repertoire of responses for coping effectively with the environment.

Finally, in positing this model, there is a clear recognition that children's outcomes evolve out of bidirectional interactions to which both parent and child make contributions (Azar, Barnes, & Twentyman, 1988; Parke & Collmer, 1975). Thus, although this chapter primarily focuses on parental responses and intervention with these responses, what the child brings to the dyadic interaction may greatly influence, either for the better or worse, the nature of parental schema, the effectiveness of their responses, and the meaning the child takes from the transactions. For example, clinically it may be easier to challenge a parent's negative interpretations regarding a child whose behavior is relatively benign, compared with one who evidences attention deficit hyperactivity disorder (ADHD) or oppositional defiant disorder (ODD). The child for his or her part also attaches meaning to parental responses, and some children may even take the worst of treatment and attach a positive meaning to it (e.g., as evidence of high parental investment in them). This last aspect of the child as constructor of reality is often overlooked in most formulations (Azar & Bober, in press).

This framework attempts to explain both the etiology of abuse and the developmental disturbances observed among affected children (Azar, 1986, 1989a). Social-cognitive theory posits that individuals develop cognitive structures to aid them in handling the thousands of pieces of information that bombard them each moment of every day, including those involved in making parenting decisions. The complexity, flexibility, and nature of the content of these schemas are seen as either facilitating or destabilizing to parental functioning both within the family (e.g., in parenting and marital transactions) and outside it (e.g., with employers, friends, store clerks, children's teachers, neighbors). The level of parents' discriminant responsivity to children's behavior also shapes the outcomes. If parents' schemas are too simplistic, inflexible, inconsistent, or biased in some way, then the parents' responses will be less adaptive and children's outcome may be affected (Azar, 1989a). These processes are core to the model that will be described.

This framework that focuses on interpretive processes in social interaction has been offered as a general model of parenting (Azar, 1989a, 1991c; Azar & Benjet, 1994) and would allow for placing the disturbances in parenting found in a myriad of at-risk family situations, not just abuse, into one framework. (For example, it would explain the intergenerational transmission of depression in terms of socialization of distorted schemas by the depressed parents.) It also leads naturally to an intervention that combines both behavioral (e.g, child management skills training) and cognitive techniques (e.g., cognitive restructuring, problem-solving training, stress-coping methods) to produce positive changes in family environments.

A COGNITIVE FRAMEWORK
FOR CONSIDERING ABUSE

In this model, child maltreatment is one of many possible signs of a family environment that has broken down in its capacity to provide an optimal socialization environment for a child (Azar, 1986, 1989a). The term *environment* includes both the direct care that children receive and the transactions that occur both within the family and with the larger outside environment that are crucial for children's development either directly through modeling or indirectly by providing the parent and family with resources. Thus, child abuse is part of a cluster of responses at one end of a continuum of parenting that leads to heightened risk; at the other end of this continuum are responses that result in optimal outcome in children (Azar & Wolfe, 1989).

Whereas psychological models of parenting generally have emphasized its affective quality or behavioral regulation (Becker, 1964; Maccoby & Martin, 1983), the proposed model has focused more heavily on the crucial role of cognitive processes in guiding parenting behavior (and as is outlined later, children's response to it). That is, socialization requires a "thinking" parent. Socialization is seen as highly dependent on parental schemas regarding role relationships, as well as a set of cognitive processes used to interpret and operate on environmental stimuli, especially problematic situations (e.g., attributional style, problem solving, perception, cognitive complexity/flexibility, decision-making skills). These cognitive schema and processes are seen as guiding moment-by-moment interpretations of the causes of children's behavior by the parent and, depending on contextual factors (e.g., stress, social support, mood state), may facilitate the occurrence of adaptive or maladaptive responses (ones that do or do not foster development). These same processes also influence a social context that does or does not promote development (e.g., one that is rich or devoid of economic, social, and emotional resources).

According to cognitive theories of motivation (Heider, 1958), when an individual encounters an action of another, an interpretation of the meaning of that action must be made for the selection of a response to occur. That is, cognitive processes are seen as mediating interpersonal emotional and behavioral responses. The appropriateness of the response made is seen as being dependent on the accuracy (or, at the very least, the adaptiveness) of the interpretation made. Adaptive responses facilitate continued contact with others, produce success in interpersonal transactions and with the environment, and maintain as much as possible a positive mood state. For example, it is adaptive for parents to focus on strengths in their children, both from a mastery perspective (e.g., "I have produced a competent child") and from the perspective of a growing child (e.g., "My parent thinks positively of me, so I must be OK"). This tendency may even be seen as a positive distortion of sorts (e.g., when a very young child runs across the street after being told not to, a parent might say or think: "Isn't he strong willed" or "He's so independent"). Interpretations such as these or ones that focus on general development (e.g., "He's only two; he doesn't know any better") keep parents calm in the face of their children's more limited self-regulation capacities and allow them to problem-solve and respond in the most adaptive manner, keeping children's developmental needs in focus, as they decide on actions.

Over time, we as people develop cognitive sets or schemas regarding basic social roles (e.g., the self, parent, child) and scripts that define the basic patterns of how people in these roles behave and relate to others (e.g., mothers attempt to put their children's needs ahead of their own; it is not the job of children to care for parents). The sources of these schemas include societal norms, subcultural beliefs, and personal experiences within one's own family. Thus, although a good deal of overlap occurs, each person has somewhat unique schema about social roles. One might argue that those schemas whose sources are most private (e.g., ones regarding family life and parent-child roles) would vary between individuals the greatest, as opposed to those schemas that are most public (e.g., ones like being a student or a professional). We also develop more specialized schemas regarding the meaning of the responses of specific individuals we encounter on a regular basis in our lives (e.g., our own mother, our children) and of the self-in-relation to these people (e.g., "People in my family try not to hurt me"). Not unlike psychodynamic theorizing, this gives a special place to familial interactions in forming unique initial frameworks for schemas, but unlike traditional formulations of attachment theory does not in and of itself suggest that such schemas are not amenable to change.

These schemas or scripts make social interaction with strangers and with those we encounter often more "automatic" and less "effortful." These schemas also guide our judgments about ourselves as we react to the feedback we receive from others and the environment. Finally, these schemas also shape our processing of the information we encounter in interpersonal situations (they may lead to selective attention to some pieces of information—that which is consistent with the schemas—and less attention to other information—that which is inconsistent). The sum of such processing colors our perspective on life generally. If our schemas about relationships and the self are positively toned and predictable, the world too is perceived as a safe and positive place where what happens is predictable.

Nowhere may such interpretive processes be more important than in the parenting of young children. Young children's motivation is often not clear and must be inferred by parents for them to take action. Under conditions of ambiguity, established schemas play the greatest role in interpretative processes. Parental interpretations, in turn, serve a developmental purpose. Parents selectively marking and responding to their children's actions is believed to be crucial in guiding them toward more sophisticated means of responding. It also provides children with elements of their own schemas that, over time, will help them operate independently in the world. Parents must develop a fine-tuned ability to identify acts in their offspring as meaningful and worthy of response and to provide accurate and predominantly positively-toned information about the self, others, and the world. Indeed, it has been demonstrated that parents see more meaningful acts in infant/toddler behavior than do nonparents (Adamson, Bakeman, Smith, & Walters, 1987). Factors that interfere with or distort these interpretive processes, therefore, would affect negatively both parenting and child outcome. Positively toned elements in schemas would include a sense of mastery, confidence in one's decisions, and a sense that the world is a relatively predictable (contingent) place. Schemas also need to be flexible, and the very processes involved in revising and reshaping one's views can also be modeled by parents.

It has been argued that abusive parents show disturbances in cognitive areas that result in disruptions in their capacity to appropriately interpret child behavior, to problem-solve in child-rearing situations, and to respond in developmentally appropriate ways to their children (Azar, 1986, 1989a). The abusive parent is posited to have rigid and disturbed schemas regarding how children operate in the world and their role in relation to parents. (Some evidence also suggests that their schema more generally may be disturbed about others and the world [Miller & Azar, 1996].)

Fundamental is the lack or reversal of the typical hierarchical relationship between parent and child, with the parent providing and the child being provided for (e.g., what early writers in this area called *role reversal;* Morris & Gould, 1963). Abusive parents evidence unrealistic expectations regarding both the social-cognitive and physical care capacities of children (e.g., believing a 3-year-old can comfort them when they are upset, that a 4-year-old can pick out the right clothing for the weather, that a teenager can help patch up their marital problems). Such expectancies differentiate them from both nonabusive parents and ones whose partners have physically abused their children (Azar, Robinson, Hekimian, & Twentyman, 1984; Azar & Rohrbeck, 1986).

Such schemas are constantly violated by children. This may be especially apparent in the early years, when child care needs are high, but they still may be present in parents of adolescents (e.g., believing it is appropriate to expect a teenager to stay home to keep them company, rather than go out with friends). Because of other cognitive disturbances observed in such parents (e.g., poor interpersonal problem solving) and their limited repertoire of social and parenting skills, difficulties that ensue cannot be easily resolved by such parents. Parenting becomes an aversive task in which the parent feels incompetent (engages in self-blaming) and, after repeated failures, begins to feel a lack of self-efficacy in that role. If further evidence of social incompetence occurs (e.g., marital problems, life issues), stress may increase further. Ultimately, the parent, in a self-protective stance, may come to blame the child for the difficulties, labeling the child as "the problem" (he or she develops a negative attributional bias toward the child). This negative bias, coupled with a more restricted repertoire of parenting responses, leads the parent either to avoid contact with the child or, when contact is necessary, react with negative verbal and physical control behaviors (see Table 4.1 for a schematic of this process). For such parents, parenting is an aversive task, and their children are aversive stimuli. These coercive responses and lack of positive ones begin to dominate the interactions, and the process of parenting becomes even less rewarding. With lowered contact, children receive less cognitive stimulation, further negatively affecting development.

IMPACT ON THE CHILD'S
SOCIOEMOTIONAL ENVIRONMENT

Parents with the cognitive problems outlined above are less able to operate within their children's "zone of proximal development" (within their children's developmental reach; Rogoff & Wertsch, 1984). Because of their disturbed interpretations of child behavior and negative biases, the parents are less able to provide their children with the kind of "scaffolding" required to allow them to gain mastery over tasks. Children's ensuing failures, coupled with parental negative feedback that follows from their negative attributional bias, would restrict the development of positive schema of the self, others, and the world. Because of their decreased desire for contact with their children, such parents would also provide children with inadequate levels of cognitive stimulation, negatively influencing the children's cognitive development. Moreover, from the children's perspective, such parents would behave in an inconsistent manner because their responses are not closely connected to the children's cues. All of this would bode poorly for the children's outcomes. Furthermore, because the cognitive disturbances of these parents may also negatively influence their other interpersonal interactions, they are poor role models for interpersonal relationships and social adjustment more generally (e.g., development of friendships), further detracting from children's development of adaptive "scripts" for operating within relationships.

As can be seen in the discussion above, the more developmental periods within which the factors described above exist, the more disturbed the feedback and the more disturbed children's constructions of the self, others,

TABLE 4.1   The Makings of an Abusive Incident: A 4-Stage Process*

Stage 1:	The parent holds unrealistic standards regarding what are appropriate behaviors in children.
Stage 2:	The parent encounters a child behavior that fails to meet her standards.
Stage 3:	The parent misattributes negative intent to the behavior and does not question her interpretation or blames herself when her interventions do not change the child's response.
Stage 4:	The parent overreacts, perhaps after making some poorly skilled effort to change the child's behavior and punishes the child excessively.

NOTE: *Movement through the stages may feel "automatized," and the process is more likely to occur under perceived conditions of stress.

and the world may become. For families in which these distorted processes are present early and are chronic, the very foundation of basic schemas may be distorted (Azar & Bober, in press). For example, such children would have fewer opportunities to see the self taken care of, others as trustworthy and meeting of their needs, and the world as a place where good things are likely to happen. In the extreme, abused children's relational schemas will be laced with elements of emotional pain, the potential for physical harm, and fears regarding survival.

This view is supported by the many negative outcomes observed among abused children, which include heightened levels of depression, poor social relationships, and negative interpersonal responses (Ammerman, Cassisi, Hersen, & VanHasselt, 1986; Azar et al., 1988; Azar & Bober, in press; Azar & Twentyman, 1986; Wolfe, 1987).

EMPIRICAL SUPPORT FOR THE PARENTAL DISTURBANCES OUTLINED AND TARGETS FOR INTERVENTION WORK

On the basis of the model described above, the most pervasive disturbance posited in abusive parents is manifest *social-cognitive problems*. These disturbances are seen as the root of each of the other skill deficits described later in the chapter. Abusive and at-risk parents show evidence of maladaptive schema regarding children and parent-child transactions (Azar et al., 1984; Azar & Rohrbeck, 1986) and a negative attributional bias in interpreting child behavior (Azar, 1988; Johnston, 1996; Larrance & Twentyman, 1983). Such parents maintain *unrealistic expectations,* such as believing that a 4-year-old knows enough not to embarrass a parent in a grocery store (Azar & Rohrbeck, 1986). They also appear to assign more responsibility to their children for negative outcomes (e.g., views that the child is intentionally misbehaving or "out to get" the parent; Larrance & Twentyman, 1983). This last point is particularly important in the light of evidence suggesting that the extent to which a child is held responsible for negative behavior influences the severity of punishment deemed appropriate by parents (Dix, Ruble, & Zambarano, 1989). Thus, such attributions would heighten the probability of harsh treatment of the child. They would also decrease the sense of joy experienced in the role of parenting (e.g., feeling that one is an important figure to this helpless child).

Further increasing parenting strain and detracting from opportunities to facilitate children's development is the fact that abusers also appear to be *poorer problem solvers* in child-rearing situations (Azar et al., 1984; Hansen, Pallotta, Tishelman, & Conaway, 1989). They are less able to generate solutions and generate fewer categories of solutions, suggesting a more limited and inflexible child-rearing repertoire. They also appear to judge child misbehavior more harshly in some domains than do nonabusive parents (Azar et al., 1984; Chilamkurti & Milner, 1993) and to perceive their children's behavior as more deviant than do outside observers (Mash, Johnston, & Kovitz, 1983). In addition, subtle difficulties in interpersonal discrimination skills may be causing parents to be poor trackers of child behavior (Wahler & Dumas, 1989). They may not pick up on children's cues of discomfort as quickly (Crittenden, 1982). For example, clinically such parents have been observed to behave in physically intrusive ways with their infants and young children (e.g., squirting water in their babies' faces in attempts to be playful, but not noticing when their babies find it aversive; tickling their preschoolers beyond the point where the children are comfortable).

Overall, these cognitive disturbances would increase the potential for anger, aggression, and inept responses in parenting and detract from the positive aspects of the experience. They would make for the maladaptive parent-child interactions described earlier (ones that feel unpredictable for the child).

These cognitive disturbances are posited to be associated with a variety of *disturbances in optimal parenting responses.* Indeed, such disturbances have been observed in abusive parents. Mothers at risk for abusing their children make less use of explanation (Barnes & Azar, 1990), which is crucial to many aspects of children's cognitive and social development (e.g., the development of empathy). This lack may be rooted in parents' distorted view that children "know" all that adults do (unrealistic expectations), making explanation unnecessary. This may be similar to the "mind reading" that distressed couples expect from each other described by Epstein and his colleagues (Eidelson & Epstein, 1982). Abusive parents also appear to engage in fewer positive verbal interactions with their children and to use more negative, coercive, and rigid control tactics than nonmaltreating mothers (Bousha & Twentyman, 1984; Burgess & Conger, 1978; Oldershaw, Walters, & Hall, 1986). These findings may reflect the narrow repertoire of parenting strategies, poor problem solving, and the negative biases toward children described above.

Some evidence suggests that these cognitive disturbances are linked with each other and with parenting responses as the model posits. Three studies have found unrealistic expectations to be positively correlated to higher levels of attributions of negative intent to children. In turn, both of these cognitive problems have been linked with higher levels of punishment assigned to aversive child behavior (Azar, 1991a, 1991b; Barnes & Azar, 1990). In one of these studies that involved at-risk teenage mothers, these cognitive factors were linked with social workers' ratings of family dysfunction and child jeopardy (Azar, 1989b). In another study, levels of unrealistic expectations were significantly negatively correlated with empathy (Azar, 1991b). Using a daily discipline diary methodology, mothers who had high levels of unrealistic expectations were also found to make more negative attributions in naturally occurring child-rearing situations and to use explanation less and coercive responses more than mothers with low levels of such expectations (Barnes & Azar, 1990).

Abusive parents also have been found to exhibit disturbances in other domains that may have similar cognitive roots and that would interfere with an optimal environment for children's development. These include *poor stress management* (e.g., Casanova, Domanic, McCanne, & Milner, 1992; Frodi & Lamb, 1980; Wolfe, Fairbanks, Kelly, & Bradlyn, 1983), *poor abilities to marshal a support network* (e.g., Burgess & Conger, 1978; Lovell, Reid, & Richey, 1992; Newberger, Hampton, Marx, & White, 1986; Salzinger, Kaplan, & Artemyeff, 1983), and *greater impulsivity* (e.g., Rohrbeck & Twentyman, 1986). Although each of these disturbances may be driven by social-cognitive problems, each may also lead to further cognitively based difficulties. For example, given the research of Easterbrook (1959) and others (see Cohen, 1980, for a review), researchers know that information-processing capacities narrow under stress. In addition, impulsivity would derail the careful consideration of information required in problem-solving situations. Similarly, social support, which facilitates parents being able to cope with child rearing by providing emotional and concrete resources, would be restricted.

Taken together, these findings suggest that the interpersonal difficulties observed in abusive parents with their children may characterize all the interpersonal transactions of the abusive parent. Indeed, some limited information suggests that the bias toward overattributing responsibility to children for aversive events may be part of a more pervasive bias in perceiving the behavior of others (Miller & Azar, 1996). Negative attributions to others' behavior, coupled with the other disturbances outlined above, therefore, may interfere not only with family transactions but also with those with other adults. This interference would be detrimental to the resources available for child rearing, and such parents would provide poor role models for adaptive social functioning.

In summary, empirical support is available suggesting validity for elements of this model. This suggests that cognitive disturbances may need to be addressed in intervention work with this population. Illustrations of how to incorporate cognitive-behavioral strategies into standard parent training work is described briefly below (Azar, 1989a; Azar, Breton, & Miller, in press; Johnston, 1996).

COGNITIVE RESTRUCTURING
WITH ABUSIVE PARENTS

Cognitive work should begin in the early stages of the therapeutic process by working on potential resistances to treatment. This technique illustrates quickly to parents the role that thoughts may have in action. Pointed discussion regarding thoughts they may have as they approach parent therapy can be discussed (e.g., "You may be worrying that you might be called *a bad parent,* and this may keep you from attending sessions"—this begins the linking of thoughts and behavior). Alternative, facilitating self-statements can then be illustrated. For example, the therapist might state: "I think there is no such thing as *a bad parent,* just as I think there is no such thing as *a bad child.* Parents do the best they can." This is a reframing that will be a core one for their working with their children—"He's only 2. He is doing the best he can."

Challenges to parental schema regarding children begin with a discussion of what children are capable of doing. Adult examples can be used to illustrate points. For example, if a parent suggests sending children to their room for the whole day as a punishment, children's different sense of time can be illustrated with the following: "Remember how long it took for Christmas to come as a child?—it took forever—and now it seems to come really quickly, right?" Such examples not only challenge the idea that children are little adults but also foster perspective taking.

In the process of doing standard child management training (e.g., defining targets for intervention, basic learning theory principles, use of rewards and punishment; Becker, 1971; Patterson, 1971), the therapist needs to be alert to examples of misattributions and unrealistic expectations in the parent's narrative. Table 4.2 illustrates some examples of phrases that may signal the need for cognitive interventions.

Directly soliciting parental thoughts regarding any behavior the parent describes as problematic is crucial. Any behavioral strategy may be doomed to failure if the parent is not motivated because the behavior is interpreted as either part of a lack of caring on the child's part (negative intent) or evidence of a child's negative personality (a stable attribute).

Cognitions can also be identified in the midst of role plays or through the use of imagery techniques using preidentified parenting situations. For example, tantrums in stores are often seen as aimed at embarrassing parents (e.g., "He was trying to make me look bad in front of people. He always waits until we are out in public!"). The therapist can "walk" parents through such a situation by using guided imagery and solicit what might be happening to the parent internally (cognitively, physically) to get at core triggers for anger.

Once self-defeating or maladaptive cognitions are identified, cognitive restructuring work can follow. It has been argued that the challenging of parents' strongly held negative expectancies needs to proceed cautiously. Confrontation may increase parental defensiveness and may activate parents to marshal confirmatory evidence, leading to further entrenchment in their maladaptive views (Johnston, 1996). Therapists again might model the self-questioning involved in challenging extreme thinking and the more favorable outcomes that parents might expect if they adopt different interpretations. Parents can then be challenged as to whether their negative internal dialogue

TABLE 4.2   Phrases in Parents' Narratives That May Signal the Need for
Cognitive Work

Phrase	*Example Statements*	*Distorted Underlying Assumption/Expectation/ Cognitive Problem*
"He/She knows"	He knew I was tired. He knows his father had a bad day. She knows I don't let her do that.	Assumption of mind reading
A string of personality-based comments	He's a sneak. She's a brat.	Stable negative internal attributions
Evidence of a power struggle	She thinks she's boss! I can't let her get away with this! He thinks he can put one over on me!	Low self-efficacy
Overly personalized explanations of causality with strong language	He knew it would get to me. He knew people were watching, and he did it anyway. She was trying to destroy me.	Misattributions
Self-deprecatory statements	He must think I'm stupid. She must really think I'm dumb!	Negative self-schema
Explanations that are similar to descriptions of others in the parent's life	He's just like his father—no good! She looks at me just like my mother did when I did something wrong. When she does that, she reminds me of me.	Discrimination failure

helps or hinders their self-concept and work as a parent. Wherever possible, their positive expectancies should also be highlighted.

Exercises and adult analogies can be used to chip away at parental beliefs that children think like adults (e.g., "He knew what he was doing"). For example, the therapist can have preschool children do Piagetian conservation tasks in a parent's presence to illustrate their immature cognitive abilities. Faulty beliefs can then be replaced with more adaptive or calming ones that allow parents to operate more successfully (e.g., "He's only 2, he doesn't know any better").

Role schemas that are inflexible or not well articulated might also be targeted. For example, parents might be asked to generate definitions of a "good" mother or a "bad" mother to identify rigid elements in their role schemas, which then can be challenged (e.g., extreme words like "a mother *always*" or "a father *should*"). If done in the initial sessions of a group, this task also helps illustrate therapists' openness to the diversity that parents present.

Occasionally, parents present evidence of role schema regarding being a parent that precludes their engaging in anything that resembles discipline of their child. Such schema may have a basis in their own child-rearing histories (e.g., "I won't be like my mother, she beat me"; "My father used to lock me in the cellar; I can't make my child stay in his room alone"). In this situation, discipline strategies presented in therapy are seen as equivalent to being harsh and a "bad" mother. The stance of the parents, however, may backfire. Restraining themselves may lead to a buildup of frustration and, ultimately, to an outburst of anger with dire consequences. New links need to be made between providing appropriate structure and feedback and their children feeling "safe," rather than "unsafe." Clinically, a useful metaphor is describing young children as developmentally "floating in space" and "pushing until they find walls, ceiling, and floor" and the importance of rules and structure being "in the same place each time so that they can feel safe."

Even in training of standard behavioral strategies, concrete examples are helpful, especially given the intellectual limitations often seen within maltreating samples. For example, in teaching the appropriate use of social rewards, parental attention can be described as children's "paychecks," and the point can be made that parents often inadvertently "pay" children for behaviors they do not want to see.

Discussions regarding punishment are particularly difficult with this population because parents may hold values that physical punishment "works best." The therapist can best open the possibility of alternative strategies by first reviewing parents' own childhood experiences with punishment, what they "learned," and how it may have affected their relationships with their caregivers. This telling of "their stories" brings into the foreground the negative self-schema that punishment may have left them with as children and how it continues to influence their views regarding relationships. By doing so, the idea that "punishment is equivalent to good parenting" comes into question, and this allows for the possibility of challenging the parents' belief system. The successful challenging of this core belief also eases the way toward discussions and role plays around more adaptive ways to invoke negative consequences that will "teach" their children the rules and preserve the relationship they have with them.

Once some trust has been built in the therapist, specific work can be done directly with anger. Typically, for parents to feel free to talk about "losing it" with their children, much ground work has to be laid early around the therapist being nonjudgmental. It is rare for parents to openly acknowledge their being abusive with their children. Guided imagery at this point can be very effective in eliciting "in vivo" signs of anger. These are referred to as "red flags" that should cue parents that they are about to "lose it." In addition, examples from the parents' own lives are elicited and dissected in discussion to identify their own personal signals and situational triggers. Problem solving can then be used to generate alternative cognitive and behavioral responses. Training in relaxation techniques can also be done to provide alternative competing responses under conditions of stress. Communication skills can also be presented with the goal of increasing parents' capacities to identify verbal and nonverbal child cues of distress in the ongoing stream of their interactions with their children and to interpret these cues more positively and/or accurately to produce more adaptive responses. This technique will also help increase parents' perspective-taking ability. It is useful to have parents play the child in role plays or to have them tell the "story of what is happening" from the child's perspective. This technique will reduce emotional and verbal abuse (e.g., name calling, intrusiveness, selectively attending only to negative cues) by bringing alive the child's perspective.

Extensive use needs to be made of problem solving. Each time parents bring new child-rearing problems into discussion, the components of this skill should be reviewed by using a Socratic method to enhance parents' capacity to engage in such questioning on their own. Parents need to be repeatedly asked to identify their thoughts about their children's behaviors, the consequences of these thoughts (if they are maladaptive), and to problem-solve to arrive at an appropriate reframing and alternative solutions.

Although these cognitive strategies may be useful in individual parenting work, group treatment with this population may be preferable for a number of reasons. First, group treatment reduces the social isolation common among maltreating parents (Salzinger et al., 1983). A second and perhaps more important rationale for group treatment from a cognitive perspective is that it is easier at times to illustrate distorted thinking to parents as they hear other parents share their interpretations of children's behavior. That is, initially parents can more readily see cognitive distortions when it is not their child and when another parent is the one verbalizing it, than if the therapist attempts to dispute their own personal distorted thinking. Finally, parent groups allow the presentation of a broad range of child problems. Because each parent has not experienced all possible types of child-rearing problems, hearing others present a variety of problems provides an opportunity for parents to consider potential future difficulties and possible solutions. They can also remain calm and practice the kind of questioning required to decrease their negative and ineffective cognitive "self-talk" and to be better prepared later if they should encounter such difficulties.

It is best to form groups in which parents have children of a common age. Keeping the group restricted to one developmental era is helpful because it allows parents to compare the kinds of typical behaviors they are all seeing and works against the idea that "only my child" does behavior X. This again fosters a decrease in overly personalized negative self-statements (e.g., "Other parents can handle this, what's wrong with me that I can't?"). Such cognitions make parenting more frustrating and isolating and reduce the probability that parents will solicit help from others. More important, such cognitions reduce self-efficacy and lessen the chance that parents will try new strategies because of fear of failure.

As an adjunct to group work, home visiting should be used. This technique allows for individualizing parenting strategies and for further practice in the home each week, promoting generalization. The child's contribution to supporting the maintenance of the distortions (e.g., severe child behavioral disorder) can also best be addressed in these one-on-one sessions. Techniques can thereby be tailored to each family's situation.

More important, because of the high risk to children in maltreating families, home visiting also allows for greater monitoring of the parent and child. Recidivism is high in such families, and therapists need to be vigilant. Furthermore, such parents may misuse strategies (e.g., locking children in closets for time-out), and the home sessions provide an added check here.

Themes that emerge in therapy with maltreaters vary. Common ones include feelings of incompetency in their role as parents (e.g., "If I was a good mother, I could get him to do it"), anger at social service agents for labeling them as abusive or at risk, resistance to advice, and difficulties in achieving compliance and attendance. These themes may need to be addressed early in group work (e.g., through the use of incentives or group problem solving) and may reemerge throughout sessions. The successful negotiation of these themes, however, may model important relational and conflict resolution skills that are lacking in such parents (e.g., interpersonal problem solving). More important, the therapist can also "talk aloud" and provide the parents with thoughts that could go through their heads and the kinds of negative actions that might follow if they have such thoughts. Then, the therapist can model the alternative "self-talk" that might lead to better outcomes. The emergence of such issues also allows for generalization of cognitive work to relationship transactions outside the parent-child dyad (e.g., with their social worker or the child's teacher), which can promote better interactions outside the family system.

Preliminary outcome data with a package that includes cognitive strategies and standard child management training appear promising. At 1-year follow-up, a cognitive-behavioral group treatment produced no recidivism, compared with 21% for a short-term, insight-oriented approach (Azar & Twentyman, 1984). The sample sizes for this study, however, were extremely small, and further work is under way to examine the model's validity and to fine-tune treatment components.

SUMMARY

Early approaches to understanding child maltreatment have not been an effective basis for treatment development. Behavioral approaches, though reducing aggressive responses and increasing parental control of difficult child behavior, may not be comprehensive enough to address the underlying relational problems between parent and child that may undermine children's social, cognitive, and emotional adjustment. A cognitive-behavioral formulation would more adequately explain many of the deficits found in maltreated children. Including the cognitive elements described above into behavioral treatments may be a first step in beginning both to address the difficulties such parents exhibit and improve the overall family environment to facilitate children's development.

REFERENCES

Adamson, L. B., Bakeman, R., Smith, C. B., & Walters, A. S. (1987). Adults' interpretation of infants' acts. *Developmental Psychology, 23,* 383-387.
Ainsworth, M. D. S. (1980). Attachment and child abuse. In G. Gerber, C. J. Ross, & E. Zigler (Eds.), *Child abuse reconsidered: An agenda for action* (pp. 35-47). New York: Oxford University Press.

Ammerman, R. T., Cassisi, J. E., Hersen, M., & Van Hasselt, V. B. (1986). Consequences of physical abuse and neglect in children. *Clinical Psychology Review, 6,* 291-310.

Azar, S. T. (1986). A framework for understanding child maltreatment: An integration of cognitive behavioral and development perspectives. *Canadian Journal of Behavioural Science, 18,* 340-355.

Azar, S. T. (1988, November). *Child-rearing stress and attributional processes: An examination of a cognitive behavioral model of child maltreatment.* Paper presented at the annual meeting of the Association for Advancement of Behavior Therapy, New York.

Azar, S. T. (1989a). Training parents of abused children. In C. E. Schaefer & J. M. Briesmeister (Eds.), *Handbook of parent training* (pp. 414-441). New York: John Wiley.

Azar, S. T. (1989b). *Unrealistic expectations and attributions of negative intent among teenage mothers at risk for child maltreatment: The validity of a cognitive view of parenting.* Paper presented at the annual meeting of the Association for Advancement of Behavior Therapy, Washington, DC.

Azar, S. T. (1991a, April). *Concern about the physical abuse of adolescents: A case of neglect.* Paper presented at the annual meeting of the Eastern Psychological Association, New York.

Azar, S. T. (1991b, November). *Is the cognitively low-functioning mother at risk for child maltreatment?* Paper presented at the annual meeting of the Association for Advancement of Behavior Therapy, New York.

Azar, S. T. (1991c). Models of physical child abuse: A metatheoretical analysis. *Criminal Justice and Behavior, 18,* 30-46.

Azar, S. T., Barnes, K. T., & Twentyman, C. T. (1988). Developmental outcomes in physically abused children: Consequences of parental abuse or the effects of a more general breakdown in caregiving behaviors? *Behavior Therapist, 11,* 27-32.

Azar, S. T., & Benjet, C. L. (1994). A cognitive perspective on ethnicity, race, and termination of parental rights. *Law and Human Behavior, 18,* 249-268.

Azar, S. T., & Bober, S. L. (in press). Developmental outcomes in abused children: The result of a breakdown in socialization environment. In W. Silverman & T. Ollendick (Eds.), *Issues in clinical treatment of children.* Needham Heights, MA: Allyn & Bacon.

Azar, S. T., Breton, S. J., & Miller, L. P. (in press). Cognitive behavioral group work and physical child abuse: Intervention and prevention. In K. C. Stoiber & T. Kratochwill (Eds.), *Group intervention in the school and the community.* Needham Heights, MA: Allyn & Bacon.

Azar, S. T., Robinson, D. R., Hekimian, E., & Twentyman, C. T. (1984). Unrealistic expectations and problem-solving ability in maltreating and comparison mothers. *Journal of Consulting and Clinical Psychology, 52,* 687-691.

Azar, S. T., & Rohrbeck, C. A. (1986). Child abuse and unrealistic expectations: Further validation of the Parent Opinion Questionnaire. *Journal of Consulting and Clinical Psychology, 54,* 867-868.

Azar, S. T., & Twentyman, C. T. (1984, November). *An evaluation of the effectiveness of behaviorally versus insight-oriented group treatments with maltreating mothers.* Paper presented at the annual meeting of the Association for Advancement of Behavior Therapy, Philadelphia.

Azar, S. T., & Twentyman, C. T. (1986). Cognitive-behavioral perspectives on the assessment and treatment of child abuse. In P. C. Kendall (Ed.), *Advances in cognitive-behavioral research and therapy* (Vol. 5, pp. 237-267). San Diego: Academic Press.

Azar, S. T., & Wolfe, D. (1989). Child abuse and neglect. In E. J. Mash & R. A. Barkley (Eds.), *Treatment of childhood disorders* (pp. 451-489). New York: Guilford.

Barnes, K. T., & Azar, S. T. (1990, August). *Maternal expectations and attributions in discipline situations: A test of a cognitive model of parenting.* Poster presented at the annual meeting of the American Psychological Association, Boston.

Becker, W. C. (1964). Consequences of different kinds of parental discipline. In M. L. Hoffman & L. W. Hoffman (Eds.), *Review of child development* (Vol. 1, pp. 169-207). New York: Russell Sage.

Becker, W. C. (1971). *Parents are teachers.* Champaign, IL: Research Press.

Bousha, D., & Twentyman, C. T. (1984). Abusing, neglectful, and comparison mother-child interactional style. *Journal of Abnormal Psychology, 93,* 106-114.

Burgess, R. L., & Conger, R. D. (1978). Family interaction in abusive, neglectful, and normal families. *Child Development, 49,* 1163-1173.

Casanova, G. M., Domanic, J., McCanne, T. R., & Milner, J. S. (1992). Physiological responses to non-child-related stressors in mothers at risk for child abuse. *Child Abuse and Neglect, 16,* 31-44.

Chilamkurti, C., & Milner, J. S. (1993). Perceptions and evaluations of child transgressions and disciplinary techniques in high- and low-risk mothers and their children. *Child Development, 64,* 1801-1814.

Cicchetti, D., & Rizley, R. (1981). Developmental perspectives on the etiology, intergenerational transmission, and sequelae of child maltreatment. *New Directions for Child Development, 11,* 31-56.

Cohen, S. (1980). After effects of stress on human performance and social behavior: A review of research and theory. *Psychological Bulletin, 88,* 82-108.

Crittenden, P. M. (1982). Abusing, neglecting, problematic, and adequate dyads: Differentiating by patterns of interaction. *Merrill-Palmer Quarterly, 27,* 201-218.

Crittenden, P. M., & Ainsworth, M. D. S. (1989). Child maltreatment and attachment theory. In D. Cicchetti & V. Carlson (Eds.), *Child maltreatment* (pp. 432-463). Cambridge, UK: Cambridge University Press.

Dix, T. H., Ruble, D. N., & Zambarano, R. J. (1989). Mothers' implicit theories of discipline: Child effects, parent effects, and the attribution process. *Child Development, 60,* 1373-1391.

D'Zurilla, T. J., & Goldfried, M. (1971). Problem solving and behavior modification. *Journal of Abnormal Psychology, 78,* 104-126.

Easterbrook, J. A. (1959). The effect of emotion on cue utilization and the organization of behavior. *Psychological Review, 66,* 183-201.

Eidelson, R. J., & Epstein, N. (1982). Cognition and relationship maladjustment: Development of a measure of dysfunctional relationship beliefs. *Journal of Consulting and Clinical Psychology, 50,* 715-720.

Epstein, N. B., Schlesinger, S., & Dryden D. (1988). *Cognitive-behavioral therapy with families.* New York: Brunner/Mazel.

Farber, E. A., & Egeland, B. (1987). Invulnerability among abused and neglected children. In E. J. Anthony & B. J. Cohler (Eds.), *The invulnerable child* (pp. 253-288). New York: Guilford.

Fiske, S. T., & Taylor, S. E. (1991). *Social cognition.* New York: McGraw-Hill.

Friedman, R., Sandler, J., Hernandez, M., & Wolfe, D. (1981). Child abuse. In E. J. Mash & L. G. Terdal (Eds.), *Behavioral assessment of childhood disorders* (pp. 221-255). New York: Guilford.

Frodi, A. M., & Lamb, M. E. (1980). Child abusers' responses to infant smiles and cries. *Child Development, 51,* 238-241.

Hansen, D. J., Pallotta, G. M., Tishelman, A. C., & Conaway, L. P. (1989). Parental problem-solving skills and child behavior problems: A comparison of physically abusive, neglectful, clinic, and community families. *Journal of Family Violence, 4,* 353-368.

Heider, F. (1958). *The psychology of interpersonal relationships.* New York: John Wiley.

Johnston, C. (1996). Addressing parent cognitions in interventions with families of disruptive children. In K. S. Dobson & K. D. Craig (Ed.), *Advances in cognitive behavioral therapy* (pp. 193-209). Thousand Oaks, CA: Sage.

Klaus, M. H., & Kennell, J. H. (1982). *Maternal-infant bonding* (2nd ed.). Cambridge, UK: Cambridge University Press.

Larrance, D. T., & Twentyman, C. T. (1983). Maternal attributions in child abuse. *Journal of Abnormal Psychology, 92,* 449-457.

Lazarus, R. A., & Folkman, S. (1984). *Stress, appraisal, and coping.* New York: Springer.

Lovell, M. L., Reid, K., & Richey, C. A. (1992). Social support training for abusive mothers. *Social Work with Groups, 15,* 95-107.

Maccoby, E. E., & Martin, J. A. (1983). Socialization in the context of the family: Parent-child interaction. In P. H. Mussen (Series Ed.) & E. Hetherington (Vol. Ed.), *Handbook of child psychology: Vol. 4. Socialization, personality, and social development* (4th ed., pp. 1-101). New York: John Wiley.

Mash, E. J., Johnston, C., & Kovitz, K. R. (1983). A comparison of the mother-child interactions of physically abused and nonabused children during play and task situations. *Journal of Clinical Child Psychology, 12,* 337-346.

McGee, R. A., & Wolfe, D. A. (1991). Psychological maltreatment: Toward an operational definition. *Development and Psychopathology, 3,* 3-18.

Miller, L. R., & Azar, S. T. (1996). The pervasiveness of maladaptive attributions in mothers at-risk for child abuse. *Family Violence & Sexual Assault Bulletin, 12,* 31-37.

Morris, M. G., & Gould, R. W. (1963). Role reversal: A necessary concept in dealing with the battered child syndrome. *American Journal of Orthopsychiatry, 33,* 298-299.

Newberger, E. H., Hampton, R. L., Marx, T. J., & White, K. M. (1986). Child abuse and pediatric social illness. *American Journal of Orthopsychiatry, 56,* 589-601.

Novaco, R. W. (1975). *Anger control: The development and evaluation of an experimental treatment.* Lexington, MA: Lexington.

Oldershaw, L., Walters, G. C., & Hall, D. K. (1986). Control strategies and noncompliance in abusive mother-child dyads: An observational study. *Child Development, 57,* 722-732.

Parke, R. D., & Collmer, C. W. (1975). Child abuse: An interdisciplinary analysis. In E. M. Hetherington (Ed.), *Review of child development research* (Vol. 5, pp. 509-590). Chicago: University of Chicago Press.

Patterson, G. R. (1971). *Families: Application of social learning theory to family life.* Champaign, IL: Research Press.

Patterson, G. R., & Reid, J. (1970). Reciprocity and coercion: Two facets of social systems. In C. Neuringer & J. Michael (Eds.), *Behavior modification in clinical psychology* (pp. 133-177). New York: Appleton-Century-Crofts.

Rogoff, B., & Wertsch, J. V. (1984). *Children's learning in the "zone of proximal development."* San Francisco: Jossey-Bass.

Rogosch, F. A., Cicchetti, D., Shields, A., & Toth, S. L. (1995). Parenting dysfunction in child maltreatment. In M. H. Bornstein (Ed.), *Handbook of parenting* (Vol. 4, pp. 127-159). Mahwah, NJ: Lawrence Erlbaum.

Rohrbeck, C. A., & Twentyman, C. T. (1986). A multimodal assessment of impulsiveness in abusing, neglectful, and nonmaltreating mothers and their preschool children. *Journal of Consulting and Clinical Psychology, 54,* 231-236.

Salzinger, S., Kaplan, S., & Artemyeff, C. (1983). Mothers' personal social networks and child maltreatment. *Journal of Abnormal Psychology, 92,* 68-76.

Spivack, G., Platt, J., & Shure, M. (1976). *The problem-solving approach to adjustment.* San Francisco: Jossey-Bass.

Wahler, R. G., & Dumas, J. E. (1989). Attentional problems in dysfunctional mother-child interactions: An interbehavioral model. *Psychological Bulletin, 105,* 116-130.

Wolfe, D. A. (1987). *Child abuse: Implications for child development and psychopathology.* Newbury Park, CA: Sage.

Wolfe, D. A., Fairbanks, J. A., Kelly, J. A., & Bradlyn, A. S. (1983). Child abusive parents' physiological responses to stressful and nonstressful behavior in children. *Behavioral Assessment, 5,* 363-371.

Wolfe, D. A., Kaufman, D., Aragona, J., & Sandler, J. (1981). *The child management program for abusive parents.* Winter Park, FL: Anna Publishing.

5

Interrupting the Cycle of Violence

EMPOWERING YOUTH TO PROMOTE
HEALTHY RELATIONSHIPS

DAVID A. WOLFE

CHRISTINE WEKERLE

DEBORAH REITZEL-JAFFE

CAROLYN GRASLEY

ANNA-LEE PITTMAN

ANDREA MacEACHRAN

Violence against women and children is rooted in sociocultural influences, many of which begin to exert their influence in childhood and adolescence (Health and Welfare Canada, 1989; National Research Council, 1993). Children with a history of family disruption and violence have an elevated risk of becoming victims or perpetrators of violence, especially during mid- to late-adolescence (Dutton, 1994; Widom, 1989). Peers who condone violence, media images tinged with sexist and violent behavior, and a lack of positive role models also contribute to the enhancement of beliefs and attitudes that foster myths and stereotypes about intimate relationships.

Developmental and social learning theories propose that harsh socialization practices lay the foundation for long-term problems in forming stable, noncoercive relationships (Cicchetti, 1989; Sroufe, 1989). Empirical studies have generally supported this view and indicate that, for both men and women, maltreatment experiences make one more likely to become subsequently involved in coercive relationships with peers, intimate partners, and children (e.g., Malamuth, Sockloskie, Koss, & Tanaka, 1991; Stith & Farley, 1993). Experiencing or witnessing violence or abuse in childhood increases the possibility of using or transmitting these same behaviors into intimate and interpersonal relationships during adolescence and adulthood.

We begin this chapter by discussing current progress in the prevention of child maltreatment, which has primarily focused on the parent-child relationship at an early age. This discussion sets the stage for subsequent discussion of the merits of involving middle adolescents (ages 14-16) in educational efforts designed to make them more aware of how patterns of violence emerge in relationships and how to prevent such events from happening. It is our belief that mid-adolescence offers a valuable window of opportunity because it is a period of development that can alter the course of current and future relationships. Knowledge gained and skills learned during mid-adolescence may transfer to youths' subsequent relationships with marital partners and children if provided at an appropriate time and level. Whether a psychoeducational program can significantly overcome the powerful developmental trajectory that is often cast by maltreatment is clearly a question that must be answered empirically. Following an overview of the Youth Relationships Project (YRP), we offer initial results of our ongoing evaluation.

AUTHORS' NOTES: This chapter was supported, in part, by a Senior Research Fellowship Award and Research Grant from the Ontario Mental Health Foundation to the first author. Requests for reprints may be sent to David Wolfe, Department of Psychology, University of Western Ontario, London, Canada, N6A 5C2.

The authors wish to thank the administration and staff of the London/Middlesex Children's Aid Society, Oxford County Children's Aid Society, and St. Thomas Family and Children's Services for their assistance in this research.

PROGRESS IN THE PREVENTION
OF CHILD MALTREATMENT

Prevention of child maltreatment has been attempted at all three levels (universal, selected, and indicated prevention approaches), although the success of these efforts has varied considerably. Prevention studies aimed at persons already identified as abusive or neglectful (services provided to specifically indicated populations, such as known child abusers) have reported some degree of success at improving child-rearing skills and knowledge of child development, although limited follow-up data, evidence of recidivism, and high cost of delivery reveal the inadequacy of delivering prevention or treatment services only after maltreatment has occurred and been identified (Wolfe & Wekerle, 1993). Selected, or secondary, prevention efforts favor assisting parents and children at an earlier point in time. These efforts usually cover a wide range of interventions, including those designed to assist parents and expectant parents who may possess one or more circumstantial "risk" factors (e.g., low income, single mothers). These wide-ranging strategies have shown considerable promise, especially when the intervention is matched closely with the needs of each individual and his or her family (Wekerle & Wolfe, 1993). Parental need for support, instruction, and linkage to important community resources seems to be met best by personalized outreach efforts involving trained home visitors, such as the Prenatal/Early Infancy Project (PEIP; Olds et al., in press).

Unfortunately, universal (or primary) prevention of child maltreatment (including the promotion of healthy families and parent-child relationships; see Daro, in press) has seldom been implemented and evaluated carefully, largely because of practical and financial restrictions and public resistance to family-based services (Melton & Barry, 1994). The few programs designed to offer universal prevention of maltreatment and related parent-child conflict have primarily relied on educational strategies to teach youth of high school age and young adults about parenthood responsibilities and developmental expectations and behaviors of young children. Evaluations of such programs are limited, although initial results suggest that adolescents do acquire relevant information about parenting and exhibit attitudinal gains consistent with positive parenting (e.g., lower authoritarian attitudes; Lewko, Carriere, Whissell, & Radford, 1986; Ritchett & Towns, 1980). Behavioral gains supporting the preventive nature of such programs in terms of child-rearing ability have yet to be evaluated, however.

From these beginnings, child maltreatment prevention efforts have begun to reorganize around the principle of building upon strengths and developing protective factors in an effort to deter violence and inadequate parenting. This principle underscores the importance of the relational context associated with child maltreatment and other child-rearing problems, as proposed by a developmental psychopathology perspective (Cicchetti, 1989). Establishing an early pattern of successful or unsuccessful relationships, according to this view, is crucial to navigating further relationship successes or failures (Crittenden & Ainsworth, 1989). Not surprisingly, as maltreated children approach adolescence, they face major challenges in forming peer and social dating relationships, which are often accompanied by poor interpersonal adjustment (e.g., wariness, mistrust, hostility) and limited personal resources (e.g., poor problem solving, lower self-efficacy, distorted beliefs about relationships), which further tax their ability to form healthy, nonviolent relationships (Wolfe & Wekerle, in press). Therefore, learning to relate to others, especially intimates, in a respectful, nonviolent manner is a crucial foundation for building effective prevention strategies for child maltreatment (Garbarino, Drew, Kostelny, & Pardo, 1992; Wekerle & Wolfe, 1993) and related forms of violence and abuse between romantic partners (Wolfe, Wekerle, & Scott, 1997). Prevention efforts are multifaceted and can incorporate various methods developed to eliminate any forms of violence (verbal, physical, or sexual) against children or other family members, in conjunction with efforts to promote healthy relationships (Wekerle & Wolfe, in press).

SIGNIFICANCE OF ADOLESCENCE IN THE PREVENTION OF RELATIONSHIP VIOLENCE

Strategy for Promoting Healthy, Nonviolent Relationships

Why are certain children and youth at risk of repeating the cycle of violence? Although this is a simple question with an obvious connection to relationship violence, we are presently dependent on explanatory theories rather than established findings. Three prominent theories are summarized below, followed by an overview of a conceptual model that places primary importance on the role of early child maltreatment in the formation of pathways to violence in future relationships.

Social learning theory proposes that children who witness or experience violence are taught that violence is a normative or acceptable behavior, as well as a valid conflict resolution strategy (e.g., Emery, 1989; Jaffe, Wolfe, & Wilson, 1990). Social learning theory acknowledges that both the media and general cultural influences are important in teaching messages about violence because they present violence as a typical and acceptable way of dealing with problems (Miedzian, 1995). Through the media, youth are exposed to violent, coercive, and sexist models of relationships (e.g., Barongan & Hall, 1995). Extensive exposure to violence, combined with the socialization pressure to conform to gender-specific roles, can significantly affect the ways intimate relationships develop during adolescence. In addition, witnessing violence between parents, being the victim of physical or sexual child abuse or both, or experiencing pronounced psychological abuse or emotional neglect from caregivers has the effect of generating adversarial, hostile beliefs and power-assertive behavior concerning male-to-female, parent-to-child, and similar intimate relationships (Wolfe & McGee, 1994). The maltreated child thus forms representational models of relationships that involve "victims and victimizers," with the maltreated child alternating between being the aggressor and being the victim (Dodge, Pettit, & Bates, 1994).

Feminist theory identifies abuse as gender-specific and attributes violence and abuse to a power imbalance in society in which men benefit from asserting their power and control over women (Walker, 1989). A feminist perspective on domestic violence focuses on the process of sex role socialization as central to men's violence against their female partners (e.g., Dobash & Dobash, 1992; Miedzian, 1995). Power inequality between the genders and active devaluation of females are considered the fundamental causes of violence against women (Sudermann, Jaffe, & Hastings, 1995). Gender role rigidity is viewed as a product of "traditional" socialization practices in which boys are raised to be strong, uncommunicative, competitive, and in control; and girls are raised to be compliant, other-oriented, and not to express anger directly (Serbin, Powlishta, & Gulko, 1993). Restriction of gender roles is believed to reinforce negative attitudes and power imbalances in male-female relationships (Dobash & Dobash, 1992). Similarly, gender-based, inflexible attitudes about each partner's role in a relationship often translate into the belief that the woman is responsible for the relationship, including the happiness and well-being of her male partner, and that the man is entitled to greater focus within a relationship. In a complementary process,

gender-role rigidity may also translate into a man's tendency toward com-
partmentalizing female partners according to the separate functions they can
perform for him (e.g., "Madonna" and "whore" view of women; Dutton,
1994).

Empowerment and health promotion efforts are closely, though not exclusively, linked with a feminist perspective. This view explores the meaning of
the permanent inequality in relationships in which one member is defined as
unequal by society on the basis of his or her sex, race, class, or other
characteristics ascribed by birth (Miller, 1986). Empowerment has a special
attraction to working with youth, especially in conjunction with an emphasis
on the importance of relationships as key methods of learning and developing
interpersonal skills. Empowerment reflects the active way we put our principles into practice, and the concept incorporates many of the implicit as well
as explicit principles underlying prevention and health promotion.

Attachment theory underscores the cross-cultural finding that adult protection and care are necessary for healthy infant development and development in relationships thereafter (Hazan & Shaver, 1994). Human attachment
is a process well designed by nature to ensure proximity, contact, and
interactions that form the foundation of the adult-child relationship. Infant
attachment is essentially complementary in nature: The infant seeks and is
provided with care, and the caregiver, in turn, receives pleasure from the
infant. In adulthood, however, attachment models are typically reciprocal in
nature, with each partner being a giver and receiver of care. How we choose
partners in our dating relationships may be directly related to the kinds of
attachment experiences we have had in childhood and early adolescence. The
need for emotional support, care, and sexual gratification are all naturally
satisfied by close social relationships, and often we are attracted to characteristics and personalities that are familiar to us (Hazan & Shaver, 1994).
Thus, abusive or unsupportive relationship experiences in childhood set up
adolescents to seek partners with similarly abusive, controlling, or submis-
sive behaviors in their dating relationships.

Developmental View of the
Cycle of Violence

Being a victim of child abuse or the victim of interparental violence has
long been associated with the perpetuation of a cycle of violence across
generations. Understandably, the above-mentioned theories, along with

many others, have been drawn on to help in explaining this documented but poorly understood phenomenon. According to Rutter's (1989) cumulative risk model, cross-generational continuity of abusive or neglectful parenting occurs largely because early negative experiences, such as maltreatment, predispose its victims to similarly negative experiences later in childhood, adolescence, and adulthood. Thus, both the amount and severity of maltreatment and the quality of attachment to others are integral concepts in explaining the continuity of maltreatment across generations (Zuravin, McMillen, DePanfilis, & Risley-Curtiss, 1996).

From an intergenerational viewpoint, child rearing can be viewed as an adaptational challenge that is influenced by prior experiences and resources (Sroufe, 1989). This viewpoint suggests that earlier forms of behavior (e.g., the use of threats and physical aggression with parents or peers) become hierarchically integrated with more complex, recent forms of behavior and remain potentially active, especially in periods of stress. For example, a teen who failed to develop self-control during childhood may fall back on using aggressive behavior when threatened or frustrated by a dating partner. Moreover, developmental researchers assume that more recently integrated patterns of behavior are most susceptible to disruption, giving way to the earlier, less differentiated forms that are often more problematic. Newly emerging attempts to resolve conflicts with dating partners will require adequate models and information, practice, reinforcement, and ongoing assistance if the youth is to successfully overcome his or her powerful background experiences.

Finally, this viewpoint implies that a disordered pattern of adaptation may lie dormant until periods of extreme stress, such as conflict with an intimate partner or the demands of child rearing, elicit the previously learned patterns. Predictably, persons who adhere rigidly to previously acquired maladaptive behavior patterns are most likely to fail the challenge of these new adaptational tasks, with tragic results. Many abusive parents and abusive partners certainly fall within the realm of such a descriptive account.

Funnel of Violence

In our model describing pathways leading to the emergence of relationship violence during adolescence (Wolfe et al., 1997), we refer to a hypothetical "funnel of violence" as a way of investigating both distal and more immediate influences on the cycle of violence (see Figure 5.1). At the mouth

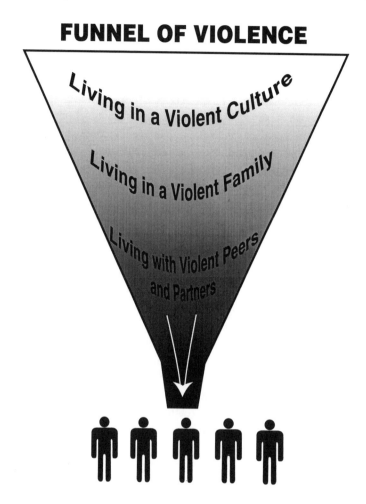

Figure 5.1. Funnel Diagram
SOURCE: Wolfe, Wekerle, & Scott (1997). Used with permission of Sage Publications, Inc.

of the funnel are common, everyday exposures to societal and cultural messages that glorify, glamorize, or exploit violent and abusive behavior. The influence of family members becomes more and more meaningful as we progress toward the narrow end of the funnel. Family members may "filter" and oppose the broader proviolent messages in our culture or model further the abuse of power and control. As discussed above, abusive experiences in the family strongly influence a child or adolescent who is in the process of forming his or her own intimate relationships (Cicchetti, 1989; Zuravin et al., 1996). Youth who have personal experiences with violence and abuse bring forward a central relationship theme and conflict resolution strategy based significantly on the abuse of power. Moreover, alternative sources of information, appropriate nonviolent models, and positive learning experiences that could oppose these forces and contribute to the development of healthy relationships are too often lacking (Coie & Jacobs, 1993; Jessor, 1993).

As depicted by the funnel, these cultural and familial influences lay the foundation for two important lessons in the creation of interpersonal violence: learning to abuse power and learning to fear others. Children and youth are attracted to those most like themselves, particularly when it comes to aggressive behavior and delinquent behavior (Dishion, Andrews, & Crosby, 1995; Patterson, DeBaryshe, & Ramsey, 1989), which further impairs their ability to master developmental tasks and to resist antisocial activity. Finally, individual limitations or challenges, such as aggression, impulsivity, and low self-esteem, interact with these prior and coexisting influences and increase the likelihood of violent relationships and antisocial activity.

We have been testing this theoretical model of relationship violence with samples of high school students (Wolfe, Wekerle, Reitzel-Jaffe, & Lefebvre, in press) to show that it applies even among youth who have not been identified by child protective services. Self-reported maltreatment history was strongly predictive of violence in current dating relationships. Notably, males with a background of maltreatment, compared with those with no maltreatment, reported significantly more coercion, abuse, and intimidation (physical, emotional, and sexual) toward a dating partner and also perceived their partners as exhibiting more coercion and emotional abuse toward them. Females with a background of maltreatment similarly reported using more coercive strategies toward their dating partners and described their partners as more coercive and emotionally abusive toward them. For males, the degree of interpersonal sensitivity or irritability (defined in terms of hostility and avoidant attachment) added significantly to the prediction of relationship violence and abuse beyond the contribution of early child maltreatment alone, accounting for 21% of the variance in such behavior. For females, the connection between early child maltreatment and current experiences of dating violence was also significant, but to a lesser extent than for males. The effects of child maltreatment on outcomes of being the *victim* of dating violence as well as the *offender* (which for females largely consisted of verbal rather than physical abuse) was mediated by females' current attachment style (in particular, avoidant and anxious/ambivalent) and degree of interpersonal sensitivity and hostility.

In sum, adolescents who have had supportive and violence-free relationships with parents and friends in the past are more likely to have a strong base from which to develop future relationships and to resolve disagreements without resorting to violence or the abuse of power. Without such a foundation and role models, a young person is more vulnerable to the powerful influences provided by the media, peers, and his or her own emotional dysregulation. The methods they choose to resolve conflict, moreover, shape the future outcomes of that relationship and many to come. On the basis of these findings and others (Wekerle & Wolfe, 1996; Wolfe & Wekerle, in press), we now turn to a closer look at the patterns of relationship conflict and violence in adolescence that might be amenable to early intervention.

THE YOUTH RELATIONSHIPS PROJECT:
INTERVENTION MATCHED TO THE
RELATIONSHIP CONTEXT

Recent studies have collected descriptive data concerning dating violence experiences of adolescents and their normative beliefs about gender roles and appropriate conflict resolution. These studies suggest that teen victims of violence behave in a manner not unlike that of battered women: They have particular difficulty recognizing the abuse and leaving abusive relationships. Sadly, only about half of teen victims terminate the relationship following a violent act, and a significant proportion of those who remain in the relationship report being unaffected by the violence (see Bethke & DeJoy, 1993). Moreover, studies indicate that between 15% and 25% of male college students (e.g., Malamuth et al., 1991) and 9% and 39% of male high school students (see Girshick, 1993) engage in some level of sexual or physical aggression toward women.

Abuse among teen dating partners is thought to be about as widespread as in adult relationships (Girshick, 1993) and resembles adult patterns of intimate violence: a building of tension, an explosion of anger, and a honeymoon period of making up (Walker, 1989). Such behavior most often appears around age 15 to 16 years (Bethke & DeJoy, 1993) and includes a broad spectrum of physically and sexually violent acts ranging from slapping and pushing to beating or threatening the other partner with severe violence.

Sudermann and Jaffe (1993) reported that, in a sample of 1,547 high school students, more than 50% of girls and 30% of boys reported some form of verbal and emotional abuse by dating partners. Among 9th and 10th graders, 40% of females reported having experienced emotional or verbal abuse from boys they were casually dating, whereas 59% reported having experienced physical abuse and 28% sexual abuse in a steady dating relationship. For these reasons, adolescent dating patterns may represent a bridge between experiences of maltreatment and witnessing wife assault in childhood and the occurrence of similar personal violence or victimization in adulthood. Consequently, adolescent dating activities offer a prime opportunity to educate teens around issues concerning relationships.

Adolescence is a time when intimate relationships and intimate conflicts begin to develop. Adolescent romantic partners increase in their importance as social support providers (Furman & Buhrmester, 1992), with the length of partnerships increasing across time (4 months for 15 year olds to 9 months for 18 year olds; Feiring, 1995). Further, most adolescent conflicts within the context of close relationships result in continued social interaction with that person (Laursen, 1993). Across sexes, when considering long-term teen relationships (1 year or greater), teens highlight reciprocity, commitment, and love as important relationship qualities, suggesting that such partnerships may be conceptualized as attachment relationships (Feiring, 1995).

For these reasons, we have chosen to match our intervention with the context of adolescent dating relationships, rather than with childhood experiences. In developing an educational program, we were interested in the nature of adolescent peer relationships and dating relationships as they pertain to the beginning stages of the abuse of power and control. Adolescence represents a crucial link in the prevention of violence in relationships because it is both an important time for relationship formation and a period in which the scars of childhood can impair normal adjustment. Yet, adolescence has been virtually ignored in terms of its dynamic importance in establishing a pattern of healthy, nonviolent relationships with intimate partners and future family members. Adolescence encompasses important learning opportunities and successful accomplishments that far outweigh the discriminatory view of youth as being antisocial or violent (Millstein, Peterson, & Nightingale, 1993). From a developmental perspective, the transitional nature and normal disequilibrium that accompany adolescent development may represent an especially sensitive and opportune time for early intervention and enhancement experiences (Kazdin, 1993).

Conceptual Model of Intervention
Targets and Methods

A key construct for understanding interpersonal violence is the power imbalance necessary for abusive behavior and victimization to occur (Dutton, 1994; Pence & Paymar, 1993; Walker, 1989). We address both sides of the issue of the abuse of power and control—offending behavior and victimization experiences—for both males and females. Also, our model targets negative behaviors to be prevented, as well as desired behaviors to be promoted; that is, relationships are considered in terms of aspects that increase the risk of violence, as well as behavior that promotes egalitarian problem solving. We argue that, although early maltreatment and negative relationship patterns are strong predeterminants of coercive physical and sexual behavior (both as victim and victimizer) in young adulthood, the developmental course can be mediated through psychoeducational intervention during adolescence that involves the following components: (a) cognitive awareness of the foundations of abusive behavior and attitudes and beliefs about relationship violence and (b) skills to help adolescents in building healthy relationships, to recognize and respond to abuse in their own relationships and in relationships of their peers, and to increase competency through community involvement and social action.

Fisher and Fisher (1992) concluded in their review of risk prevention programs with adolescents that modifying "risk behaviors" is best achieved by simultaneously attending to participants' needs for accurate information, motivational influences, and behavioral skills. Coupled with the experiences and settings linked with relationship violence noted above, we have based our conceptual framework for intervention on these three intervention components. This prevention model was also developed in conjunction with other health promotion efforts with youth, such as sexual activity, weight control, smoking, and exercise, where considerable progress has been made by capitalizing on the natural interest and motivation of youth to learn about lifestyle issues (Dryfoos, 1990). For example, Millstein et al. (1993) describe major considerations for health promotion with youth: (a) Greater self-understanding can be fostered through interventions in which teens learn to express personal points of view while keeping an open mind to alternative perspectives; (b) active exploration of alternative roles can be supported by community-based projects, apprenticeships, and other learning experiences; (c) youth may build self-esteem by experiencing opportunities to feel competent and behave successfully; (d) self-efficacy and potency are bolstered by improving their life skills and by providing opportunities for community service; and (e) support from peers can be increased by interventions or educational opportunities aimed at these social-cognitive-behavioral skills. These considerations were integrated into the following intervention components.

To accompany this model, we developed the Conflict in Relationships Questionnaire (CIRQ; Wolfe, Reitzel-Jaffe, Gough, & Wekerle, 1994) as a way to measure more precisely the nature and scope of verbal and physical abuse/violence in adolescent dating relationships, both as an offender and as a victim. A pilot study of 76 youth (33 males; 43 females) from Child Protective Services (CPS) reported their experiences on this measure, as shown in Table 5.1. These findings demonstrate the nature and extent of problems among these high-risk youth (those who grew up with documented and severe episodes of violence). What is first apparent from Table 5.1 is the high victimization reporting rate among (mostly younger) girls of forced sex (56%) and of being slapped or having hair pulled (47%) by a dating partner, and among males of being kicked, hit, or punched by a dating partner (24%). In contrast, "offender" behavior appears to be emergent for both genders, with girls more likely than boys to report having thrown something ($\chi^2 = 5.96$, $p < .01$) or kicked, hit, or punched their partners ($\chi^2 = 2.24$, $p < .13$).[1] Males did not commonly report any offender behaviors, with only three males accounting for the offenses shown in Table 5.1. Our high school samples, as well as CPS samples, however, have revealed relatively high male "offender behaviors" reported by girls, consistent with other findings (that such behavior may be common; Follingstad, Wright, Lloyd, & Sebastian, 1991). Thus, although research has suggested that males "drive" an adult domestically violent system (Hotaling & Sugarman, 1986), the dynamics and transformations of adolescent partnerships are less understood.

Curriculum and Participants of the Youth Relationships Project

The Youth Relationships Project (YRP) curriculum is based on aspects of attachment theory, social learning theory, and feminist explanations of relationship violence among youth. In brief, our model hypothesizes that coercive sexual and physical patterns (both as victim and victimizer) are linked with early maltreatment and attachment experiences, mediated by such

TABLE 5.1. Frequency of Offender and Victim Experiences Among Youth
Receiving Child Protective Services

	Males (n = 33)		Females (n = 43)	
	Offender	Victim	Offender	Victim
Violent Act Against Partner[a]				
Pushed, shoved, or shook	2 (6%)	1 (3%)	0 (0%)	6 (14%)
Slapped or pulled hair	2 (6%)	4 (12%)	5 (12%)	20 (47%)[b]
Forced partner to have sex	1 (3%)	0 (0%)	0 (0%)	24 (56%)[b]
Kicked, hit, or punched	2 (6%)	8 (24%)	9 (21%)[c]	8 (19%)
Threw something at partner	0 (0%)	4 (12%)	9 (21%)	0 (0%)

NOTES: a. 16% (N = 12) of the sample were not dating and were included as a non-occurrence.
b. These behaviors were more common among youth < 15 years old.
c. These behaviors were more common among older youth ≥ 15 years old.

variables as interpersonal relating, normative beliefs and attitudes, and
problem-solving/decision-making strategies (Wolfe et al., 1996). The YRP
is a youth-centered education program that focuses on education regarding
interpersonal violence and abuse, communication and healthy relationship
skills development, and social action. We base our approach on the belief
that a positive foundation in relationship-enhancing skills will facilitate
ongoing development as adolescents move into adult-partner and parent-
child roles (Holtzworth-Munroe et al., in press).

The program was designed for adolescents 14 to 16 years old who have
experienced maltreatment in childhood. We focus on this age range because
this is the age when adolescents are beginning to develop intimate relationships and are therefore intrinsically interested in relationship issues directly
relevant to their lives. It is hoped that we can provide them with the skills to
develop healthy relationships as they begin to date. Currently, adolescents
who are in the care of, or have association with, CPS agencies are the primary
recipients of the program largely because they have experienced past events
that place them at greater risk of relationship violence. Application of the
program in high schools is underway with youth who have a wide range of
maltreatment experiences but are not identified on this basis. The program
is conducted by two cofacilitators, a male and a female who model appropriate sharing of power in their relationship with each other and with the
adolescents. Teens participating in the program meet in groups of 10 to 12
for 2 hours each week for 18 weeks.

The YRP was organized around the four major objectives noted in Table 5.2. Briefly, group discussions and field group activities have been designed to promote nonaggressive attitudes and beliefs concerning women, to strengthen social competence in areas related to relationships, to strengthen noncontrolling conflict resolution and communication skills, and to enhance teens' perceptions of their ability to use such skills. Five stages are incorporated into each lesson: teach, show, practice, reinforce, and apply (McWhirter, McWhirter, McWhirter, & McWhirter, 1993). All skills are role-modeled by the cofacilitators, opportunities are given for rehearsal, and ways to practice outside the group are suggested. Prevention of relationship violence, therefore, is achieved through education and information, skill development, and an opportunity for social action—the chance to make a difference and to educate others. Skills are taught through role-playing exercises, demonstrations and panel discussions offered by community advocates (e.g., former batterers), video-based demonstrations of abusive and nonabusive communication, and similar exercises and small-group discussions (see Wolfe et al., 1996). We focus on the development of positive, prosocial alternatives to aggression-based interpersonal problem solving that replace narrow, gender-based role expectations. Ways in which attitudes and subtle forms of coercion can develop into patterns of violence or victimization are shown. This intervention is unique in that it is offered within a social context, is both attitudinal and skill-oriented, and allows for considerable input from the adolescents themselves.

Section I: Violence in Close Relationships

The first three sessions of the program are aimed at developing youth-centered group cohesion and examining power imbalances in society. Youth define power and violence and look at the many ways the abuse of power may be expressed. In addition, youth are given the opportunity to identify and explore their personal rights and to learn ways to express their feelings, both positively and assertively.

Section II: Breaking the Cycle of Violence

The next three sessions focus specifically on learning about power dynamics in relationships. Youth are given the opportunity to reflect on how a person breaks out of a cycle of violence that may span many generations. Guest speakers, a former batterer and a former victim of abuse, share their experiences with the group. These "real life" testimonials about intimate violence

TABLE 5.2 Aims and Objectives of the Youth Relationships Project

Intervention Aims and Constructs	*Intervention Objectives (Sessions)*
Section I: Violence in Close Relationships: It's All About Power	1. Establishing a safe, teen-centered environment
Aim 1: Understanding power and its role in relationship violence	2. Power in relationships: Explosions and assertions
Constructs: Power and control; Myths about abuse; Personal power and safety; Communication	3. Defining relationship violence: Power abuses
Section II: Breaking the Cycle of Violence: What We Can Do and What We Can Choose Not To Do	4. Defining powerful relationships: Equality, empathy, and emotional expressiveness
Aim 2: Developing skills needed to help adolescents build healthy relationships and to recognize and respond to abuse in their own relationships	5. Defining powerful relationships: Assertiveness instead of aggressiveness
Constructs: Role stereotypes; Choosing partners; Sexism	6. Understanding power processes: Victim and batterer
Section III: The Contexts of Relationship Violence	7. Peer pressure and the case of date rape
Aim 3: To understand the societal influences and pressures that can lead to violence and to develop skills to respond to these influences	8. Gender socialization and societal pressures
	9. Choosing partners and sex role stereotypes
Constructs: Sexism; Gender differences; Media influences; Assertiveness	10. Sexism
	11. Media and sexism
Section IV: Making a Difference: Working Toward Breaking the Cycle of Violence	12. Confronting sexism and violence against women
Aim 4: Increasing competency through community involvement and social action	13. Getting to know community helpers for relationship violence
Constructs: Help seeking; Community action	14-16. Getting out and about in the community
	17. Social action event
	18. End of group celebration

SOURCE: From Wolfe, Wekerle, & Scott (1997).

enable the youth to ask questions about violence and to recognize the power and control issues they have examined in the first few sessions of the group. Positive communication skills, including active listening, empathy, and emotional expressiveness, are developed in these sessions. A strategy for approaching interpersonal problems is also introduced and used throughout the remainder of the group, involving exercises that develop attending skills, empathy skills, and listening skills. The DESC protocol developed by Bower and Bower (1976) is used to practice the 4-step breakdown of an assertive statement: Describe, Express, Specify, Consequences. This assertiveness script includes such statements as "When you . . ." (describes the problem), "I feel . . ." (expresses how this behavior affects me), "I want you to . . ." (specify the behavior I want the other person to do), "Then I would, and you would . . ." (the consequences, what I would be prepared to do in return). Opportunity is provided to practice these steps based on recent conflicts, as well as a means of providing compliments. Specific communication skills are enhanced, such as the need for young men to ensure consent in sexual relations and the importance of young women being clear, assertive, and safe.

Section III: The Contexts of Relationship Violence

These five sessions bring the societal contexts of relationship violence into focus by examining the role of gender socialization, peer pressure, and media influences. This section allows youth to look critically at how violence is encouraged in our society through subtle and not so subtle messages transmitted from a number of sources. Videos are used in explaining and portraying issues of date rape, marital violence, power in relationships, and in the portrayal of sexism in the media. Discussions center on how such gender-based negative attitudes are at the foundation of the way maleness and femaleness are defined by society and how this fact challenges one's ability to develop healthy intimate relationships. While exploring gender socialization and societal pressure, youth are encouraged to role-play scenarios by using the listening skills they have developed to date. A training video is used to depict scenes involving different power relationships, followed by ways of rehearsing healthy communication skills. An opportunity to practice giving compliments is provided in this section because it is also important for teens to learn that healthy communication skills do not focus only on listening and being assertive.

Section IV: Making a Difference

The final group of sessions focus on learning how to find and use community resources that can help when one is experiencing relationship violence. Youth learn to identify community resources that can help in particular situations, and they visit local community agencies to learn about the services offered. Scenarios are provided, some from personal experiences and some from videos, in which the actors are in trouble (e.g., pregnancy, date rape). For each scenario, group participants have to determine what the problems are and the best ways to solve them. Initial steps are taken, such as consulting a telephone book to find out what services are available in the community. Then, follow-up is made with these agencies by way of an appointment. Youth go to the agency to learn about the services offered and perhaps receive a tour in pairs or small groups. Afterward, they share with other members what they learned at the agency.

These activities are combined with the planning of a social action event designed to raise awareness regarding dating violence in the community and perhaps to raise money for a particular community agency. This event helps provide group cohesiveness and allows youth to go public with their new knowledge regarding relationship violence. It is intended that, through these various experiences with the community-at-large, teens will feel a greater sense of empowerment to deal effectively with violence in their own lives, as well as believe in their effectiveness to make a contribution to ending the cycle of violence in society.

Evaluation Progress

To evaluate the effectiveness of a prevention program, we often focus on measuring how much individuals have changed in their attitudes and beliefs, their use of new skills, and their behavior with dating partners. Prochaska, DiClemente, and Norcross (1992) described the stages of change as being a cyclical or spiral process including five major stages: precontemplation, contemplation, preparation, action, and maintenance. Education-based prevention is likely to be most successful at motivating change from the precontemplation to the contemplation stage. Skills-based prevention focusing on developing coping and competency skills is most likely to shift an individual from the contemplation stage to the preparation stage. And action-based activities are most likely to move an individual to the action and maintenance stages of change. Because many attempts are often needed to change behavior patterns and because relapse is an expected part of the change process, we make an effort to continually expose youth to education, skills, and action to help them achieve and maintain desired change.

Modeling Growth Within Sessions

We are undergoing a full evaluation of the YRP, and we present herein some process data that support the program model and "fit" with youth. This example provides a useful description of how hierarchical linear modeling (HLM) can be used to measure growth in relationship skills, awareness, and knowledge among youth. Much of the research on measuring change has been based on individual status at two time points—pre- and posttest—thereby collecting two waves of data on each subject. In general, two time points provide an inadequate basis for studying change because they provide only minimum information regarding growth (Bryk & Raudenbush, 1987). HLM uses multiple waves of data collected on groups or individuals over time to establish a longitudinal growth record as a model of change (Willett, Ayoub, & Robinson, 1991). The advantages to this approach over repeated measures and covariance procedures are clear, including better handling of missing data, stronger parameter estimates of growth, and flexibility in collecting multiple waves of data (Gottman & Rushe, 1993).

One of our first objectives was to determine the level of interest and understanding shown by youth who participate in the YRP. Group cofacilitators used a descriptive rating form to evaluate each participant's involvement and change in the program each week, using a 7-point scale (1 = lowest level of attainment; 7 = highest level of attainment). The four principal categories were (a) *support:* the extent to which the participant made statements of prosocial support to another member; (b) *interest:* the degree to which the participant attended to the material; (c) *expression of negative attitudes and beliefs about relationship violence;* and (d) *cognitive understanding* of the material. Although such ratings can be subject to reporter bias, they form a useful in vivo measure of change without introducing a highly intrusive observer to the group. Interrater consistency was achieved through independent ratings by cofacilitators, followed by comparison and discussion of differences greater than two points (independent reliability calculations were not available using this method, however).

An HLM Level 1 (unconditional) growth modeling analysis was used to assess growth in interest in the program content and decline in negative attitudes and beliefs about relationship violence over the 18 weeks.[2] Using a multiwave approach (weekly ratings of change), we represented each individual growth trajectory by a linear growth model to describe true status as a function of time (Willett et al., 1991). The straight line growth model applied herein looked at one key growth parameter: the slope of each line, which represented weekly rate of change for each participant.

Significant positive growth across 18 assessment waves was shown for "support given to others" ($\beta_1 = 0.12$, $t = 4.22$, $p < .001$; see Table 5.3, Part A). With multiwave data, a consistent estimate of the correlation of true initial status and true change can be obtained (Tau). The Tau correlation of -0.46 for these data indicates that teens who had limited supportive skills at entry tended to gain at a faster rate. A significant decline was also found in negative attitudes and beliefs ($\beta_1 = -4.87$, $t = -2.25$, $p < .05$; see Table 5.3, Part B). The estimated mean intercept, β_1, and mean growth rate, β_0, for attitudes and beliefs indicate that the average accumulated rating score for negative attitudes and beliefs was 76.83 at the beginning of group sessions and that the teens decreased an average score of 4.87 per session. In terms of individual variance in growth (random effect), the χ^2 for the intercept parameter suggests that participants varied significantly in their negative attitudes and beliefs at entry into the program, and the χ^2 for growth rate also suggests significant variation in the participants' acquisition of positive attitudes and beliefs. Thus, preliminary within-group evaluation suggests that intervention is initially interesting to youth and remains so throughout the 18 weeks; moreover, the program results in observable changes in youths' involvement with the topic and support given to other participants. Positive growth was realized in attitudes and awareness, which are necessary for the initial stages of change in promoting healthy relationships (precontemplation and contemplation).

Modeling Growth Between Groups

Comparative analyses were conducted on rates of growth in selected outcome measures between subjects randomly assigned to receive either the intervention or control condition (regular CPS). Level-2 HLM analyses were conducted across four time points (pregroup to 6-month follow-up), which involved a comparison of growth curves for participants in each condition.

TABLE 5.3   Linear Model of Growth, Based on Cofacilitator Ratings, of
"Support Given to Others" (Part A) and Decline in "Negative
Attitudes and Beliefs" (Part B)

Part A: Growth in Ratings of Support Given to Others[a]

Fixed Effect	Coefficient	SE	t ratio	p value
Mean initial status, β_0	2.30	0.35	6.67	< .001
Mean growth rate, β_1	0.12	0.03	4.22	< .001

Part B: Decline in Negative Attitudes and Beliefs[a]

Fixed Effect	Coefficient	SE	t ratio	p value
Mean initial status, β_0	76.83	6.43	11.94	< .001
Mean growth rate, β_1	–4.87	2.16	–2.25	< .05
Random Effect	*Variance*	*df*	χ^2	*p value*
Initial status, r_0	659.13	27	62.59	< .001
Growth rate, r_1	64.43	27	53.09	< .01
Level-1 error	333.36			

[a]Behavior ratings on a 7-point scale ranging from 1 (*very low*) to 7 (*very high*).

Based on a sample of 58 (30 YRP participants and 28 controls), a trend ($p <$ .20) was found for the intervention group to exceed that of controls in terms of their decline in use of coercive tactics with a dating partner, using the CIRQ (Wekerle & Wolfe, in press). These results are preliminary and are presented for illustrative purposes only; additional data points and subjects are required to detect growth across conditions (readers interested in the richness of HLM analyses are referred to Bryk & Raudenbush, 1987; Osgood & Smith, 1995; and Willett et al., 1991).

Testing the YRP in a High School Setting (Universal Prevention)

The above study involved youth from CPS agencies with known maltreatment backgrounds (a targeted sample). We are also investigating whether the YRP program can be delivered effectively as a universal prevention effort for all youth, or perhaps those with "normative" exposure to maltreatment and family violence. We tested this idea by randomly assigning 45 high school students to receive the program and another 45 high school students as controls (see Table 5.4).

Briefly, we found that, at posttest, the intervention group showed significant gains in *positive* aspects of relationships and knowledge, relative to controls. Significant treatment effects were associated with knowledge and awareness on an attitudinal measure (Inventory of Knowledge and Attitudes; Rybarik, Dosch, Gilmore, & Krajewski, 1995), and significant gains in positive relations and friends (on the Peer Relations Inventory; Wolfe, Grasley, & Wekerle, 1994). Not surprisingly, the CIRQ data showed trends for improvement in terms of positive communication as well (although changes in *negative* behaviors were not found in this sample). Because this high school sample did not report the degree of relationship conflict in the beginning of the intervention, as did our CPS sample, it is not surprising that this measure is less effective in measuring change over a short time period (the impact of the program in terms of violence prevention takes months or years to evaluate).

Our ongoing evaluation of the YRP involves a battery of measures regarding peer relations, trauma experiences, dating background, and conflict experiences during dating relationships, which are completed at the beginning of the group program, at mid-point, at the end of the program, and every 6 months thereafter for a period of 2 years. Brief telephone interviews are held with the subjects on a bimonthly basis to maintain contact and to determine whether the subjects are dating and how the relationship is progressing. When subjects are engaged in a dating relationship, a video interaction is obtained of the couple attempting to solve a problem that exists in their relationship. Dating partners complete questionnaires about each other regarding social competence and conflicts they experience in their relationships.

CONCLUSIONS

Adolescence is a time of considerable choices, and the importance of relationship formation has been largely underplayed in relation to violence prevention and health promotion. Instead, solutions to problems of youth violence and youth conflict have tended to overfocus on youth as the cause and on detection and punishment as the solution. It is not surprising, therefore, that youth have felt overly criticized and disempowered (Millstein et al., 1993).

TABLE 5.4   Means and Standard Deviations (*SD*) for Treatment (*n* = 45) and Control (*n* = 45) Groups of High School Students at Posttest (Analysis of Covariance Findings)

	Treatment		*Control*		*F (1,87)*	*Sig. of F*
Measure[a]	*M*	*SD*	*M*	*SD*		
1. Attitudes and Knowledge	54.33	12.10	66.67	15.45	4.20	< .05
2. Peer Relations Inventory						
a. Positive Relations	1.65	.47	2.21	.71	12.73	< .001
b. Aggression	1.59	.40	1.82	.49	2.27	< .15
c. Negative Jokes	2.23	.92	2.55	.90	1.31	< .25
d. Peer Network	29.55	5.38	34.09	5.99	9.12	< .01
3. Conflict in Relationships (Behavior toward partner)						
Males					*F (1,29)*	*Sig. of F*
Coercion:	8.44	1.33	8.13	.46	< 1.	ns
Intimidation:	13.78	1.72	15.00	2.86	1.89	< .18
Positive Communication:	18.71	2.43	22.83	3.93	10.43	< .01
Females					*F (1,41)*	*Sig. of F*
Coercion:	15.35	3.10	15.43	2.18	< 1.	ns
Intimidation:	10.19	1.93	9.71	1.55	< 1.	ns
Positive Communication:	10.48	1.79	12.90	1.84	3.14	< .10

SOURCES: Measures are from the Inventory of Knowledge and Attitudes (Rybarik, Dosch, Gilmore, & Krajewski, 1995); the Peer Relations Inventory (Wolfe, Grasley, & Wekerle, 1994); and the Conflicts in Relationships Questionnaire (Wolfe, Reitzel-Jaffe, Gough, & Wekerle, 1994).

NOTE: [a]higher score = worse adjustment for *all measures* (e.g, a high score on positive peer relations indicates worse relations).

Within-group growth analyses reported herein revealed that participants, who were considered to be at-risk of relationship violence because of their histories of maltreatment and their current self-reported beliefs and behaviors concerning dating relationships, attended to the materials without significant disruption and showed interest in the topic throughout the 18 weeks of the program. The content, moreover, seems appropriately pitched to their cognitive level and learning abilities. We are encouraged by these findings indicating that the materials are of interest to this age-group and are relevant to the interests and needs of both male and female adolescents. As well, current between-group comparisons show promise in the ability of the program to produce growth and change in both healthy relationship skills and decline in harsh and abusive behavior toward and by dating partners, although these findings are only preliminary until the complete sample of 400 is available for analysis.

In addition to an effective criminal justice response, the strategy to reduce violence against women and children begins with a view that youth are not merely targets of intervention, but rather are part of a planned approach. Youth need to learn more about power and status to avoid such abuses in the future. Educational and cultural experiences in which power is understood and not abused would assist in this matter. Youth, especially those at greater risk of relationship-based violence and abuse, need education and skills to promote healthy, nonviolent relationships, to develop peer support, and to establish social action aimed at ending violence in relationships.

NOTES

1. Unfortunately, there is no way to determine the degree to which these behaviors were committed in self-defense among young women in our study, and these rates should not be misconstrued as evidence that young women are more violent than young men. Adult women also report high rates of verbal and physical aggression toward their male partners; however, these behaviors occur largely as a function of their fear and self-defense, rather than provocation (Jacobson et al., 1994).

2. Only these two rated dimensions are presented here because analyses of the other two dimensions (understanding and interest in the material) revealed that acceptable levels were reported at the beginning of the program and remained acceptable across the 18 weeks.

REFERENCES

Barongan, C., & Hall, G. C. N. (1995). The influence of misogynous rap music on sexual aggression against women. *Psychology of Women Quarterly, 19,* 195-207.

Bethke, T. M., & DeJoy, D. M. (1993). An experimental study of factors influencing the acceptability of dating violence. *Journal of Interpersonal Violence, 8,* 36-51.

Bower, S. A., & Bower, G. H. (1976). *Asserting yourself: A practical guide for positive change.* Reading, MA: Addison-Wesley.

Bryk, A. S., & Raudenbush, S. W. (1987). Application of hierarchical linear models to assessing change. *Psychological Bulletin, 101,* 147-158.

Cicchetti, D. (1989). How research on child maltreatment has informed the study of child development: Perspectives from developmental psychopathology. In D. Cicchetti & V. Carlson (Eds.), *Child maltreatment: Theory and research on the causes and consequences of child abuse and neglect* (pp. 377-431). New York: Cambridge University Press.

Coie, J. D., & Jacobs, M. R. (1993). The role of social context in the prevention of conduct disorder. *Development and Psychopathology, 5,* 263-275.

Crittenden, P. M., & Ainsworth, M. D. S. (1989). Child maltreatment and attachment theory. In D. Cicchetti & V. Carlson (Eds.), *Child maltreatment: Theory and research on the causes and consequences of child abuse and neglect* (pp. 432-463). Cambridge, UK: Cambridge University Press.

Daro, D. (in press). *Child abuse prevention: New strategies for a new era.* Lincoln: University of Nebraska Press.

Dishion, T. J., Andrews, D. W., & Crosby, L. (1995). Antisocial boys and their friends in early adolescence: Relationship characteristics, quality, and interactional process. *Child Development, 66,* 139-151.

Dobash, R. E., & Dobash, R. P. (1992). *Women, violence, and social change.* New York: Routledge.

Dodge, K. A., Pettit, G. S., & Bates, J. E. (1994). Effects of physical maltreatment on the development of peer relations. *Development and Psychopathology, 6,* 43-55.

Dryfoos, J. G. (1990). *Adolescents at risk: Current prevalence and intervention.* New York: Oxford University Press.

Dutton, D. G. (1994). *The domestic assault of women: Psychological and criminal justice perspectives.* Vancouver, Canada: University of British Columbia Press.

Emery, R. E. (1989). Family violence. *American Psychologist, 44,* 321-328.

Feiring, C. (1995, April). *Lovers as friends: Developing conscious views of romance in adolescence.* Paper presented at the biennial meeting of the Society for Research in Child Development, Indianapolis, IN.

Fisher, J. D., & Fisher, W. A. (1992). Changing AIDS risk behavior. *Psychological Bulletin, 111,* 455-474.

Follingstad, D. R., Wright, S., Lloyd, S., & Sebastian, J. A. (1991). Sex differences in motivations and effects in dating violence. *Family Relations, 40,* 51-57.

Furman, W., & Buhrmester, D. (1992). Age and sex differences in perceptions of networks of personal relationships. *Child Development, 63,* 103-115.

Garbarino, J., Drew, N., Kostelny, K., & Pardo, C. (1992). *Children in danger.* San Francisco: Jossey-Bass.

Girshick, L. B. (1993). Teen dating violence. *Violence Update, 3,* 1-2, 4, 6.

Gottman, J. M., & Rushe, R. H. (1993). The analysis of change: Issues, fallacies, and new ideas. *Journal of Consulting and Clinical Psychology, 61,* 907-910.

Hazan, C., & Shaver, P. (1994). Attachment as an organizational framework for research on close relationships. *Psychological Inquiry, 5,* 1-22.

Health and Welfare Canada. (1989). *Family violence: A review of theoretical and clinical literature* (Cat. No. H21-103/1989E). Ottowa: Minister of Support Services Canada.

Holtzworth-Munroe, A., Markman, H., O'Leary, K. D., Leber, D., Heyman, R. E., Hulbert, D., & Smutzler, N. (in press). The need for marital violence prevention efforts: A behavioral-cognitive secondary prevention program for engaged and newly married couples. *Applied & Preventive Psychology: Current Scientific Perspectives.*

Hotaling, G. T., & Sugarman, D. B. (1986). An analysis of risk markers in husband to wife violence: The current state of knowledge. *Violence and Victims, 1,* 101-124.

Jacobson, N. S., Gottman, J. M., Waltz, J., Rushe, R., Babcock, J., & Holtzworth-Munroe, A. (1994). Affect, verbal content, and psychophysiology in the arguments of couples with a violent husband. *Journal of Consulting and Clinical Psychology, 62,* 982-988.

Jaffe, P., Wolfe, D. A., & Wilson, S. (1990). *Children of battered women.* Newbury Park, CA: Sage.

Jessor, R. (1993). Successful adolescent development among youth in high-risk settings. *American Psychologist, 48,* 117-126.

Kazdin, A. E. (1993). Adolescent mental health: Prevention and treatment programs. *American Psychologist, 48,* 127-141.

Laursen, B. (1993). Conflict management among close peers. *New Directions for Child Development, 60,* 39-54.

Lewko, J., Carriere, R., Whissell, C., & Radford, J. (1986). *Final report of the study investigating the long-term effectiveness of the Parenting for Teens and Children Project.* Sudbury, Canada: Laurentian University, Center for Research in Human Development.

Malamuth, N. M., Sockloskie, R. J., Koss, M. P., & Tanaka, J. S. (1991). Characteristics of aggressors against women: Testing a model using a national sample of college students. *Journal of Consulting and Clinical Psychology, 59,* 670-681.

McWhirter, J. J., McWhirter, B. T., McWhirter, A. M., & McWhirter, E. H. (1993). *At-risk youth: A comprehensive approach.* Pacific Grove, CA: Brooks/Cole.

Melton, G. B., & Barry, F. D. (1994). Neighbors helping neighbors: The vision of the U.S. Advisory Board on Child Abuse and Neglect. In G. B. Melton & F. D. Barry (Eds.), *Protecting children from abuse and neglect: Foundations for a new national strategy (pp. 1-13).* New York: Guilford.

Miedzian, M. (1995). Learning to be violent. In E. Peled, P. G. Jaffe, & J. L. Edelson (Eds.), *Ending the cycle of violence: Community responses to children of battered women* (pp. 10-24). Thousand Oaks, CA: Sage.

Miller, J. B. (1986). *Toward a new psychology of women.* Boston: Beacon.

Millstein, S. G., Peterson, A. C., & Nightingale, E. O. (1993). *Promoting the health of adolescents: New directions for the 21st century.* New York: Oxford University Press.

National Research Council. (1993). *Understanding and preventing violence* (Panel on the Understanding and Control of Violent Behavior). Washington, DC: National Academy Press.

Olds, D., Pettit, L. M., Robinson, J., Eckenrode, J., Kitzman, H., Cole, B., & Powers, J. (in press). The potential for reducing antisocial behavior with a program of prenatal and early childhood home visitation. *American Journal of Community Psychology.*

Osgood, D. W., & Smith, G. L. (1995). Applying hierarchical linear modeling to extended longitudinal evaluations. *Evaluation Review, 19,* 3-38.

Patterson, G. R., DeBaryshe, B. D., & Ramsey, E. (1989). A developmental perspective on antisocial behavior. *American Psychologist, 44,* 329-335.

Pence, E., & Paymar, M. (1993). *Education groups for men who batter: The Duluth model.* New York: Springer.

Prochaska, J., DiClemente, C., & Norcross, J. (1992). In search of how people change. *American Psychologist, 47,* 1102-1114.

Ritchett, D., & Towns, K. (1980, April). *Education for parenthood: Eighth graders change child-rearing attitudes.* Paper presented at the annual meeting of the American Educational Research Association, Boston, MA.

Rutter, M. (1989). Intergenerational continuities and discontinuities in serious parenting difficulties. In D. Cicchetti & V. Carlson (Eds.), *Child maltreatment: Theory and research on the causes and consequences of child abuse and neglect* (pp. 317-348). Cambridge, UK: Cambridge University Press.

Rybarik, M. F., Dosch, M. F., Gilmore, G., & Krajewski, S. S. (1995). Violence in relationships: A seventh-grade inventory of knowledge and attitudes. *Journal of Family Violence, 10,* 223-251.

Serbin, L. A., Powlishta, K. K., & Gulko, J. (1993). The development of sex typing in middle childhood. *Monographs of the Society for Research in Child Development, 58*(Serial No. 232).

Sroufe, L. A. (1989). Relationships, self, and individual adaptation. In A. J. Sameroff & R. N. Emde (Eds.), *Relationship disturbances in early childhood: A developmental approach* (pp. 70-94). New York: Basic Books.

Stith, S. M., & Farley, S. C. (1993). A predictive model of male spousal violence. *Journal of Family Violence, 8,* 183-201.

Sudermann, M., & Jaffe, P. (1993, August). *Dating violence among a sample of 1,567 high school students.* Paper presented at the annual meeting of the American Psychological Association, Toronto.

Sudermann, M., Jaffe, P. G., & Hastings, E. (1995). Violence prevention programs in secondary (high) schools. In E. Peled, P. G. Jaffe, & J. L. Edleson (Eds.), *Ending the cycle of violence: Community responses to children of battered women* (pp. 232-254). Thousand Oaks, CA: Sage.

Walker, L. E. A. (1989). Psychology and violence against women. *American Psychologist, 2044,* 695-702.

Wekerle, C., & Wolfe, D. A. (1993). Prevention of child physical abuse and neglect: Promising new directions. *Clinical Psychology Review, 13,* 501-540.

Wekerle, C., & Wolfe, D. A. (in press). *History of child maltreatment and adolescent insecure attachment models. Development and Psychopathology.*

Wekerle, C., & Wolfe, D. A. (in press). Windows for preventing child and partner abuse: Early childhood and adolescence. In P. K. Trickett & C. Schellenbach (Eds.), *Violence against children in the family and the community.* Washington, DC: APA Books.

Widom, C. S. (1989). Does violence beget violence? A critical examination of the literature. *Psychological Bulletin, 106,* 3-28.

Willett, J. B., Ayoub, C. C., & Robinson, D. (1991). Using growth modeling to examine systematic differences in growth: An example of change in the functioning of families at risk of maladaptive parenting, child abuse, or neglect. *Journal of Consulting and Clinical Psychology, 59,* 38-47.

Wolfe, D. A., Grasley, C., & Wekerle, C. (1994). *The Peer Relations Inventory.* (Available from the Youth Relationships Project, Department of Psychology, University of Western Ontario, London, Canada, N6A 5C2)

Wolfe, D. A., & McGee, R. (1994). Dimensions of child maltreatment and their relationship to adolescent adjustment. *Development and Psychopathology, 6,* 165-181.

Wolfe, D. A., Reitzel-Jaffe, D., Gough, R., & Wekerle, C. (1994). *The Conflicts in Relationships Questionnaire: Measuring physical and sexual coercion among youth.* (Available from the Youth Relationships Project, Department of Psychology, University of Western Ontario, London, Canada, N6A 5C2)

Wolfe, D. A., & Wekerle, C. (1993). Treatment strategies for child physical abuse and neglect: A critical progress report. *Clinical Psychology Review, 13,* 473-500.

Wolfe, D. A., & Wekerle, C. (in press). Pathways to violence in teen dating relationships. In D. Cicchetti & S. L. Toth (Eds.), *Rochester Symposium on Developmental Psychopathology: Vol. 8. The effects of trauma on the developmental process.* Rochester, NY: University of Rochester Press.

Wolfe, D., Wekerle, C., Gough, R., Reitzel-Jaffe, D., Grasley, C., Pittman, A. L., Lefebvre, L., & Stumpf, J. (1996). *The Youth Relationships Project manual: A group approach with adolescents for the prevention of woman abuse and the promotion of healthy relationships.* Thousand Oaks, CA: Sage.

Wolfe, D. A., Wekerle, C., Reitzel-Jaffe, D., & Lefebvre, L. (in press). Factors associated with abusive relationships among maltreated and nonmaltreated youth. *Development and Psychopathology.*

Wolfe, D., Wekerle, C., & Scott. K. (1997). *Alternatives to violence: Empowering youth to develop healthy relationships.* Thousand Oaks, CA: Sage.

Zuravin, S., McMillen, C., DePanfilis, D., & Risley-Curtiss, C. (1996). The intergenerational cycle of child maltreatment: Continuity versus discontinuity. *Journal of Interpersonal Violence, 11,* 315-334.

6

The Prenatal Early Infancy Project

PREVENTING CHILD ABUSE AND NEGLECT
IN THE CONTEXT OF PROMOTING
MATERNAL AND CHILD HEALTH

DAVID OLDS

For the past 20 years, my colleagues and I have been conducting random-ized clinical trials of a program designed to prevent a host of maternal and child health problems that are important in their own right but that create substantial risks for child abuse and neglect and later crime and delinquency. The prevention of child maltreatment is approached in the context of our preventing a wide range of associated health and developmental problems in mothers and children. Some of these problems are listed below:

- Nine infants out of every 1,000 in the United States die before their 1st birthday. As a result of high rates of low birthweight (< 2,500 g), the U.S. infant mortality rate is worse than that of 19 other nations despite dramatic reductions in infant mortality in the last two decades because of improvements in newborn intensive care (Children's Defense Fund, 1992; National Center for Health Statistics, 1991). Low birthweight babies who survive are 50%

more likely to use special education services once they enter school than are normal birthweight controls (Chaikind & Corman, 1991).

- More than 2.5 million children were reported as being abused or neglected in 1990, and one in three of the victims of physical abuse were infants less than 1 year of age. Between 1,200 and 1,500 children die each year as a result of parental or caregiver maltreatment (Daro & McCurdy, 1990). Not only is maltreatment morally unacceptable, but the social consequences are so devastating that the U.S. Advisory Panel on Child Abuse and Neglect has called child maltreatment a national emergency (U.S. Advisory Board on Child Abuse and Neglect, 1990).

- Childhood injuries are the leading cause of death among children aged 1 through 14 (National Center for Health Statistics, 1991).

- High rates of violence among adolescents, both as victims and as perpetrators, threaten the safety and well-being of neighborhoods. Among young people aged 15 to 24, homicide is a leading cause of death, and for African Americans, it is number one (National Center for Health Statistics, 1991).

Although these problems cut across all segments of U.S. society, they are more common among children born to poor, teenaged, and single parents and among women who have rapid, successive pregnancies (Furstenberg, Brooks-Gunn, & Morgan, 1987). A significant portion of these problems can be traced to parental behavior—in particular, to women's health-related behaviors during pregnancy and to the qualities of care that parents provide to their children. Low-income, single, adolescent mothers can have good pregnancy outcomes and children who do well, but their capacity to care for themselves and for their children is often compromised by histories of maltreatment in their own childhoods, psychological immaturity or depression, stressful living conditions, and inadequate social support. These conditions contribute to the greater likelihood that socially disadvantaged parents will abuse cigarettes and other drugs during pregnancy (leading to compromised neurological functioning on the part of the children) and that parents will simultaneously fail to provide adequate care for their children, often with devastating results.

Women who smoke cigarettes and use other substances during pregnancy, for example, are at considerable risk for bearing low birthweight newborns, and their children are at heightened risk for neurodevelopmental impairment (Kramer, 1987; Olds, Henderson, & Tatelbaum, 1994a; Weitzman, Gortmaker, & Sobol, 1992). Even subtle damage to the fetal brain can undermine a child's intellectual functioning and capacity for emotional and behavioral regulation. Compromised neurological functioning on the part of the child makes it more difficult for parents to read and respond effectively to their child's needs, and for their child to experience the kind of trust that forms the basis of healthy development. Parents' capacities to read and respond to their infants' communicative signals form the basis for children's sense of security and trust in the world and their belief in their capacity to influence that world (Ainsworth, 1979). Breaches of that trust have long-term consequences, especially when caregiving dysfunction is combined with neurodevelopmental impairment on the part of the child.

A recently reported longitudinal study of a large Danish sample of children and their families found that children who experienced the combination of birth complications and parental rejection in the 1st year of life were at substantially increased risk for violent criminality at age 18, in comparison with children who experienced only birth complications or parental rejection alone. Although only 4.5% of the sample experienced both birth complications and parental rejection, that group accounted for 18% of all violent crimes among the 18-year-olds. Parental rejection or birth trauma by itself did not increase the risk for violence (Raine, Brennan, & Mednick, 1994). When risk factors accumulate, the risk for adverse outcomes increases, often in synergistically vicious ways.

Although the problems listed have been resistive to government intervention during the past 30 years, scientific evidence is accumulating that it is possible to improve the outcomes of pregnancy, to improve parents' abilities to care for their children, and to reduce welfare dependence with programs of prenatal and early childhood home visitation—but it is not easy. Our optimism stands in contrast with earlier research on home visitation (Combs-Orme, Reis, & Ward, 1985). The earlier research was difficult to interpret because the programs studied were often not designed to address the needs of parents in sensible and powerful ways, and the research itself frequently lacked scientific rigor (Olds & Kitzman, 1990, 1993).

In the following sections, we review the program of prenatal and early childhood home visitation that has been tested in randomized clinical trials and that has been shown to improve the outcomes of pregnancy, the qualities of care that parents provide to their children, and families' economic self-sufficiency when it was provided to low-income, European American families in and around Elmira, New York. An economic evaluation of the program, from the standpoint of government spending, has shown that its cost, when focused on low-income families, was recovered with dividends by the time the children were 4 years of age. More recently, we have replicated the program of research in Memphis, Tennessee (where it was tested with African American families living in an urban area), and Denver, Colorado (where nurses and paraprofessionals were compared to determine their unique contributions as home visitors). The results from these trials are not yet available.

In the course of conducting the program in new settings, the program content and methods have been refined over time. We start by describing the program model, giving particular emphasis to its theoretical foundations.

PROGRAM MODEL

The home-visitation program was designed to improve three aspects of maternal and child functioning: (a) outcomes of pregnancy, (b) qualities of parental caregiving (including reducing associated child health and developmental problems), and (c) maternal life-course development (helping women return to school, find work, and plan future pregnancies). In the Elmira program, the nurses completed an average of 9 ($SD = 3$) visits during the mother's pregnancy and 23 ($SD = 15$) visits from birth through the 2nd year of the child's life. The content and methods of the program, though adhering to a common core and set of theoretical foundations, have evolved over time. This evolution is described below and is articulated in greater depth elsewhere (Olds, Kitzman, Cole, & Robinson, in press).

The program has been grounded in theories of human ecology (Bronfenbrenner, 1979, 1992), self-efficacy (Bandura, 1977), and human attachment (Bowlby, 1969). The earliest formulations of the program gave greatest emphasis to human ecology, but as the program has evolved, it has been grounded more explicitly in theories of self-efficacy and human attachment.

Human Ecology Theory

The original formulation of this program was derived, in large part, from Bronfenbrenner's theory of human ecology (Bronfenbrenner, 1979). Human ecology theory emphasizes the importance of social contexts as influences on human development. Parents' care of their infants, from this perspective, is influenced by characteristics of their families, social networks, neighborhoods, communities, and cultures and interrelations among these structures. Bronfenbrenner's original theoretical framework has been elaborated more recently (with greater attention to individual influences) in his person-process-context model of research on human development (Bronfenbrenner, 1992).

Figure 6.1 displays how this model applies to the current program of research. The *person* elements of the model are reflected in the boxes that refer to "parent" and "child" and have to do with behavioral and psychological characteristics of each. In the formulation of the theoretical foundations of the program, parents, and especially mothers, are considered to be both developing persons and the primary focus of the preventive intervention. Particular attention is focused on parents' progressive mastery of their roles as parents and as adults responsible for their own health and economic self-sufficiency. This program emphasizes parental development because parents' behavior constitutes the most powerful and potentially alterable influence on the developing child, particularly given parents' control over their children's prenatal environment, their face-to-face interaction with their children post-natally, and their influence on the family's home environment.

The concept of *process,* articulated here and denoted by the arrows in Figure 6.1, encompasses parents' interaction with their environment, as well as the intrapsychic changes that characterize their mastery of their roles as parents and providers. Three aspects of process emphasized here relate to individuals' functioning: (a) program processes (e.g., the ways home visitors work with parents to strengthen parents' competencies); (b) processes that take place within parents (the influence of their psychological resources—developmental histories, mental health, and coping styles—on behavioral adaptation); and (c) parents' interaction with their children, other family members, friends, and health and human service providers. For the sake of simplicity, the discussion of these processes has been integrated below into the person (parent) part of the model.

The focus on parents elaborated here is not intended to minimize the role that contextual factors such as economic conditions, cultural patterns, racism, and sexism play in shaping the opportunities that parents are afforded (Olds, 1991). Most of those features of the environment, however, are outside the influence of preventive interventions provided through health and human service systems. Certain contexts, nevertheless, are affected by parents' adaptive competencies. These are the features of the environment that the current program attempts to affect, primarily by enhancing parents' social skills. This is why, in Figure 6.1, the effect of the program on context is mediated by parents' behavior. The aspects of context that we are most concerned about have to do with informal and formal sources of support for

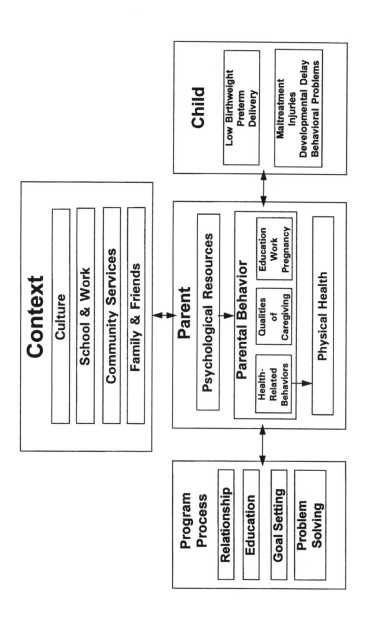

Figure 6.1. Person-Process-Context Model of Program Influences on Pregnancy Outcomes, Child Health and Development, and Maternal Life Course

the family, characteristics of communities that can support or undermine the functioning of the program and families, the impact of going to school or participating in work on family life, as well as cultural conditions that need to be taken into consideration in the design and implementation of the program.

One central hypothesis of ecologic theory is that the capacity of the parent-child relationship to function effectively as a context for development depends on the existence and nature of other relationships the parent may have. The parent-child relationship is enhanced as a context for development to the extent that each of these other relationships involves mutual positive feelings and that the other parties are supportive of the developmental activities carried on in the parent-child relationship. Conversely, the developmental potential of the parent-child relationship is impaired to the extent that each of the other relationships in which the parent is involved consists of mutual antagonism or interference with the developmental activities carried on in the parent-child relationship (Bronfenbrenner, 1979, p. 77).

Program Implications

Human ecology theory has played an important role in identifying which families would be enrolled in the study and when. We chose to work with women who had no previous live births and thus were undergoing a major role change that Bronfenbrenner calls an *ecological transition*. We began the program during pregnancy and the early years of the child's life because, during pregnancy, women have not yet formally assumed the parental role. In providing support to young people prior to and while learning about being parents, we reasoned that the home visitors would enhance their influence on parents' enduring orientation to their roles as parents and providers. The skills and resources that parents develop around the care of the first child would also carry over to later children. And to the extent that the program was successful in helping parents plan for their futures (including planning subsequent pregnancies), parents would have fewer unintended children. This would ease some of the challenges of caring for the first child.

Human ecology theory also focused the home visitors' attention on the systematic evaluation and enhancement of the material and social environment of the family. As indicated in Figure 6.1, the visitors assess and promote informal social support (individuals within the family and friend network who can serve as reliable sources of material and emotional support for the mother in her efforts to care for her children) and families' use of formal community services.

Human ecologists would hypothesize that women's capacity to improve their health-related behaviors is influenced by their levels of informal support for change. Women's efforts to reduce cigarette smoking during pregnancy, for example, are affected by the extent to which individuals close to them believe that smoking is bad for pregnant women and the fetus and to the extent that they actively support the women's efforts to quit. Consequently, the home visitors encourage mothers during pregnancy to invite other family members and friends to the visits in an effort to enhance friends' and family members' support of the mothers' efforts to improve their health-related behaviors and to prepare for labor, delivery, and early care of the child.

The involvement of other family members, friends, and mothers' partners is especially important in helping women practice contraception, finish their education, and find work. In discussions of family planning and contraception, the home visitors make every effort to conduct some of those visits when mothers' partners are present. In addition, returning to school after delivery or finding work usually requires finding appropriate child care; in low-income families, this usually means the mother must find someone in her household or network of friends who might be able to provide reliable and safe care for the baby. The nurses help mothers identify safe and nurturant care within their network of family members and friends and, if none can be found, help them find appropriate subsidized center-based care. To the extent that the home visitors have been successful in helping women complete their education and participate in the workforce, they have altered the ecology of the family by placing additional demands on other family members and friends. Moreover, in spending more time in educational or work settings, women are integrated into social contexts where there are greater pressures to conform to societal expectations. These activities change the ecology of the family in fundamental ways.

Human ecology theory also focuses the home visitors' attention on the identification of family stressors and needed health and human services. The visitors assess the needs of the families and then systematically help them make use of other needed services in an attempt to reduce the situational stressors that many low-income families encounter. Families are helped to obtain such services as Medicaid, Aid to Families with Dependent Children (AFDC), subsidized housing, family counseling, nutritional supplementation, substance abuse counseling, and assistance with finding clothing and furniture.

An important part of the program involves the home visitors helping women interact effectively with the office-based nursing staff and physicians who provide their primary care. In this way, the visitors can clarify and reinforce recommendations made by the office staff and thus help ensure greater compliance with physician and nurse recommendations. During the women's pregnancies, the visitors remind the women about such things as maintaining regular antepartum visits, finishing prescribed medications, and strict bed rest for the early signs of hypertensive disorders.

After the babies are born, the home visitors continue to inform mothers and other family members about the availability of formal community services and provide mothers with the skills to use those services more effectively. As during pregnancy, the visitors communicate with the children's physicians and their office staffs to reinforce the medical staffs' recommendations and to enable the staffs to provide more informed and sensitive care in the office. Parents are taught to observe their children's indicators of health and illness, to use thermometers, and to call the physician's office with appropriate signs of their children's illnesses. The expectation is that this approach will increase the appropriate use and decrease the inappropriate use of emergency departments.

As the program model was transferred from Elmira (where it served a primarily European American population) to Memphis and Denver, it was reviewed from the standpoint of its congruence with the cultural beliefs of the African American and Mexican American families it increasingly served. This work was facilitated by the creation of community advisory committees that reviewed the protocols. The reassuring message in both Memphis and Denver was that the protocols were essentially culturally competent. This sanctioning of the program was based, in part, on its inclusion of other family members and friends in the program and its creation of racially and ethnically diverse teams of visitors and supervisors.

Limitations of Human Ecology Theory

Compared with other developmental theories, Bronfenbrenner's framework (1979, 1992) provides a more extended and elaborated conception of the environment. The original formulation of the theory, however, tended to treat the immediate settings in which children and families find themselves as shaped by cultural and structural characteristics of the society, with little consideration given to the role that adults (in particular, parents) can play in selecting and shaping the settings in which they find themselves.

Consequently, self-efficacy and attachment theories were integrated into the model to provide a broader conception of the parent-setting relationship. The integration of these theories allows for a conceptualization of development that encompasses truly reciprocal relationships in which settings, children, and other adults influence parental behavior and in which parents simultaneously select and shape their settings and interpersonal relationships.

Self-Efficacy Theory

Self-efficacy theory provides a useful framework for promoting women's health-related behavior during pregnancy, their care of their children, and their own personal development. According to Bandura (1977), differences in motivation, behavior, and persistence in efforts to change a wide range of social behaviors are a function of individuals' beliefs about the connection between their efforts and their desired results. According to this view, cognitive processes play a central role in the acquisition and retention of new behavioral patterns. In self-efficacy theory, Bandura distinguishes efficacy expectations from outcome expectations. *Outcome expectations* are individuals' estimates that a given behavior will lead to a given outcome. *Efficacy expectations* are individuals' beliefs that they can successfully carry out the behavior required to produce the outcome. Efficacy expectations affect both the initiation and the persistence of coping behavior. Individuals' perceptions of self-efficacy can influence their choice of activities and settings and can determine how much effort they will put forth in the face of obstacles.

Program Implications

Although self-efficacy theory played a role in the design of the Elmira program through an emphasis on helping women set small, achievable objectives for themselves that would strengthen their confidence in their capacity for behavioral change, it was not emphasized explicitly as a theoretical foundation in Elmira to the same degree as it was in Memphis and Denver. The increased focus on self-efficacy in the later trials grew out of our observation that several of the most important program effects in Elmira (in particular, the reduction in child maltreatment and emergency-department encounters for injuries) were concentrated among women who, at registration, had little sense of control over their life circumstances (Olds, Henderson, Chamberlin, & Tatelbaum, 1986). We hypothesized that the promotion of self-efficacy played a central role in enabling at-risk women to reduce their prenatal cigarette smoking, rates of subsequent pregnancy, and rates of unemployment (Olds, Henderson, Tatelbaum, & Chamberlin, 1986, 1988), given that the nurses used these methods in helping women manage these aspects of their lives. We reasoned that the nurses' emphasis on helping women gain control over specific life circumstances such as these promoted women's generalized self-efficacy.

As a result of these observations, in the Memphis and Denver trials the home visitors were trained explicitly in self-efficacy theory and its applications, and the program protocols were written in a way that distinguishes efficacy expectations from outcome expectations. For instance, women may acknowledge that smoking is harmful for themselves and their babies (an outcome expectation) but not believe that they will be able to quit (an efficacy expectation). Distinguishing these two aspects of the problem helps in the specification of smoking reduction efforts and other individualized interventions.

Much of the educational content of the program was focused on helping women understand what is known (or thought) about the influence of particular behaviors on the health and growth of the fetus, on a woman's own health, and on the subsequent health and development of the child. The educational program represents an effort to bring women's outcome expectations into alignment with the best evidence available.

Improvements in behavior depend on the confidence of individuals in their ability to change. According to Bandura (1982), helping services like those carried out in the current program achieve their primary effect by creating and strengthening the individual's expectation of personal efficacy. Self-efficacy theory has direct implications for the methods the home visitors use to promote mothers' healthy behavior, optimal caregiving, family planning, and economic self-sufficiency.

First, because the power of efficacy information is greater if it is based on the individual's personal accomplishments than if it derives from vicarious experiences and verbal persuasion (Bandura, 1977), the home visitors emphasize methods of enhancing self-efficacy that rely on women's actually carrying out parts of the desired behavior. Verbal persuasion methods are used, of course, but whenever possible they serve as guides and reinforcers for behaviors the women already have enacted. Women who already display some adequate prenatal behaviors are encouraged for what they are doing well. Similarly, the visitors reinforce caregiving behaviors that are close to the goals of the program—such as the sensitive identification of and response to the child's cries, or the removal of safety hazards in the home environment. This identification of family strengths helps build the confidence of mothers and other family members in their roles as parents and provides incentives for their acquiring new caregiving skills.

Second, the home visitors employ methods of behavioral and problem analysis that emphasize the establishment of realistic goals and behavioral objectives in which the chances for successful performance are increased. The same principles apply whether the individual is trying to quit drinking, correct her diet, or improve her relationship with her boyfriend. Because perceptions of self-efficacy predict coping and self-regulatory behavior, the home visitors periodically ask women about their beliefs concerning their abilities to manage all types of problems related to the overall goals of the program or to the concerns of the women themselves. This information is used to help the visitors focus their efforts on creating opportunities for women to accomplish small, achievable objectives related to particular goals. As a result of these observations, visitors in the Memphis program developed a series of questionnaires used clinically to assess women's and other family members' beliefs (outcome and efficacy expectations) and behaviors about their health-related behavior, their care of their children, and their life course. These assessments now provide visitors with a basis on which to begin their educational work with mothers and other family members.

Our articulation of self-efficacy in the program protocols has evolved over each of the three trials. In the Memphis trial, we augmented the emphasis on setting small, realistic objectives with a program of goal setting and problem solving (Haley, 1991; Wasik, Bryant, Ramey, & Sparling, 1992). The theory of self-efficacy was built into the training program more formally, and we began teaching the problem-solving method (defining the problem, generating sets of possible solutions, trying certain solutions, and evaluating the results) as a general approach to coping (Haley, 1991; Wasik et al., 1992). In addition, assessments of efficacy and outcome expectations with respect to critical behaviors were added to the formal test of program effects. In the Denver trial, the program model was further refined with solution-focused methods that emphasize the competence of family members and that are focused on parents' successes (O'Brien & Baca, 1997).

Limitations of Self-Efficacy Theory

Although self-efficacy theory provides powerful insights into human motivation and behavior, it is limited in several respects. The first limitation is that it is primarily a cognitive-behavioral theory. It attends to the emotional life of the mother and other family members only through the impact of behavior on women's beliefs or expectations, which in turn affect emotions. Many people have experienced multiple adversities in the form of overly harsh parenting, rejection, or neglect that often contribute to a sense of worthlessness, depression, and cynicism about relationships. Self-efficacy gives inadequate attention to methods of helping parents cope with these features of their personal history or the impact of those early experiences on their care of their children. We have augmented the theoretical underpinnings of the program regarding these social and emotional issues with attachment theory (discussed below).

The second limitation is that self-efficacy attends to environmental influences in a cursory way. People can give up because they do not believe they can do what is required, but they can also give up because they expect that their efforts will meet with punitiveness, resistance, or unresponsiveness. Although Bandura (1982) acknowledges that adversity and intractable environmental conditions are important factors in the development of individuals' sense of futility, the structure of those environmental forces is not the subject of Bandura's theory. In other words, individuals' feelings of helplessness and futility are not simply intrapsychic phenomena, but rather are connected to environmental contexts that provide limited opportunities and that fail to nurture individuals' growth and well-being. The structure of those environmental influences is the primary subject of human ecology theory, discussed above.

Finally, although Bandura (1982) discusses self-efficacy in terms of groups, communities, and nations, the focus of the theory tends to be on the individual. In this sense, the theory may be less relevant for cultural groups that place greater emphasis on group accomplishments (or survival)—such as kin networks, families, and communities.

Attachment Theory

Historically, our program owes much to Bowlby's (1969) theory of attachment. Attachment theory posits that human beings (and other primates) have evolved a repertoire of behaviors that promote interaction between caregivers and their infants (e.g., crying, clinging, smiling, signaling) and that these behaviors tend to keep specific caregivers in proximity to defenseless youngsters, thus promoting their survival, especially in emergencies. Humans (as well as many other species) are biologically predisposed to seek proximity to specific caregivers under times of stress, illness, or fatigue to promote survival. This organization of behavior directed toward the caregiver is *attachment*.

A growing body of evidence indicates that caregivers' levels of responsivity to their children can be traced to the caregivers' own child-rearing histories and attachment-related experiences (Main, Kaplan, & Cassidy, 1985). Caregivers' attachment-related experiences are thought to be encoded in "internal working models" of self and others that create styles of emotional communication and relationships that either buffer the individual in times of stress or lead to maladaptive patterns of affect regulation and create feelings of worthlessness (Carlson & Sroufe, 1995). Differences in internal working models, according to attachment theorists, have enormous implications for mothers' capacities for developing sensitive and responsive relationships, especially with their own children.

Program Implications

Attachment theory has affected the design of the home-visitation programs in three fundamental ways. The first has to do with its emphasis on the home visitors developing an empathic relationship with the mothers (and other family members where possible). The second has to do with the emphasis of the program on helping mothers and other caregivers review their own child-rearing histories. And the third has to do with the program's explicit promotion of sensitive, responsive, and engaged caregiving in the early years of a child's life.

A fundamental element of the program has been the home visitors developing close, therapeutic alliances with the mothers and other family members beginning during pregnancy. The establishment of such a relationship, consisting of empathy and respect, was expected to help modify women's internal working models of themselves and their social relationships (most important, their developing relationship with their children).

It is important for the home visitors to know about the women's child-rearing histories and their internal working models of relationships because, without intervention, destructive models are likely to undermine the quality of care that parents provide to their own children. By assessing women's beliefs and attitudes toward their children's behavior during pregnancy, the visitors were able to help women and other caregivers develop accurate conceptions about infants' motivations and methods of communicating.

Program protocols have been designed to present systematically how infants communicate, giving special attention to nonverbal cues, crying behavior, and colic and how parents can meet their infants' and toddlers' emotional needs. An emphasis on the mother and other caregivers correctly reading and responding to the infant's cues begins during pregnancy and continues through the end of the program.

To promote sensitive and responsive caregiving, increasingly comprehensive parent-infant curricula were incorporated into the program in each of the three trials. For example, in the Elmira program, all the nurses were trained in the Brazelton newborn examination (Brazelton, 1973). The nurses in the Elmira program, however, thought the primarily didactic nature of the parent-child curriculum failed to provide them with the kind of guidance they needed to promote emotionally responsive caregiving. We realized that we had too few activities incorporated into the program to promote parents' sense of success in interacting with their children. In the Memphis program, the number of standardized materials employed to promote sensitive and responsive caregiving was expanded to include such activities as Barnard's Keys to Caregiving program, her NCAST feeding scale (Barnard, 1979), and an adaptation of Sparling's Partners for Learning program (Sparling & Lewis, 1984). In the Denver program, a curriculum has been incorporated explicitly to promote parents' emotional availability and joy in interacting with their children. Known as the Partners in Parenting Education (PIPE), the program was designed originally for adolescents in classroom settings (Dolezal, Butterfield, & Grimshaw, 1994) but has been adapted for home visitors in the Denver trial. Like Partners for Learning, it uses recommended activities for caregivers and children. One key difference is its focus on shared positive emotions as the goal of the activity. Although we have only preliminary feedback from staff supporting the value of this component of the program, as we have reflected on the development and shortcomings of the home-visitation program to date, we are increasingly convinced that the emphasis on the emotional features of the relationship is fundamental.

Limitations of Attachment Theory

Although attachment theory provides a rich set of insights into the origins of dysfunctional caregiving and possible preventive interventions focused on parent-visitor and parent-child relationships, it gives scant attention to the role of individual differences in infants as independent influences on parental behavior and provides inadequate attention to issues of parental motivation for change in caregiving. Moreover, it minimizes the importance of the current social and material environment in which the family is functioning as influences on parents' capacities to care for their children. For more systematic treatments of these issues, we turned to self-efficacy and human ecology theories (discussed above).

Given that the results of the program based on the Memphis and Denver trails have not yet been published, we now turn to a discussion of the effects of the program employing data from the Elmira trial.

THE ELMIRA STUDY

Starting in 1977, we carried out a study of the program described above in and around Elmira, New York (Olds, Henderson, Chamberlin, & Tatelbaum, 1986; Olds, Henderson, & Kitzman, 1994; Olds, Henderson, Tatelbaum, & Chamberlin, 1986, 1988; Olds et al., 1994a, 1994b). We enrolled 400 women before the 30th week of pregnancy, 85% of whom were either low income, unmarried, or teenaged. None had a previous live birth. Caucasians made up 89% of the sample, and the findings reported below apply to the Caucasians. We randomly assigned the participating women to receive either home visits by nurses (from pregnancy through the child's 2nd year of life) plus transportation for health care and screening for health problems or to a comparison group that received transportation and screening alone. Details of the research design can be found in our original empirical reports (Olds, Henderson, Chamberlin, & Tatelbaum, 1986; Olds, Henderson, Tatelbaum, & Chamberlin, 1986, 1988).

Prenatal Findings

We found that, during pregnancy, nurse-visited women improved the quality of their diets and that those identified as smokers at the beginning of pregnancy smoked 25% fewer cigarettes by the end of pregnancy than did their counterparts in the comparison group. By the end of pregnancy, nurse-visited women had fewer kidney infections, experienced greater informal social support, and made better use of formal community services. Among women who smoked, those who were nurse-visited had 75% fewer preterm deliveries, and among very young adolescents (ages 14-16), those who were nurse-visited had babies who were nearly 400 g heavier, in contrast with their counterparts assigned to the comparison group (Olds, Henderson, Tatelbaum, & Chamberlin, 1986).

Infancy and Early Childhood Findings

Child Maltreatment, Injuries, and Qualities of Caregiving

During the first 2 years after delivery, according to state records, 19% of poor, unmarried teens in the comparison group abused or neglected their children, as compared with 4% of poor, unmarried teens visited by a nurse. This result was corroborated by independent observations of maternal-child interaction and conditions in the home and reviews of medical records. It is important to note that the impact of the program on child maltreatment was further moderated by women's sense of control (or mastery) over their life circumstances when they registered in the program during pregnancy (Figure 6.2). For poor, unmarried teenagers in the comparison group, the rates of child maltreatment were substantially higher for those with little sense of control. The program moderated this risk. We see in Figure 6.3 the same pattern of results for emergency department (ED) encounters during the 2nd year of the children's lives for the sample as a whole (Olds, Henderson, Chamberlin, & Tatelbaum, 1986). (This same pattern was reflected in ED encounters for injuries.) The concentration of effects in the 2nd year of the child's life makes sense, given the dramatic increase in injuries at that time, when children become more mobile and the rates of injuries increase.

In addition, between their 24th and 48th month of life, children of nurse-visited women were 40% less likely to visit a physician for an injury or ingestion than were their comparison-group counterparts. Although no differences were found in the rates of state-verified cases of child maltreatment during the 2-year period after the end of the program (Olds et al., 1994), secondary analyses of the comparison and nurse-visited children identified through state records as having been maltreated indicated that those who had been in the nurse-visited condition were at substantially lower risk for harm than were their maltreated counterparts in the comparison group. They paid 87% fewer visits to the physician for injuries and ingestions during the 2-year period after the program ended, they lived in homes with fewer safety hazards, and their homes were more conducive to their intellectual and

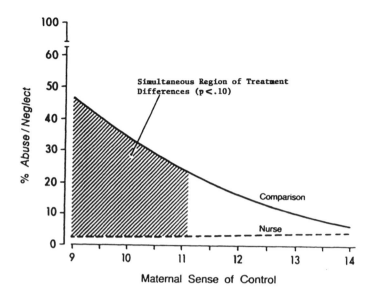

Figure 6.2. Child Maltreatment as a Function of Maternal Sense of Control and Treatment Condition

SOURCE: From "Preventing Child Abuse and Neglect: A Randomized Trial of Nurse Home Visitation," by D. L. Olds, C. R. Henderson, Jr., R. Chamberlin, & R. Tatelbaum, 1986, *Pediatrics, 78*, p. 75. Copyright 1986 by the American Academy of Pediatrics. Reproduced by permission of *Pediatrics*.

emotional development as measured through home-based assessments using the HOME scale (Olds, Henderson, Kitzman, & Cole, 1995). These differences between "maltreated" children in the nurse-visited group and those in the comparison group were so large that they are not likely to be solely a result of the beneficial effects of the program on parents' qualities of caregiving, but rather are likely to be a result of greater detection of maltreatment in the nurse-visited families (Olds et al., 1995). The rate of actual maltreatment is likely to be higher in the comparison group than was reflected in the state central registries because milder forms of maltreatment were less likely to be detected in the comparison-group families.

Maternal Cigarette Smoking During Pregnancy and Children's Intellectual Functioning

Children born to women visited during pregnancy and who smoked 10 or more cigarettes when they registered in the program had IQ scores at 3 and

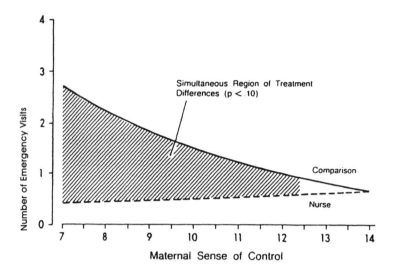

Figure 6.3. Emergency Room Contacts as a Function of Maternal Sense of Control and Treatment Condition

SOURCE: From "Preventing Child Abuse and Neglect: A Randomized Trial of Nurse Home Visitation," by D. L. Olds, C. R. Henderson, Jr., R. Chamberlin, & R. Tatelbaum, 1986, *Pediatrics, 78,* p. 75. Copyright 1986 by the American Academy of Pediatrics. Reproduced by permission of *Pediatrics.*

4 years of age that were 4 to 5 points higher than did their counterparts in the comparison group (Olds et al., 1994b). This is, in part, because of a decline in intellectual functioning over the first 4 years of life among children born to comparison-group women who smoked 10 or more cigarettes during pregnancy, which we think is because of neurodevelopmental impairment resulting from prenatal exposure to the adverse effects of cigarettes (Olds et al., 1994a). The protective effect of the program was most likely because of the nurse-visited women's reduction in cigarette smoking and improvement in quality of diet during pregnancy (Olds et al., 1994b).

Maternal Life Course

During the 4-year period after delivery of the first child, among low-income, unmarried women, the rate of subsequent pregnancy was reduced by 42% and the number of months that nurse-visited women participated in the workforce was increased by 83%. Moreover, much of the impact of the program on workforce participation among the adolescent portion of the sample did not occur until the 2-year period after the program ended, when the teens were old enough to obtain jobs (Olds et al., 1988).

Cost Analysis Through Age 4

We examined the impact of the program on families' use (and corresponding cost) of other government services (Olds, Henderson, Phelps, Kitzman, & Hanks, 1993). In 1980 dollars, the program cost $3,173 for 2 ½ years of intervention. We conceived of government savings as the difference in government spending for these other services between the group that received home visitation and the comparison group. Savings also were expressed in 1980 dollars and were adjusted by using a 3% discount rate. By the time the children were 4 years of age, low-income families who received a nurse during pregnancy and through the 2nd year of the child's life cost the government $3,313 less than did their counterparts in the comparison group. When focused on low-income families, the investment in the service was recovered with a discounted dividend of about $180 per family within 2 years after the program ended.

NEW RESEARCH ENDEAVORS

As a result of these promising findings, we set in motion three additional studies. The first consisted of a 15-year follow-up of the Elmira sample to determine the extent to which the trajectories set in motion early in the life cycle would propel nurse-visited families toward more adaptive functioning later in life. With funds from the National Institute of Mental Health, we are completing an evaluation of the children's adaptive functioning in school, at home, and in society, as well as the mothers' long-term rates of welfare dependence, substance abuse, child maltreatment, and additional children to which they have given birth. We have hypothesized that the program will reduce the rates of children's disruptive behavior, given the impact of the program on (a) neurodevelopmental impairment of the child because of the reduction in cigarette smoking and improvement in diet during pregnancy (Olds et al., 1994a, 1994b); (b) abuse and neglect of the child at earlier phases (Olds, Henderson, Chamberlin, & Tatelbaum, 1986; Olds et al., 1994; Olds et al., 1995); and (c) rates of subsequent children, welfare dependence, and economic self-sufficiency measured in the first 4 years after delivery of the first child (Olds et al., 1988; Olds et al., 1993).

The second study consisted of an urban replication of the Elmira trial conducted in Memphis, Tennessee. The Memphis trial was designed to find out whether the promising effects of the Elmira program could be replicated with a large sample of low-income African American families living in a major urban area and when the program was carried out through an existing health department. We recruited from the obstetrical clinic at the Regional Medical Center in Memphis 1,125 women who were less than 29 weeks pregnant; 92% of the women were African American, 97% were unmarried, 65% were age 18 or younger at registration, 85% came from households with incomes at or below the federal poverty guidelines, and 22% smoked cigarettes at registration. These women were randomized to receive either (a) home visitation plus transportation for prenatal care and developmental screening for their children at 6, 12, and 24 months of age or (b) transportation for prenatal care and developmental screening alone. We are conducting a 5-year follow-up of the families in the Memphis trial to determine the long-term effects in that community. At the time this chapter was written, the findings from the Memphis trial had not been published, although it is safe to say that many of the most important findings from the Elmira trial were replicated and, in some cases, extended and refined (Olds, 1995).

The third study was undertaken in Denver with support from the Colorado Trust. The Denver trial was designed to determine the extent to which the positive results produced by nurse home visitors can be reproduced with paraprofessional home visitors. This study was motivated by the observation that many home-visitation programs are staffed by visitors who often reside in the communities they serve and who have no professional training in health or human services, although there is no good scientific evidence of the efficacy of this approach (Olds & Kitzman, 1990, 1993). The Denver trial enrolled 736 pregnant women; 45% of the women were Mexican American, 35% European American, 16% African American, and 4% Asian American or American Indian. All either received Medicaid or had no private health insurance, 84% were unmarried, and 30% smoked cigarettes at registration during pregnancy. They were randomly assigned to one of three treatment conditions: (a) paraprofessional home visitation, (b) nurse home visitation, or (c) comparison services. Families in all three groups were provided with sensory and developmental services for the children at 6, 15, and 24 months of age. Suspected problems were referred for further clinical evaluations and treatment. The nurse and paraprofessional visitors in each program followed essentially the same program protocol that was developed in Elmira and refined in Memphis.

PROGRAMMATIC
DISSEMINATION EFFORTS

As data accumulate that this program of prenatal and early childhood home visitation can improve the outcomes of pregnancy, qualities of parental caregiving (and children's corresponding health and development), as well as mothers' own personal development, we have begun to lay the groundwork for dissemination of the program in new settings for programmatic purposes. Legitimate questions can be raised, however, about the extent to which results from randomized trials can be used to predict results from programs that are implemented in nonresearch settings. Replicated programs often fail to resemble adequately the models on which they are based. Consequently, effectiveness may, and frequently does, fall short of expectations. Compromising the model in the process of replicating or institutionalizing it is apt to compromise its performance (Blakely et al., 1987). In the light of these experiences and observations, we have begun a series of new research-related activities to strengthen the applicability of our findings for policy and program planners.

Studies of Program Dissemination

In the winter of 1994-95, we were approached by leaders in the Department of Justice about disseminating our program to some of its "Operation Weed and Seed" sites. Operation Weed and Seed is a multiagency strategy that attempts to "weed out" violent crime, gang, and drug activity in targeted high-crime neighborhoods and then "seed" the area by restoring these neighborhoods through social and economic revitalization.

Our program was selected for dissemination in selected Weed and Seed sites because of its scientific foundations, its effects on child maltreatment and welfare dependence, and its potential for reducing the rates of delinquency, crime, and violence among children as they mature (Olds, Pettitt, et al., in press). We accepted the invitation from the staff of Operation Weed and Seed because it will give us an opportunity to study the dissemination process and thus learn how to help new communities develop a successful replication. A grant to provide training and technical assistance to Weed and Seed sites was awarded in the winter of 1995-96.

In the Weed and Seed initiative, we are not conducting additional randomized trials, but instead are conducting process studies. These inquiries will enable us to explore those factors at the levels of communities, organizations, staffs, and populations served that influence how effectively the program is carried out in accordance with the original program model. Given that many programs lose their vitality once they are institutionalized, we hope to learn something about what it will take to maintain that vitality, including the influence of our own role as developers of the model and coordinators of the dissemination.

CONCLUSIONS

Evidence from our series of trials now indicates that it is possible to reduce the rates of adverse health-related behaviors during pregnancy, child mal-treatment, and risks for welfare dependence, conduct disorder, and violence with this program of prenatal and early childhood home visitation. Although the program described here is expensive, evidence indicates that the long-term costs to government of failing to provide these services exceed the initial investment in the service. One of our next challenges is to understand how to scale up this program so that it might be carried out in many more settings while preserving the vitality and essential elements of the original model.

REFERENCES

Ainsworth, M. D. S. (1979). Attachment as related to mother-infant interaction. In J. S. Rosenblatt, R. A. Hinde, C. Beer, & M. Busnel (Eds.), *Advances in the study of behavior* (Vol. 9, pp. 1-51). San Diego: Academic Press.

Bandura, A. (1977). Self-efficacy: Toward a unifying theory of behavioral change. *Psychological Review, 84,* 191-215.

Bandura, A. (1982). Self-efficacy mechanism in human agency. *American Journal of Psychology, 37,* 122-147.

Barnard, K. E. (1979). *Nursing child assessment satellite teaching manual.* Seattle: University of Washington.

Blakely, C. H., Mayer, J. P., Gottschalk, R. G., Schmitt, N., Davidson, W. S., Roitman, D. B., & Emshoff, J. G. (1987). The fidelity-adaptation debate: Implications for the implementation of Public Sector Social Program. *American Journal of Community Psychology, 15,* 253-268.

Bowlby, J. (1969). *Attachment and loss: Vol. 1. Attachment.* New York: Basic Books.

Brazelton, T. B. (1973). Neonatal Behavioral Assessment Scale. *Clinics in Developmental Medicine, 50.*

Bronfenbrenner, U. (1979). *The ecology of human development: Experiments by nature and design.* Cambridge, MA: Harvard University Press.

Bronfenbrenner, U. (1992). *The process-person-context model in developmental research principles, applications, and implications.* Unpublished manuscript, Cornell University, Ithaca, NY.

Carlson, E. A., & Sroufe, L. A. (1995). Contribution of attachment theory to developmental psychopathology. In D. Cicchetti & D. J. Cohen (Eds.), *Developmental psychopathology: Theory and method* (Vol. 1, pp. 581-617). New York: John Wiley.

Chaikind, S., & Corman, H. (1991). The impact of low birthweight on special education costs. *Journal of Health Economics, 10,* 291-311.

Children's Defense Fund. (1992). *The state of America's children.* Washington, DC: Author.

Combs-Orme, T., Reis J., & Ward, L. D. (1985). Effectiveness of home visits by public health nurses in maternal and child health: An empirical review. *Public Health Reports, 100,* 490-499.

Daro, D., & McCurdy, K. (1990). *Current trends in abuse reporting and fatalities: The results of the 1990 annual 50-state survey.* Chicago: National Committee for the Prevention of Child Abuse.

Dolezal, S., Butterfield, P. M., & Grinsahw, J. (1994). *Listen, listen, listen: A curriculum for Partners in Parenting Education.* Denver: Partners in Parenting Education.

Furstenberg, F. F., Brooks-Gunn, J., & Morgan, S. P. (1987). *Adolescent mothers in later life.* New York: Cambridge University Press.

Haley, J. (1991). *Problem-solving therapy* (2nd ed.). San Francisco: Jossey-Bass.

Kramer, M. S. (1987). Intrauterine growth and gestational duration determinants. *Pediatrics, 80,* 502-511.

Main, M., Kaplan, N., & Cassidy, J. (1985). Security in infancy, childhood, and adulthood: A move to the level of representation. In I. Bretherton & E. Waters (Eds.), Growing points of attachment theory and research. *Monographs of the Society for Research in Child Development, 50* (1-2, Serial No. 209), 66-104.

National Center for Health Statistics. (1991). Advance report of final mortality statistics 1991. *Vital statistics of the United States* (Vol. 1). Washington, DC: U.S. Department of Health and Human Services.

O'Brien, R. A., & Baca, R. P. (1997). Application of solution-focused interventions to nurse home visitation for pregnant women and parents of young children. *Journal of Community Psychology, 25* (1), 47-58.

Olds, D. (1991). The prenatal/early infancy project: An ecological approach to prevention of developmental disabilities. In J. Belsky (Ed.), *In the beginning: Readings in infancy* (pp. 270-285). New York: Columbia University Press.

Olds, D. (1995, May). *Effect of home visitation by nurses on caregiving and maternal life-course.* Paper presented at the 35th annual meeting of the Ambulatory Pediatric Association, San Diego.

Olds, D., Henderson, C., Chamberlin, R., & Tatelbaum, R. (1986). Preventing child abuse and neglect: A randomized trial of nurse home visitation. *Pediatrics, 78,* 65-78.

Olds, D., Henderson, C., Chamberlin, R., & Tatelbaum, R. (1988). Improving the life-course development of socially disadvantaged mothers: A randomized trial of nurse home visitation. *American Journal of Public Health, 78,* 1436-1445.

Olds, D., Henderson, C. R., & Kitzman, H. (1994). Does prenatal and infancy nurse home visitation have enduring effects on qualities of parental caregiving and child health and 25 to 50 months of life? *Pediatrics, 93,* 89-98.

Olds, D., Henderson, C. R., Kitzman, H., & Cole, R. (1995). Effects of prenatal and infancy nurse home visitation on surveillance of child maltreatment. *Pediatrics, 95,* 365-372.

Olds, D. L., Henderson, C. R., Phelps, C., Kitzman, H., & Hanks, C. (1993). Effect of prenatal and infancy nurse home visitation on government spending. *Medical Care, 3,* 1-20.

Olds, D. L., Henderson, C. R., & Tatelbaum, R. (1994a). Intellectual impairment in children of women who smoke cigarettes during pregnancy. *Pediatrics, 93,* 221-227.

Olds, D. L., Henderson, C. R., & Tatelbaum, R. (1994b). Prevention of intellectual impairment in children of women who smoke cigarettes during pregnancy. *Pediatrics, 93,* 228-233.

Olds, D. L., Henderson, C. R., Tatelbaum, R., & Chamberlin, R. (1986). Improving the life-course development of socially disadvantaged mothers: A randomized trial of nurse home visitation. *Pediatrics, 77,* 16-28.

Olds, D. L., & Kitzman, H. (1990). Can home visitation improve the health of women and children at environmental risk? *Pediatrics, 86,* 108-116.

Olds, D. L., & Kitzman, H. (1993). Review of research on home visiting. *The Future of Children, 3*(4), 51-92.

Olds, D. L., Kitzman, H., Cole, R. C., & Robinson, J. (in press). Theoretical and empirical foundations of a program of home visitation for pregnant women and parents of young children. *Journal of Community Psychology.*

Olds, D. L., Pettitt, L. M., Robinson, J., Eckenrode, J., Kitzman, H., Cole, R. C., & Powers, J. (in press). Reducing risks for antisocial behavior with a program of prenatal and early childhood home visitation. *Journal of Community Psychology.*

Raine, A., Brennan, P., & Mednick, S. A. (1994). Birth complications combined with early maternal rejection at age 1 year predispose to violent crime at age 18 years. *Archives of General Psychiatry, 51,* 984-988.

Sparling, J., & Lewis, I. (1979). *Learning Games for the first 3 years: A guide to parent-child play.* New York: Walker.

U.S. Advisory Board on Child Abuse and Neglect. (1990). *Child abuse and neglect: Critical first steps in response to a national emergency.* Washington, DC: Government Printing Office.

Wasik, B. H., Bryant, D. M., Ramey, C. T., & Sparling, J. J. (1992). Mediating variables: Maternal problem solving. In R. T. Gross, D. Spiker, & C. Hayes (Eds.), *The Infant Health and Development program.* Palo Alto, CA: Stanford University.

Weitzman, M., Gortmaker, S., & Sobol, A. (1992). Maternal smoking and behavior problems of children. *Pediatrics, 90,* 342-349.

PART II

Prevention and Treatment of Child Sexual Abuse

7

Trauma-Specific Therapy
for Sexually Abused Children

LUCY BERLINER

A trauma-specific approach to treating children who have been sexually abused has become the convention in the years since large numbers of abused children have been referred for treatment. The approach rests on two basic assumptions: (a) Abuse experiences have specific negative psychosocial effects, and (b) treatment effectiveness is enhanced when abuse-related outcomes are explicitly linked with the abuse experience as part of the therapeutic process. There is substantial support for the premise that sexual abuse is associated with negative psychological consequences (for reviews, see Beitchman, Zucker, Hood, da Costa, & Akman, 1991; Kendall-Tackett, Williams, & Finkelhor, 1993). Evidence for the effectiveness of treatment for sexually abused children is sparser, in part, because relatively few studies have been conducted yet (for reviews, see Beutler, Williams, & Zetzer, 1994; Finkelhor & Berliner, 1995; O'Donohue & Elliott, 1992).

Trauma-specific and *abuse-focused* are terms used to refer to organizing treatment around the abuse experience. Therapy is conceptualized and practiced as an effort to promote successful emotional and cognitive processing of the event(s) (Berliner & Wheeler, 1987). Education is provided about the nature of sexual abuse and the expected consequences, and children are supported in the appropriate expression of legitimate emotions and behavioral responses. Interventions are directly related to changing maladaptive thoughts, feelings, and behaviors associated with the traumatic event. The goals are to reduce the acute abuse-related impacts, to restore or maintain normal developmental progress, and to reduce risk for subsequent maladjustment.

Several theoretical and empirical arguments can be made in support of a trauma-specific approach. The first is that the experience of abuse per se causes emotional and behavioral problems. Although it is clear that children are differentially affected and that no symptom or set of symptoms occurs in even the majority of abused children, almost all studies find that sexually abused children as a group exhibit a greater prevalence of at least some problems than other clinical and nonclinical samples. Some logically related outcomes, such as sexual behavior problems, consistently discriminate sexually abused children and clinical and nonclinical groups of children who have not been sexually abused (Friedrich, 1993). Post-traumatic stress disorder (PTSD), a diagnosis that requires the presence of a specific stressor that produces the symptoms, is found in a substantial proportion of sexually abused children (McLeer, Deblinger, Henry, & Orvaschel, 1992). Certain differences between sexually abused and nonabused children emerge even when levels of family dysfunction are controlled (Hotte & Rafman, 1992). Abuse experiences, like other aversive events, are expected to produce at least temporary distress. As with other disorders that have a specific etiological factor, it is routine practice to make the source of symptoms (e.g., fears following a dog bite) the focus of attention as a means of creating understanding and enhancing coping with the naturally occurring consequences.

It is not just that in most cases the experience is inherently disturbing that justifies a specific treatment approach. A second argument is that attributions for the event and coping responses may lead to the more serious and longer-term negative outcomes. Janoff-Bulman (1989) advances a trauma theory positing that significant, disturbing events that threaten bodily integrity have the potential to alter basic assumptions about self, others, and the world. Psychological adaptation to negative cognitive schemata for safety, trust, power, esteem, and intimacy that are acquired as the result of traumatic experiences can lead to psychiatric disorders and interfere with normal functioning (McCann, Sakheim, & Abrahamson, 1988). Spaccarelli (1994) proposes a model in which the stressful effects of sexual abuse and abuse-related events are mediated by "the formation of negative cognitive appraisals . . . and the use of problematic coping strategies that are the immediate causes of increased symptomatology" (p. 343).

The negative attributions may derive from aspects of the event itself or be related to the ascribed meaning of the event. For example, certain attributions might result from efforts to explain why the abuse occurred, whereas others reflect changes in outlook occasioned by having been abused. Mannarino, Cohen, and Berman (1994) find support for the presence of attributional differences between sexually abused and nonabused children on the dimensions of feeling different from peers, interpersonal trust, and personal attributions for negative events. Among sexually abused children, these attributions are correlated with child self-report measures of depression, anxiety, and self-esteem. Abuse-related attributions have been found to predict the level of children's self-reports of psychological symptomatology (Mannarino & Cohen, 1996; Spaccarelli, 1995). The unique contribution of abuse-related attributions to outcome is demonstrated by the fact that they are not associated with parent-report of behavior or sexual problems (Spacarelli, 1995) and that only general attributions are correlated with symptomatology in nonabused children (Mannarino & Cohen, 1996). Relationships between different kinds of attributions and outcomes, however, are not yet completely understood. In one study, feeling guilty about what happened was associated with meeting diagnostic criteria for PTSD, whereas self-blame for the sexual abuse was correlated with not having PTSD (Wolfe, Sas, & Wekerle, 1994). Correcting distorted cognitions, of necessity, is trauma specific.

Briere (1992) argues that avoidance coping strategies are commonly invoked to reduce the negative affect associated with remembering the event or processing its meaning. Behavioral and cognitive avoidance, both of which are contained in the diagnostic criteria for PTSD, may be employed. Dissociation, usually thought of as a less conscious avoidance process, is also present to a greater degree in sexually abused children (Putnam, Helmers, & Trickett, 1993). Although these strategies may be considered adaptive during the event or when more active strategies are not possible or are ineffective, avoidance coping has been associated with increased symptomatology. Adolescent girl victims of incest who relied on wishful thinking and endorsed tension reduction coping strategies had higher levels of self-reported distress (Johnson & Kenkel, 1991). In a retrospective study of adult survivors, Leitenberg, Greenwald, and Cado (1992) found that denial and emotional suppression were the most frequently reported coping strategies. Although they were correlated with poorer psychological adjustment, the victims reported that these coping styles were helpful. Only one study has examined abuse coping in young children (Chaffin, Wherry, & Dykman,

1997). Interestingly, avoidant coping has associated with fewer behavior problems, angry coping with more behavior problems, and active/social coping was unrelated to outcome. Consequently, helping victims recognize the presence and function of coping is an important component of trauma-specific treatment.

The argument for trauma-specific treatment applies to caretakers as well as to children because parental response to abuse disclosure has been shown to be a significant factor in child outcome. The levels of belief and support for the children are correlated with less distress (Everson, Hunter, Runyan, Edelsohn, & Coulter, 1989), and the presence of a supportive relationship with an adult mediates abuse effects (Conte & Schuerman, 1987). These results are consistent with evidence that resilience in children who suffer from a variety of adversities is associated with having positive relationships with parents or other caregivers (Masten, Best, & Garmezy, 1991). A treatment focus on explaining the nature and effects of abuse experiences and teaching skills to manage abuse consequences is likely to be necessary to engender helpful parental responses, especially where support is compromised. Strengthening parental capacities to understand and deal with abuse effects is key to creating the environment where children can recover.

A trauma-specific treatment approach can be successfully integrated with other important theoretical perspectives that contribute to understanding abuse impact and informing therapeutic responses. Two commonly advanced frameworks for understanding the effects of abuse are attachment theory and developmental psychopathology. For example, Erickson, Egeland, and Pianta (1989) used an attachment paradigm in their prospective study of high-risk mothers and found that the attachments that abused children form with caretakers were more likely to be insecure. Although relatively less is known about the relationship of attachment and sexual abuse than other types of child maltreatment, sexually abused children with confused patterns of relatedness were significantly more likely to be depressed (Toth & Cicchetti, 1996). Alexander (1992) has proposed that insecure attachment can place children at risk for sexual abuse or can be the result of sexual abuse because internal working models for self and relationships with others are influenced by the experience. Where insecure attachment is present or where children are acquiring negative attributions for relationships with others, trauma-specific therapy can address these concerns through interventions focused on enhancing the quality of caretaker-child relationships and the developing internal working models.

A developmental perspective (Finkelhor, 1995) assumes that the stage at which victimization occurs is correlated with the type of response and that these responses, in turn, can interfere with the successful completion of normal developmental tasks. Traumatic experiences may be implicated in a wide variety of disruptions of physical, social, emotional, and cognitive development with cascading effects throughout childhood (Cicchetti & Lynch, 1993; Pynoos, Steinberg, & Wraith, 1995). For example, children's biochemistry, information processing, and memory may be altered in significant ways; children who cannot concentrate or dissociate may fall behind at school; children who constrict emotional responses or who do not learn to regulate negative abuse-related affects may not develop the capacity to experience the full range of emotions or engage in satisfying interpersonal relationships; and children who feel stigmatized or cannot cope with the reactions of others may avoid peers or interact in inappropriate ways.

The complex interplay among abuse, attachment status, and development produces many and varied impacts in children's lives (Cicchetti & Toth, 1995). Interventions with children after abuse experiences must always attend to identifying abuse effects that are compromising important developmental tasks and to promoting normal developmental processes and accomplishments as a primary method of reducing the risk of long-term negative consequences.

Trauma-specific therapy does not assume that every sexual abuse experience results in significant disruption or requires extensive therapeutic intervention. It is quite possible that relatively less serious abuse that involves sexual touching on one or a few occasions, committed by a person who is not particularly important, with a well-adjusted child living with supportive parents, may occasion only minor distress. However, because the internalized attributions and coping responses to the event may be the important sources of subsequent negative outcomes, even when the objective characteristics of the situation do not signal potential problems, some amount of focused evaluation and treatment is indicated. It can provide children and parents with a foundation for understanding the potential later impacts of abuse and support for how they are handling the experience. Because the standard abuse-specific approach ordinarily consists of education and support and is often time-limited, it is well suited for situations even in which negative impact is minimal. At the same time, it is important not to create an expectancy of serious problems in the future.

It might be argued that simply reinforcing the abusive nature of sexual abuse is in itself a source of the traumatic impact. Some evidence suggests that labeling abusive behavior as abusive is associated with increased distress. Carlin et al. (1994) found that, among adult women in a family medicine clinic who described being physically assaulted as children, those who characterized themselves as having been abused had more psychological distress than those who simply reported the assaultive behaviors. These results speak to the importance of attributions as a causal factor, although it is important to recognize that, even among the women who did not define themselves as having been abused, those who suffered abusive assaults as children were more distressed than those who did not have the experiences at all. In contrast, Varia, Abidin, and Dass (1996) found that adults who did not label childhood violence as abusive were more likely to be symptomatic. Leifer, Shapiro, Martone, and Kassem (1991) found that higher levels of cognitive coping, intelligence, and academic achievement were correlated with more distress in sexually abused girls. The researchers concluded that the relationship may be explained by a greater capacity to comprehend the meaning of abuse experiences.

It might be possible, especially for young children whose understanding of the meaning of sexual abuse experiences is derived almost entirely from adult explanations, to minimize initial impact by not explicating the wrongness of the behavior. However, by failing to convey to children that the behavior is wrong and why, children may be at increased risk for sexual misbehavior or may not understand certain disturbing aspects of the experience (e.g., secretiveness). Eventually, children will learn that sexual abuse is illegal and wrong. Early intervention that includes acknowledging the abusive nature of sexual abuse may indeed produce additional initial distress but will also allow for the opportunity to process the events in a supportive environment and to mitigate some of the subsequent negative consequences.

A final issue related to trauma-specific therapy is that many children entering treatment for a history of sexual abuse will have experienced other traumatic events, live in disorganized or dysfunctional family environments, and suffer from nonabuse-related disorders. It sometimes seems that sexual abuse experiences, however minor, are more likely to lead to a treatment referral and psychotherapy for the presumed traumatic effects than are other types of abuse. For example, typical interventions in cases of physical abuse focus primarily on parents with the goal of preventing future abuse and tend to be directed only at children when they develop behavioral problems (Kolko, 1996). The notion that physically abused children might benefit from a type of trauma-specific treatment even without substantial parental change has only recently been advanced (Graziano & Mills, 1992). The danger here is that overfocusing on the sexual abuse or failing to recognize the contribution of other factors to the difficulties of sexually abused children may exaggerate the significance of the sexual abuse in the larger context of troubled children's lives and miss other important targets for therapeutic interventions.

A related problem in these situations is how to carry out trauma-specific treatment when children and families suffer from the associated consequences of a myriad of environmental, physical, and psychological conditions, including poverty, illness, substance abuse, and criminality. These families often seem to lurch from crisis to crisis and to be overwhelmed by the exigencies of simply surviving. Poverty, ethnicity, perception of need, and system involvement are related to whether families follow through on referral for sexual abuse treatment (Haskett, Nowlan, Hutchesone, & Whitworth, 1991; Tingus, Heger, Foy, & Leskin, 1996). Although focusing on the sexual abuse experiences may present clinical challenges, success in addressing sexual abuse sequelae might have the effect of increasing a sense of self-efficacy for both parents and children and serve to motivate treatment compliance for other problems.

TREATMENT OUTCOME LITERATURE

The extant sexual abuse treatment outcome literature has usually not directly addressed the question of whether a trauma-specific model is more effective than other approaches. Although most studies do not provide a detailed description of the content of therapy, all the treatments can be characterized as abuse-focused in the sense that the treatment is provided for the express purpose of reducing or preventing abuse-related outcomes. The results of these studies reveal that children's symptoms generally decline over the course of treatment (Finkelhor & Berliner, 1995). The majority of studies are pre-/posttreatment designs, however, that do not have comparison groups. Because most sexually abused children improve with or without treatment (Gomes-Schwartz, Horowitz, & Cardarelli, 1990; Oates, O'Toole, Lynch, Stern, & Cooney, 1994), definitive conclusions cannot be drawn about the contribution of treatment to the reported outcomes. A few studies do use repeated pretreatment baseline evaluations and find that improvement only occurs following treatment, suggesting that the intervention is accounting for the results (e.g., Deblinger, McLeer, & Henry, 1990; Stauffer & Deblinger, 1996). The quasi-experimental studies that include some treated and some untreated children show no benefit for treatment per se (e.g., Oates et al., 1994). In these studies, however, the nature and amount of the treatments vary significantly. There appears to be little difference in outcomes when a group approach is compared with individual or family therapy (Hyde, Bentovim, & Monck, 1995; Perez, 1988).

Two examples of studies of trauma-specific treatment find preliminary evidence for an abuse-specific treatment effect. Both studies tested a cognitive-behavioral-based, abuse-specific treatment approach. Cohen and Mannarino (1996) randomly assigned abused preschool children to either a nondirective supportive treatment or a structured abuse-specific condition. Parent-reported behavior and sexual problems only improved significantly for children in the abuse-specific intervention. Similarly, Deblinger, Lippman, and Steer (1996) reported that children or parents or both receiving a structured abuse-specific treatment improved, compared with children in a community comparison group. Although most of the comparison children received little if any treatment, the study design permits some conclusions to be drawn about the specific nature of the experimental intervention. There were three conditions in terms of who received treatment: child only, parent only, and parent and child. When parents received treatment either alone or with the children in treatment, they reported that their children's emotional and behavioral problems improved; when the children received treatment either alone or with their parents in treatment, the children reported significant decreases in self-reported post-traumatic stress. Children's self-reports of psychological distress did not improve unless they were direct recipients of treatment.

These studies have important implications for treatment of sexually abused children. They demonstrate that the content and target of treatment, not just the fact of treatment, is related to outcome. In both studies, the treatment component for the parents in the experimental conditions included specific behavior management training, as well as abuse-related education and support. Although it is not possible to determine whether the active ingredient was the cognitive-behavior management strategies or the abuse-related education and support, or whether both contributed, an argument can be made for treatment that specifically provides parents with knowledge and skills to deal with their children's behavior following sexual abuse. These results may also explain why many of the evaluated treatments that did not include such components failed to show improvements in children's sexual or behavior problems (e.g., Nelki & Watters, 1989).

Just as important is the finding that children's self-reported distress did not improve unless the children themselves were the recipients of treatment, although fewer conclusions can be drawn about the role of trauma-specific treatment. For school-age children, trauma-specific treatment is more effective than no treatment or parent-only treatment (Deblinger et al.,1996). These results do not entirely answer the question whether trauma-specific treatment has advantages over other child therapy approaches. A comparison of trauma-specific and nonspecific treatments with children old enough to complete self-report measures is required. In the preschool study (Cohen & Mannarino, 1996), no differences were found on the child self-report instruments. It may be that, for this age-group, parent treatment is sufficient as long as it is specific. The difficulties associated with assessing young children's internal states or identifying adequate self-report measures may be addressed by using measures of knowledge gains about abuse, recognition and appropriate expression of feelings, and improvements in self-protection skills to assess whether benefits accrue from the trauma-specific condition. Sorting out the active ingredient of the parent treatment might be achieved with a design that compares different treatment regimens for the parents.

The process of trauma-specific therapy may also be important in understanding outcome. Lanktree and Briere (1995) note that certain symptoms subside early on in treatment (e.g., depression, anxiety), whereas others do not show improvement until many months later or fail to improve (e.g., sexual concerns, anger). Such results suggest that certain symptoms or abuse reactions respond differentially to treatment content and process, depending on a variety of factors such as abuse characteristics, comorbid symptoms, and the presence of other stressors.

These findings highlight the difficulties that treatment outcome studies with sexually abused children encounter that are not present in other child psychotherapy trials. As discussed by Finkelhor and Berliner (1995), most significant is that sexual abuse is an event, not a disorder. Although sexual abuse is associated with emotional and behavioral problems, there is significant variation in the severity and nature of the outcome. Children are often referred for treatment when abuse is discovered, whether they are exhibiting problems or not. Because sexual abuse is a risk factor for later psychological difficulties (Beitchman et al., 1992; Mullen, Martin, Anderson, Romans, & Herbison, 1996; Saunders, Villeponteaux, Lipovsky, Kilpatrick, & Veronen,

1992) and the exact mechanism leading to poor adult outcome has not been determined, treatment is considered prophylactic as well as palliative. These factors complicate the task of measuring treatment effectiveness in many ways. When children do not present with significant distress or the benefits of treatment may not be known for years, posttreatment assessments may not tell the whole story.

However, there is much to be learned from child psychotherapy outcome research in general that can be applied to sexual abuse treatment. The development of sexual abuse treatment approaches has often seemed to be atheoretical or to have failed to take advantage of a large literature demonstrating the characteristics of effective treatment. With the exception of PTSD, a disorder that has not previously been the subject of child treatment outcome studies, many of the other symptoms reported in sexually abused children, such as anxiety, depression, and conduct problem behaviors, have proven treatments.

Meta-analyses of child psychotherapy treatment outcome studies have shown significant treatment effects (e.g., Casey & Berman, 1985; Weisz, Weiss, Han, Granger, & Morton, 1995). Several lessons from these studies have particular relevance for trauma-specific treatment. Behavioral treatments are somewhat more effective than other approaches. Treatment appears to be equally effective with internalizing and externalizing symptoms, although parent report is more highly correlated with outcome for externalizing problems and child self-report with internalizing difficulties. Therapy effects are strongest when outcome measures specifically match the problems targeted in treatment. Scant evidence favors one modality of treatment over another, such as play, group, or individual approaches.

Certain proven approaches have direct application for symptoms of concern in sexually abused children. For example, Kendall (1994) reported success in reducing anxiety and depressive symptoms with a 16-week cognitive-behavioral intervention that consisted of assisting the children to recognize anxious feelings, clarifying negative or unrealistic attributions or expectations, teaching effective coping strategies, and practicing the new skills. This approach is very similar to the education and gradual exposure model developed by Deblinger and Heflin (1996) and uses treatment materials that might easily be applied to abuse-related anxiety. There is substantial support for cognitive-behavioral interventions for externalizing behavior problems as well (e.g., Kazdin, Siegel, & Bass, 1992).

Adult psychotherapy studies also suggest important ingredients for treatment success with sexually abused children. Two treatment outcome studies with adults suffering from PTSD found that exposure, stress inoculation, and a cognitive processing approach are effective for PTSD and trauma-related cognitive distortions (Foa, Rothbaum, Riggs, & Murdock, 1991; Resick & Schnicke, 1992). Adaptations of these models for children would be consistent with the approach to treating trauma in children advanced by Pynoos et al. (1995):

> The goal of cognitive reprocessing is an enhanced age-appropriate understanding of the circumstances and meaning of the traumatic event(s). It includes efforts to formulate constructive prevention and intervention strategies in relation both to what has occurred and to future situations. Emotional reprocessing represents an effort to understand the origins, legitimacy, and content of negative emotional reactions generated by the experience in order to increase tolerance, diminish self-punitive attributions or repair the subject sense of relatedness. (p. 83)

Because shorter-term treatments are likely to be the norm, it is useful to know that brief treatments are most effective when there is awareness on the part of the client of the problem focus and the rapid formation of a treatment alliance (Steenbarger, 1994). Trauma-specific therapy that focuses on the abuse experiences and its consequences is well suited for achieving maximum gain in relatively short periods, especially because most children will not exhibit the diffuse, broad, and poorly understood patterns that may require a longer period of treatment. Longer-term treatments may well be necessary for adult survivors who have developed more generalized disturbances.

One problem in applying research-based treatment interventions in clinical settings is that therapists and patients do not necessarily conform to the expectations of strict adherence to manualized treatments that is standard in rigorous treatment outcome studies. For example, evidence suggests significant dropout or failure to follow through with sexual abuse treatment (Haskett et al., 1991; Lanktree & Briere, 1995). Some symptoms appear to be more refractory or not show improvement until many months of treatment (Lanktree & Briere, 1995). Families may have practical problems that interfere with compliance, they may be avoidant or perceive their children as having resolved the abuse-related trauma, and there may be other more pressing family concerns or crises. Therapists may either not have access to the children and families or find it necessary to respond to immediate concerns that require a treatment focus. Therapists may question the value of specific interventions because they are novices and unfamiliar with the treatment approach or because clinical judgment dictates a different response.

Real-life clinical situations present challenges and circumstances not usually present in controlled studies, and it is important to understand which factors contribute to the finding that treatment effects are generally stronger in research, as compared with clinic settings. A recent effort to uncover explanations provides some useful direction. Weisz, Donenberg, Han, and Kauneckis (1995) investigated a number of hypotheses and found that the differences in outcome were significantly associated with the fact that research studies more often use behavioral versus nonbehavioral methods, take a more structured approach, and involve specific focused treatment. They did not find the differences accounted for by the clinic setting, the effectiveness of the clinicians, special pretreatment training of clinicians, the severity or nature of the children's problems, or the length of treatment. These findings are consistent with the typical way that trauma-specific treatment is delivered.

Taken together, the results of the treatment studies with sexually abused children and psychotherapy in general provide support for the type of treatment approach described by Deblinger and Heflin (1996) and Cohen and Mannarino (1993). These are relatively brief, structured, cognitive-behavioral treatments that include both child victims and their caretakers. Specific exposure-based and active coping-oriented interventions are used to combat abuse-related anxiety and cognitive distortions. Parents receive education and support and are taught specific behavior management strategies to use with typical behavioral abuse consequences such as sexual behavior problems or sleep difficulties. A supportive therapeutic alliance with the children and parents is emphasized, and both children and parents are engaged in a joint process of tackling abuse-related consequences.

TRAUMA-SPECIFIC
TREATMENT APPROACHES

Assessment

It is essential that trauma-specific treatment approaches begin with a systematic assessment of the child and family. The use of at least some standardized assessment measures has the benefit of allowing comparison of sexually abused children with established clinical and nonclinical norms. An important advance for trauma-specific treatment is the advent of trauma-specific measures. Self-report measures for children over 7 or 8 years of age include the Trauma Symptom Checklist for Children (Briere, 1996), the Children's Impact of Traumatic Events Scale-Revised (Wolfe, Wolfe, Gentile, & Larose, 1986), and the Children's Attributions and Perceptions Scale (Mannarino et al., 1994). The Child Sexual Behavior Inventory (Friedrich et al., 1992) is a parent-completed instrument for children 2 to 12 years of age that is specific to sexual behaviors in children and has normative and clinical comparisons available. These instruments are not designed to assess whether children have been abused; instead, they measure specific abuse-related domains that have been identified as common consequences of abuse. Use of trauma-specific measures may provide the structure that encourages therapists to apply more specific treatments and thus enhance treatment effects.

In addition, measures of parental response may be useful in determining the extent of parental belief and support or abuse-related distress. The Parental Response to Abuse Disclosure (Everson et al., 1989) and the Parent Emotional Reaction Questionnaire (Mannarino & Cohen, 1993) have both been shown to correlate with children's level of distress. They may be useful in identifying deficits in parental response or sources of parental distress that require therapeutic attention, and in measuring progress on these dimensions.

Systematic assessment is crucial to establishing the pretreatment level of emotional and behavioral functioning and to identifying treatment targets. Repeated assessment throughout the course of treatment, as opposed to only at termination, permits ongoing evaluation of the effectiveness of the treatment effort. As Lanktree and Briere (1995) have shown, different symptoms appear to respond to intervention at different points in time. Identification of symptoms or problematic cognitions that are persisting suggests where and what interventions may need to be employed. Pretreatment and ongoing treatment assessment data that are shared with the children and parents provide the framework and justification for treatment and promote a therapeutic alliance. Experienced progress may have the benefit of enhancing a sense of self-efficacy and encouraging treatment compliance and effort.

Many therapists in clinical settings are finding that insurance companies, Crime Victims Compensation programs, Medicaid, and other funding sources increasingly expect or require objective evidence for problem identification and treatment progress. The use of abuse-specific and standardized measures will make continued support for treatment more likely. Even when the clinician does not have access to or prefers not to use standardized measures, some form of systematic assessment and repeat assessment of clients will inevitably become necessary to meet quality assurance and accountability criteria.

Interventions

The usual components of trauma-specific treatment include educating children and parents about the nature of child sexual abuse and offenders, encouraging the expression of a range of abuse-related feelings, identifying and correcting distorted cognitions, teaching anxiety management and gradual exposure to the abuse experience, promoting abuse-response skills, and providing support. Each of these elements can easily be described, assessed, and reassessed for evidence of increased knowledge and skills. This treatment may be administered individually or in group settings. Parents may receive a form of parallel treatment or participate in conjoint sessions with the child.

One particular complication for trauma-specific treatments is how to handle extreme avoidance or resistance. Briere (1989) has argued that, with adult survivors, it may be important to respect the avoidance coping strategies and to titrate therapy at dosage levels that are tolerable for the patient. The clinical conundrum for therapists working with children is to not collude in avoidance while at the same time not make therapy so aversive that it is ineffective. The solution most often invoked with adults is to explain the rationale for directive treatments and to rely on their cognitive and emotional capacity to accept temporary distress in the service of ultimate resolution (e.g., Resick & Schnicke, 1993). For younger children especially, there are limitations to such a strategy, although it may have use with many child clients. This may mean that, for the youngest age group, less emphasis is placed on the exposure component. It remains to be seen whether children's less well developed cognitive capabilities mean that such approaches are less helpful or that they must wait until later to be useful.

In addition, mothers of abused children are highly distressed (Newberger, Gremy, Waternaux, & Newberger, 1993), and although an abuse history in mothers is not associated with diminished support, these mothers have more psychological distress (Deblinger, Hathaway, Lippman, & Steer, 1993). It may be that the caretakers require attention for their own emotional distress and/or abuse experiences to be better able to assist their children in recovery.

The available clinical literature is replete with descriptions of treatment strategies and techniques that can be incorporated within the framework of a structured trauma-specific treatment approach. Some approaches are cognitive-behavioral in orientation (Berliner, 1991; Cohen & Mannarino; 1993; Deblinger & Heflin, 1996; Ruma, 1993). Others are derived from integrated approaches relying on attachment theory, family systems, and psychodynamic formulations (Friedrich, 1990, 1995). Still others consist of compilations of specific exercises for use with traumatized children (James, 1989; Mandell et al., 1989). Case studies are available that provide extended examples of therapies with individual children (Becker, Skinner, & Abel, 1982; Friedrich, 1991; Gil, 1991; Kolko, 1986). Specific interventions have been developed to help prepare children for court experiences (Sas, 1991). Clinicians can find many and varied interventions in this rich clinical literature, as well as incorporate methods developed for other problems that may be modified for use with child victims. Behavior management approaches for parents can draw on currently available resources to help them in understanding and applying the principles to abuse-related problems in their children (e.g., Patterson, 1976). Of course, clinicians should have a rationale for the use of particular interventions in specific cases.

The desirable outcomes of successful trauma-specific treatment include the following: (a) The children understand that what happened was abuse, that it was wrong, and that it may have caused them some temporary problems; (b) they no longer suffer from abuse-related emotional and behavioral problems and have the knowledge and skills to recognize and handle future difficulties; (c) supportive relationships with adults, preferably parents or caretakers, vis-à-vis the abuse experience are in place; (d) and they are on track with normal developmental processes and experiences.

CONCLUSIONS

Sexual abuse experiences are not likely to be forgotten, but there is no reason to believe that most children cannot successfully process the experience on both emotional and cognitive levels (Berliner & Wheeler, 1987). It need not become the defining event of a lifetime or leave children with residual problems. Like other frightening, disturbing, or disruptive events, sexual abuse can be placed in perspective as an adversity that may be overcome. This is particularly true for the majority of children whose abuse experiences do not involve extreme violence, are not lengthy, and do not involve significant caretakers as offenders.

There will, of course, be children for whom the abuse is so severe or has compromised so much of their normal development that more serious outcomes are to be expected and longer-term therapies are necessary. Sometimes maladaptive responses have become ingrained or are refractory in brief, focused treatment. Many children will have experienced other significant stressors and have nonabuse-related difficulties that require additional or different kinds of interventions. Once the specific effects of the abuse experience are resolved, it may be desirable to explicitly shift the treatment focus to convey a sense of accomplishment and to not allow attribution of unrelated problems to the abuse experience.

The effectiveness and support for trauma-specific therapy will be enhanced when practitioners can articulate a theoretical framework, make use of the findings from treatment outcome studies, and demonstrate that abuse-related difficulties are improving over the course of treatment. A structured, relatively brief approach that incorporates cognitive-behavioral strategies has the strongest theoretical and empirical evidence for effectiveness at this time.

REFERENCES

Alexander, P. C. (1992). Application of attachment theory to the study of sexual abuse. *Journal of Consulting and Clinical Psychology, 60*, 185-195.

Becker, J. V., Skinner, L. J., & Abel, G. G. (1982). Treatment of a 4-year-old victim of incest. *American Journal of Family Therapy, 10*, 41-46.

Beitchman, J. H., Zucker, K. J., Hood, J. E., da Costa, G. A., & Akman, D. (1991). A review of the short-term effects of child sexual abuse. *Child Abuse & Neglect, 15*, 537-556.

Beitchman, J. H., Zucker, K. J., Hood, J. E., da Costa, G. A., Akman, D., & Cassavia, E. (1992). A review of the long-term effects of child sexual abuse. *Child Abuse & Neglect, 16*, 101-118.

Berliner, L. (1991). Clinical work with sexually abused children. In C. R. Hollin & K. Howells (Eds.), *Clinical approaches to sex offenders and their victims* (pp. 209-228). Chichester, UK: Wiley.

Berliner, L., & Wheeler, R. J. (1987). Treating the effects of sexual abuse on children. *Journal of Interpersonal Violence, 2*, 415-434.

Beutler, L. E., Williams, R. E., & Zetzer, H. A. (1994). Efficacy of treatment for victims of child sexual abuse. *Future of Children, 4*, 156-175.

Briere, J. (1989). *Therapy for adults molested as children: Beyond survival.* New York: Springer.

Briere, J. N. (1992). *Child abuse trauma: Theory and treatment of the lasting effects.* Newbury Park, CA: Sage.

Briere, J. N. (1996). *Trauma Symptom Checklist for Children (TSCC).* Odessa, FL: Psychological Assessment Resources (PAR).

Carlin, A. S., Kemper, K., Ward, N. G., Sowell, H., Gustafson, B., & Stevens, N. (1994). The effect of differences in objective and subjective definitions of childhood physical abuse on estimates of its incidence and relationship to psychopathology. *Child Abuse & Neglect, 18,* 393-399.

Casey, R. J., & Berman, J. S. (1985). The outcome of psychotherapy with children. *Psychological Bulletin, 98,* 388-400.

Chaffin, M., Wherry, J. N., & Dykman, R. (1997). School age children's coping with sexual abuse: Abuse stresses and symptoms associated with four coping strategies. *Child Abuse and Neglect,* 21, 227-240.

Cicchetti, D., & Lynch, M. (1993). Toward an ecological/transactional model of community violence and child maltreatment: Consequences for children's development. *Psychiatry: Interpersonal & Biological Processes, 56,* 96-118.

Cicchetti, D., & Toth, S. L. (1995). A developmental psychopathology perspective on child abuse and neglect. *Journal of the American Academy of Child and Adolescent Psychiatry, 34,* 541-565.

Cohen, J. A., & Mannarino, A. P. (1993). A treatment model for sexually abused preschoolers. *Journal of Interpersonal Violence, 8,* 115-131.

Cohen, J. A., & Mannarino, A. P. (1996). A treatment outcome study for sexually abused preschool children: Initial findings. *Journal of the American Academy of Child and Adolescent Psychiatry, 35,* 42-50.

Conte, J. R., & Schuerman, J. R. (1987). Factors associated with an increased impact of child sexual abuse. *Child Abuse & Neglect, 11,* 201-212.

Deblinger, E., Hathaway, R., Lippman, J., & Steer, R. (1993). Psychosocial characteristics and correlates of symptom distress in nonoffending mothers of sexually abused children. *Journal of Interpersonal Violence, 8,* 155-168.

Deblinger, E., & Heflin, A. H. (1996). *Cognitive behavioral interventions for treating sexually abused children.* Thousand Oaks, CA: Sage.

Deblinger, E., Lippman, J. T., & Steer, R. (1996). Sexually abused children suffering post-traumatic stress symptoms: Initial treatment outcome findings. *Child Maltreatment.*

Deblinger, E., McLeer, M. D., & Henry, D. (1990). Cognitive behavioral treatment for sexually abused children suffering post-traumatic stress: Preliminary findings. *Journal of the American Academy of Child and Adolescent Psychiatry, 29,* 747-752.

Erickson, M. F., Egeland, B., & Pianta, R. (1989). The effects of maltreatment on the development of young children. In D. Cicchetti & V. Carlson (Eds.), *Research and theory: Child maltreatment* (pp. 647-684). London: Cambridge Press.

Everson, M. D., Hunter, W. M., Runyan, D. K., Edelsohn, G. A., & Coulter, M. L. (1989). Maternal support following disclosure of incest. *American Journal of Orthopsychiatry, 59,* 197-207.

Finkelhor, D. (1995). The victimization of children: A developmental perspective. *American Journal of Orthopsychiatry, 65,* 176-193.

Finkelhor, D., & Berliner, L. (1995). Research on the treatment of sexually abuse children: A review and recommendations. *Journal of the American Academy of Child and Adolescent Psychiatry, 34,* 1408-1423.

Foa, E. B., Rothbaum, B. O., Riggs, D. S., & Murdock, T. B. (1991). Treatment of post-traumatic stress disorder in rape victims: A comparison between cognitive-behavioral procedures and counseling. *Journal of Consulting and Clinical Psychology, 59,* 715-723.

Friedrich, W. N. (1990). *Psychotherapy of sexually abused children and their families.* New York: Norton.

Friedrich, W. N. (1991). *Casebook of sexual abuse treatment.* New York: Norton.

Friedrich, W. N. (1993). Sexual victimization and sexual behavior in children: A review of recent literature. *Child Abuse & Neglect, 17,* 59-66.

Friedrich, W. N. (1995). *Treatment of sexually abused boys.* Thousand Oaks, CA: Sage.

Friedrich, W. N., Grambsch, P., Damon, L., Hewitt, S. K., Koverola, C., Lang, R. A., Wolfe, V., & Broughton, D. (1992). Child Sexual Behavior Inventory: Normative and clinical comparisons. *Psychological Assessment, 4,* 303-311.

Gil, E. (1991). *The healing power of play.* New York: Guilford.

Gomes-Schwartz, B., Horowitz, J. M., & Cardarelli, A. P. (1990). *Child sexual abuse: The initial effects.* Newbury Park, CA: Sage.

Graziano, A. M., & Mills, J. R. (1992). Treatment of abused children: When is a partial solution acceptable? *Child Abuse & Neglect, 16,* 217-228.

Haskett, M. E., Nowlan, N. P., Hutchesone, J. S., & Whitworth, J. M. (1991). Factors associated with successful entry into therapy in child sexual abuse cases. *Child Abuse & Neglect, 15,* 467-476.

Hotte, J. P., & Rafman, S. (1992). The specific effects of incest on prepubertal girls from dysfunctional families. *Child Abuse & Neglect, 16,* 273-283.

Hyde, C., Bentovim, A., & Monck, E. (1995). Some clinical & methodological implications of a treatment outcome study of sexually abused children. *Child Abuse & Neglect, 19,* 1387-1399.

James, B. (1989). *Treating traumatized children.* Lexington, MA: Lexington.

Janoff-Bulman, R. (1989). Assumptive worlds and the stress of traumatic events: Applications of the schema construct. *Social Cognition, 7,* 113-136.

Johnson, B. K., & Kenkel, M. B. (1991). Stress, coping, and adjustment in female adolescent incest victims. *Child Abuse & Neglect, 15,* 293-305.

Kazdin, A. E., Siegel, T. C., & Bass, D. (1992). Cognitive problem-solving skills training and parent management training in the treatment of antisocial behavior in children. *Journal of Consulting and Clinical Psychology, 60,* 733-747.

Kendall, P. C. (1994). Treating anxiety disorders in children: Results of a randomized clinical trial. *Journal of Consulting and Clinical Psychology, 62,* 100-110.

Kendall-Tackett, K. A., Williams, L. M., & Finkelhor, D. (1993). Impact of sexual abuse on children: A review and synthesis of recent empirical studies. *Psychological Bulletin, 113,* 164-180.

Kolko, D. (1986). Social-cognitive skills training with a sexually abused and abusive child psychiatric inpatient: Training, generalization, and follow-up. *Journal of Family Violence, 1,* 149-165.

Kolko, D. J. (1996). Child physical abuse. In J. Briere, L. Berliner, C. Jenny, J. Bulkley, & T. Reid (Eds.), *APSAC handbook of child maltreatment* (pp. 21-50). Thousand Oaks, CA: Sage.

Lanktree, C. B., & Briere, J. (1995). Outcome of therapy for sexually abused children: A repeated measures study. *Child Abuse & Neglect, 19,* 1145-1156.

Leifer, M., Shapiro, J. P., Martone, M. W., & Kassem, L. (1991). Rorschach assessment of psychological functioning in sexually abused girls. *Journal of Personality Assessment, 56,* 14-28.

Leitenberg, H., Greenwald, E., & Cado, S. (1992). A retrospective study of long-term methods of coping with having been sexually abused during childhood. *Child Abuse & Neglect, 16,* 399-407.

Mandell, J. G., Damon, L., Castaldo, P. C., Tauber, E. S., Monise, L., & Larsen, N. F. (1989). *Group treatment for sexually abused children.* New York: Guilford.

Mannarino, A. P., & Cohen, J. A. (1993). A treatment model for sexually abused preschoolers. *Journal of Interpersonal Violence, 8,* 115-131.

Mannarino, A. P., & Cohen, J. A. (1996). Abuse-related attributions and perceptions, general attributions, and locus of control in sexually abused girls. *Journal of Interpersonal Violence, 11,* 162-180.

Mannarino, A. P., Cohen, J. A., & Berman, S. R. (1994). The Children's Attributions and Perceptions Scale: A new measure of sexual abuse-related factors. *Journal of Clinical Child Psychology, 23,* 204-211.

Masten, A. S., Best, K. M., & Garmezy, N. (1991). Resilience and development: Contributions from the study of children who overcome adversity. *Development and Psychopathology, 2,* 425-444.

McCann, I. L., Sakheim, D. K., & Abrahamson, D. J. (1988). Trauma and victimization: A model of psychological adaptation. *Counseling Psychologist, 16,* 531-594.

McLeer, S. V., Deblinger, E., Henry, D., & Orvaschel, H. (1992). Sexually abused children at high risk for post-traumatic stress disorder. *Journal of the American Academy of Child and Adolescent Psychiatry, 31,* 875-879.

Mullen, P. E., Martin, J. L., Anderson, J. C., Romans, S. E., & Herbison, G. P. (1996). The long-term impact of the physical, emotional, and sexual abuse of children: A community study. *Child Abuse & Neglect, 20,* 7-21.

Nelki, J. S., & Watters, J. (1989). A group for sexually abused young children: Unravelling the web. *Child Abuse & Neglect, 13,* 369-377.

Newberger, C. M., Gremy, I. M., Waternaux, C. M., & Newberger, E. H. (1993). Mothers of sexually abused children: Trauma and repair in longitudinal perspective. *American Journal of Orthopsychiatry, 63,* 92-102.

Oates, R. K., O'Toole, B. I., Lynch, D. L., Stern, A., & Cooney, G. (1994). Stability and change in outcomes for sexually abused children. *Journal of the American Academy of Child and Adolescent Psychiatry, 33,* 945-953.

O'Donohue, W. T., & Elliott, A. N. (1992). Treatment of the sexually abused child: A review. *Journal of Clinical Child Psychology, 21,* 218-228.

Patterson, G. R. (1976). *Living with children: New methods for parents and teachers.* Champaign, IL: Research Press.

Perez, C. L. (1988). A comparison of group play therapy and individual therapy for sexually abused children. *Dissertation Abstracts International, 48,* 3079.

Putnam, F. W., Helmers, K., & Trickett, P. K. (1993). Development, reliability, and validity of a child dissociation scale. *Child Abuse & Neglect, 17,* 731-741.

Pynoos, R. S., Steinberg, A. M., & Wraith, R. (1995). A developmental model of childhood traumatic stress. In D. Cicchetti & D. Cohen (Eds.), *Developmental psychopathology: Vol. 2. Risk, disorder, and adaptation* (pp. 72-95). New York: John Wiley.

Resick, P. A., & Schnicke, M. K. (1992). Cognitive processing therapy for sexual assault victims. *Journal of Consulting and Clinical Psychology, 60,* 748-756.

Resick, P. A., & Schnicke, M. K. (1993). *Cognitive processing therapy for rape victims: A treatment manual.* Newbury Park, CA: Sage.

Ruma, C. D. (1993). Cognitive-behavioral play therapy with sexually abused children. In S. M. Knell (Eds.), *Cognitive-behavioral play therapy* (pp. 197-230). Northvale, NJ: Jason Aronson.

Sas, L. (1991). *Reducing the system-induced trauma for child sexual abuse victims through court preparation, assessment, and follow-up* (No. #4555-1-125). Ottawa, Canada: Health and Welfare Canada, National Welfare Grants Division.

Saunders, B. E., Villeponteaux, L. A., Lipovsky, J. A., Kilpatrick, D. G., & Veronen, L. J. (1992). Child sexual assault as a risk factor for mental disorders among women: A community survey. *Journal of Interpersonal Violence, 7,* 189-204.

Spaccarelli, S. (1994). Stress, appraisal, and coping in child sexual abuse: A theoretical and empirical review. *Psychological Bulletin, 116,* 340-362.

Spaccarelli, S. (1995). Measuring abuse stress and negative cognitive appraisals in child sexual abuse: Validity data on two new scales. *Journal of Abnormal Psychology, 23,* 703-727.

Stauffer, L. B., & Deblinger, E. (1996). Cognitive behavioral groups for nonoffending mothers and their young sexually abused children: A preliminary treatment outcome study. *Child Maltreatment, 1,* 65-76.

Steenbarger, B. N. (1994). Duration and outcome in psychotherapy: An integrative review. *Professional Psychology: Research and Practice, 25,* 111-119.

Tingus, K. D., Heger, A. H., Foy, D. W., & Leskin, G. A. (1996). Factors associated with entry into therapy in children evaluated for sexual abuse. *Child Abuse & Neglect, 20,* 63-68.

Toth, S. L., & Cicchetti, D. (1996). Patterns of relatedness, depressive symptomatology, and perceived competence in maltreated children. *Journal of Consulting and Clinical Psychology, 64,* 32-41.

Varia, R., Abidin, R. R., & Dass, P. (1996). Perceptions of abuse: Effects on adult psychological and social adjustment. *Child Abuse & Neglect, 20,* 511-526.

Weisz, J. R., Donenberg, G. R., Han, S. S., & Kauneckis, D. (1995). Child and adolescent psychotherapy outcomes in experiments versus clinics: Why the disparity? *Journal of Abnormal Child Psychology, 23,* 83-106.

Weisz, J. R., Weiss, B., Han, S. S., Granger, D. A., & Morton, T. (1995). Effects of psychotherapy with children and adolescents revisited: A meta-analysis of treatment outcome studies. *Psychological Bulletin, 117,* 450-468.

Wolfe, D. A., Sas, L., & Wekerle, C. (1994). Factors associated with the development of post-traumatic stress disorder among child victims of sexual abuse. *Child Abuse & Neglect, 18,* 37-50.

Wolfe, V. V., Wolfe, D. A., Gentile, C., & Larose, L. (1986). *Children's Impact of Traumatic Events Scale.* London, Ontario, Canada: Children's Hospital of Western Ontario, Department of Psychology.

8

Treating Adults Severely Abused as Children

THE SELF-TRAUMA MODEL

JOHN BRIERE

This chapter outlines an integrated approach to the treatment of adults severely abused or neglected as children. The theory on which it is based, hereafter referred to as the *self-trauma model,* incorporates aspects of trauma theory, self psychology, cognitive therapy, and behavioral therapy within a developmental perspective. The implications of this model are presented in terms of the specific process, content, and goals of abuse-relevant psychotherapy. It should be noted, however, that the long-term psychological effects of severe childhood abuse are often complex and frequently include difficulties beyond the trauma and self-disturbance addressed in this chapter. For additional information on abuse effects and treatment approaches, the reader is referred to recent books by, among others, Briere (1992, 1996b), Classen (1995), Courtois (1988), Davies and Frawley (1994), Jehu (1988), Meiselman (1990), Mendel (1995), Paddison (1993), and Salter (1996).

AUTHOR'S NOTE: Adapted from Briere (1996a) with permission of the publisher.

THEORY OF SYMPTOM
DEVELOPMENT

A central tenet of modern trauma theory concerns the individual's need to accommodate traumatic distress though the application of internal resources (e.g., McCann & Pearlman, 1990). The extent to which a given event is traumatic is thought to be a function of the degree to which it challenges the ability of the individual to "handle" it through internal coping strategies, generally referred to as *self-resources and capacities*. Self-trauma theory hypothesizes that the relative mismatch between internal capacities and especially overwhelming trauma produces a psychological imbalance that, in turn, triggers intrusive posttraumatic responses such as flashbacks, nightmares, and other reexperiencing phenomena. In contradistinction to more classical pathology models, the self-trauma model suggests that these intrusive responses are not merely symptoms of dysfunction, but instead are biological mechanisms evolved to serve an important psychological function—that of processing traumatic stress to the point that it can eventually be accommodated by existing self capacities.

Self Functions and Capacities

Although a variety of self capacities and resources have been posited, three are most relevant to the individual's response to aversive events: identity, boundary, and affect regulation.

Identity refers to a consistent sense of personal existence, of an internal locus of conscious awareness. A strong sense of personal identity is helpful in the face of potentially traumatic events because it allows the individual to respond from a secure internal base, wherein challenging stimuli can be readily organized and contextualized without excessive confusion or disorientation. Individuals whose sense of identity is less stable or who "lose track" of themselves in the face of upsetting events may easily become overwhelmed; they may become less internally organized at those very times when awareness of their own needs, perspectives, entitlements, and goals are most necessary.

Boundary is closely related to identity, in that it refers to an individual's awareness of the demarcation between self and other. People said to have poor or weak boundaries have difficulty knowing where their identities, needs, and perspectives end and others' begin, such that either they allow others to intrude on them or they inappropriately transgress on others (Elliott,

1994). An absence of boundaries when confronted with a stressor can reduce the individual's ability to negotiate interpersonal interactions, leading to, for example, difficulties in self-other discrimination, effective help seeking, and self-assertion in the face of victimization.

The third self function described here, that of *affect regulation*, has been viewed as quite important to the individual's management of potentially traumatic experiences (Friedrich, 1995; Linehan, 1993). Affect regulation may be divided into two subfunctions: affect modulation and affect tolerance. *Affect modulation* refers to the ability of an individual to engage in internal activities that in some way allow him or her to reduce or change negative affective states (McCann & Pearlman, 1990). Activities thought to assist in affect modulation include self-soothing, positive self-talk, placing upsetting events in perspective, and self-distraction. *Affect tolerance,* in contrast, refers to the individual's relative ability to experience sustained negative affects without having to resort to external activities that distract or soothe, or avoidance through the use of disassociation or psychoactive substances. For example, people with good affect tolerance may be able to experience considerable frustration, anxiety, or anger without engaging in aggression, self-injurious activities, sexual "acting out," or other forms of externalization.

Normal Development of Self Functions

The self functions described above are thought to arise from normal childhood development, primarily in the early years of life (Cole & Putnam, 1992). Identity and boundary awareness, for example, appear to unfold in the context of normal parent-child attachment experiences (Alexander, 1992). As the child interacts in the context of one or more consistent, loving, and supportive caretakers, a sense of self in contradistinction to others develops. This sense of self incorporates the sustained and reliable positive responses of the caregiver, typically leading to self-esteem, self-efficacy, and a view of others and the interpersonal environment as essentially benign. In combination, these and related processes result in a sense of internal stability: a secure psychological base from which to interact with the world (Bowlby, 1982).

As the child develops in a generally positive environment, he or she nevertheless encounters a variety of surmountable obstacles or challenges—ranging from small frustrations and minor discomfort to momentarily unavailable caretakers. In the context of sustained external security, the child learns to deal with the associated uncomfortable (but not overwhelming) internal states through trial and error, slowly building a progressively more sophisticated repertoire of internal coping strategies as he or she grows and confronts increasingly more challenging and stressful experiences. At the same time, because the associated discomfort does not exceed the growing internal resources of the child, he or she is able to become increasingly more at home with some level of distress and to tolerate greater levels of emotional pain. This process is thought to be self-sustaining: As the individual becomes better able to modulate and tolerate distress or dysphoria, such discomfort becomes less destabilizing and the individual is able to seek more challenging and complex interactions with the environment without being derailed by concomitant increases in stress and anxiety.

Effects of Abuse and Neglect on Self Functions

Because the development of self capacities and functions occurs during childhood, child abuse or neglect is an unfortunately potent source of later self difficulties (Cole & Putnam, 1992; Elliott, 1994). For ease of explication, such maltreatment and its impacts of self-development are divided into two categories: acts of omission and acts of commission.

Acts of Omission

Most typically, child maltreatment in the category of acts of omission consists of psychological neglect. *Psychological neglect of children* generally refers to sustained parental nonresponsiveness and psychological unavailability, such that the child is deprived of the normal psychological stimulation and support described in the previous section (see Erickson & Egeland, 1995). One of the most obvious impacts of child neglect is its tendency to decrease the extent to which secure parent-child attachment can occur. As a result, the child may not be as likely to encounter social experiences that teach self-confidence, self-efficacy, complex social skills, and regulated affective responses to manageable interpersonal challenges.

In addition to the obvious effects of parental nonavailability on intra- and interpersonal learning, neglect is thought to produce acute psychological distress (Bowlby, 1988). Because children are social beings with profound biopsychological needs for contact comfort, nurturance, and love, sustained psychological neglect can result in painful core feelings of deprivation and abandonment. This acute distress, in turn, may affect a child's development in many of the same ways described below for caretaker acts of commission. Also present, however, may be a growing sense of psychological emptiness and neediness and a general tendency later in life to be especially sensitive to the possibility of abandonment or rejection.

Acts of Commission

In contrast with acts of omission, acts of commission involve actual abusive behaviors directed toward the child. These acts can produce long-standing difficulties in self functioning and can directly stimulate trauma-related symptoms (Friedrich, 1995; Pynoos, 1993). As opposed to acts of omission, acts of commission during early childhood are injurious by virtue of their ability to disrupt normal development, produce intrusive reexperiencing, and motivate relatively primitive avoidance strategies.

Implicit in positive, normal development is the child's growing sense of safety and security—a base from which he or she can remain maximally open to experience and from which he or she can explore intra- and interpersonal environments and develop increasingly sophisticated self skills (Bowlby, 1988). In the case of child abuse, however, safety is diminished or disappears altogether. Faced with parental violence, the child may develop an avoidant style of relating, wherein he or she psychologically attenuates or avoids attachment interactions with a given abusive caretaker. Although this defense protects the child, to some extent, from pain and distorted environmental input, it also tends to reduce his or her responsivity to any positive attachment stimuli or figures that might be available in the environment. This response, in turn, further deprives the child of normal attachment-related learning and development, reinforces avoidance as a primary response style, and may partially replicate the self difficulties associated with neglect-related attachment deprivation.

It is likely that one primary way in which the child avoids is through *dissociation.* A defensive alteration in the normal links between thoughts, feelings, and memory (Briere, 1992), dissociation can be called on to reduce distress by decreasing awareness of upsetting events and by numbing or attenuating perception of painful internal states. Thus, the child may dissociatively exclude complete awareness of negative events in an attempt to survive relatively uncontrollable childhood trauma and may divert or suppress normal (probably biological) attachment responses. As noted earlier, this is likely to generalize in severe cases to the point that it reduces the amount of normal attachment-specific learning and development that can occur. Except for the most profound cases, however, this dissociation is less than continual or complete. As a result, some abuse-related material continues to be internalized rather than deflected or compartmentalized, presenting later as negative views of self, others, and the environment.

Beyond its impacts on attachment, dissociation during early abuse would seemingly reduce opportunities for learning how to tolerate painful affect without avoidance. Dissociation is also likely to preclude the need to develop other, more complex and conscious affect regulation skills. This forced reliance on dissociation during early childhood thus motivates the continued need for dissociation and other primitive avoidance strategies later in life.

Finally, child abuse distorts the victim's perceptions and understanding of self. As described by various writers (e.g., Janoff-Bulman, 1985; Jehu, 1988; Peterson & Seligman, 1983), abuse may teach the child that he or she is helpless, inadequate, or loathsome: lessons that the individual may continue to apply later in life. A chaotic and painful childhood may also easily inform the child regarding what to expect of relationships, persons in authority, and vulnerability. In this regard, attachment dynamics provide an unfortunately direct channel through which parental abuse can become internalized as enduring negative cognitive schemata.

Psychological Trauma

Intrusive Symptoms

Beyond its impacts on self-development, the violence of child abuse can produce posttraumatic intrusive symptoms. The self-trauma model posits, as noted in the introduction, that the flashbacks, nightmares, rumination, and other intrusive symptoms of posttraumatic stress are triggered when traumatic experience stresses the individual by challenging the self's capacities to accommodate or integrate such stimuli. This may occur as a result of preexisting inadequate self capacities or in the face of extreme trauma regardless of self resources.

Given that overwhelming stressors commonly produce repetitive intrusive experiences, an important question is what psychological purpose, if any, such painful and disruptive phenomena might serve. Integrating Horowitz's (1976, 1986) ideas with behavioral exposure models (e.g., Rothblum & Foa,

1992) and Rachman's (1980) notion of emotional processing, I propose that posttraumatic intrusion is an inborn self-healing activity. Specifically, symptoms such as flashbacks, intrusive thoughts, and nightmares, even rumination in some instances, may represent the mind's automatic attempt to desensitize and integrate affectively-laden material by repeatedly exposing itself to small, moderately distressing fragments of an otherwise overwhelming trauma (e.g., brief sensations, visions, repetitive thoughts, or incomplete autobiographic memories of the event). The avoidant symptoms of posttraumatic stress, in contrast, may serve to regulate the impact of intrusive symptoms by titrating the actual amount of exposure to reexperienced traumatic material that the individual encounters. From this perspective, flashbacks and related intrusive experiences, as well as avoidant symptoms such as numbing and cognitive disengagement, represent the mind's desensitization and processing activities more than they reflect underlying pathology per se.

This view of repetitive intrusion as a desensitization device is, in some ways, similar to Horowitz's (1976, 1986) cognitive stress response theory. Horowitz suggests, however, that posttraumatic intrusions represent the mind's ongoing attempt to integrate traumatic material into a preexisting cognitive schema that did not include the trauma or its implications. Horowitz hypothesizes that the traumatized individual automatically cycles through periods of intrusion and avoidance in an attempt to cognitively process and accommodate new, trauma-related material.

Although acknowledging the importance of gradual accommodation of cognitively unacceptable material, self-trauma theory suggests that these cycles also represent (perhaps more directly) the stepwise exposure and consolidation associated with an inborn form of systematic desensitization of *affect*. In this regard, many traumatic memories appear to be too anxiety-producing to be cognitively accommodated prior to some reduction in their stress-producing capacity (Foa & Riggs, 1993) and therefore must be at least partially desensitized before the equally important cognitive processes that Horowitz suggests can occur.

Unfortunately, some survivors of severe child maltreatment (and later adult traumas) are not able to fully desensitize and accommodate trauma through intrusive reexperiencing of affects, memories, or cognitions alone and hence present with chronic posttraumatic stress. This may occur because the severity of the trauma or the extent of impaired self capacities motivates excessive use of cognitive and emotional avoidance strategies (Rachman,

1980). The presence of excessive dissociation or other avoidance responses lessens the survivor's self-exposure to traumatic material—and the availability of the associated anxious arousal to habituation—and thus reduces the efficacy of the intrusion-desensitization process (Koss & Harvey, 1991; Resick & Schnicke, 1993). In support of this notion, it appears that individuals who tend to avoid internal access to traumatic material, through either cognitive avoidance or dissociation, suffer more psychological distress than those with less avoidant tendencies (e.g., Holen, 1993; Koopman, Classen, & Spiegel, 1994; Wirtz & Harrell, 1987). In contrast, even superficial exploration and emotional expression regarding previous traumatic events has been shown to significantly decrease psychological symptoms in university students, as well as increase indices of physical health (Murray & Segal, 1994; Pennebaker, Kiecolt-Glaser, & Glaser, 1988; Petrie, Booth, Pennebaker, Davison, & Thomas, 1995). This seeming competition between two relatively automatic trauma-related processes—intrusion/processing and avoidance/dissociation—is considered in the upcoming section on treatment.

Summary of the Self-Trauma Model

The self-trauma model suggests that early and severe child maltreatment interrupts normal child development and the usual acquisition of self skills. This reduced self functioning places the individual at risk for being easily overwhelmed by current and later trauma-related affects, thereby leading to further dissociation and other methods of avoidance in adolescence and adulthood. In this way, impaired self functioning leads to reliance on avoidance strategies, which, in turn, further preclude the development of self capacities. This negative cycle is exacerbated by the concomitant need of the traumatized individual to desensitize and accommodate trauma by repetitively reexperiencing fragments of the original traumatic event—a process that presents as intrusive symptomatology and that can further stress self capacities.

Unfortunately, if the individual is sufficiently dissociated or otherwise avoidant, this intrusion-desensitization process will not include enough direct exposure to upsetting material to reduce the survivor's trauma level. As a result, the individual will continue to have flashbacks and other intrusive symptoms indefinitely and will continue to rely on avoidance responses such as dissociation, tension reduction, or substance abuse. This process may lead the abuse survivor in therapy to present as chronically dissociated, besieged by overwhelming yet unending intrusive symptomatology, and as having "characterologic" difficulties associated with identity, boundary, and affect regulation difficulties.

TREATMENT IMPLICATIONS OF
THE SELF-TRAUMA MODEL

The model outlined above has implications for the treatment of adults severely abused as children. These include suggestions regarding (a) the correct focus, pace, and intensity of psychotherapy; (b) how one might intervene in the self and cognitive difficulties of abuse survivors; and (c) possible approaches to the resolution of the chronic posttraumatic symptomatology found in this population.

Treatment Process Issues and the Therapeutic Window

A major implication of the self-trauma model is that many untreated adult survivors of severe childhood abuse expend considerable energy addressing trauma-related distress and insufficient self capacities with avoidance mechanisms. In other words, the survivor whose trauma generally exceeds his or her internal affect regulation capacities is forced to continually invoke dissociation, tension-reduction behaviors, and other avoidance responses to maintain internal equilibrium. In the absence of such protective mechanisms, the individual is likely to become overwhelmed by anxiety and other negative affects. As a result, avoidance defenses are viewed as necessary survival responses by some clients, and overly enthusiastic or heavy-handed attempts by the therapist to remove such "symptoms" may be seen as potential threats to the client's internal equilibrium. For this reason, the psychotherapeutic process must proceed slowly and carefully to avoid overwhelming the client and to keep from stimulating additional avoidance responses that otherwise would further impede therapeutic progress.

I have found it useful to frame the process of effective psychotherapy in terms of a *therapeutic window*. This window refers to that psychological "place" during treatment wherein appropriate therapeutic interventions are cast. Such interventions are neither so nondemanding as to be useless nor so evocative or powerful that the client's delicate balance between trauma and self capacity is tipped toward the former. In other words, interventions correctly pitched into the therapeutic window are those that challenge and motivate psychological growth, accommodation, and desensitization but that do not overwhelm internal protective systems and thereby motivate unwanted avoidance responses.

Interventions that undershoot the therapeutic window are those that either (a) completely and consistently avoid traumatic material, including any exploration of childhood abuse, or (b) are focused solely on support and validation in a client who could, in fact, tolerate some processing of traumatic experience or affect. Undershooting interventions are rarely dangerous; they can, however, waste time and resources at times when more effective therapeutic interventions might be possible.

Overshooting the window occurs when interventions provide too much intensity or focus on material that requires additional work before it can be safely addressed. In addition, interventions that are too fast paced may overshoot the window because they do not allow the client to adequately accommodate and otherwise process previously activated material before adding new stressful stimuli. When therapy consistently overshoots the window, the survivor must engage in avoidance maneuvers to keep from being overwhelmed and, in some cases, actually hurt by the therapy process. Most often, the client will increase his or her level of dissociation during the session (Cornell & Olio, 1991) or will interrupt the focus or pace of therapy through arguments, "not getting" obvious therapeutic points, or radically changing the subject of the session. Although these behaviors may be seen as "resistance" by the therapist, they are often appropriate protective responses to, among other things, therapist process errors. Unfortunately, the client's need for such avoidance strategies can easily impede therapy by decreasing her or his exposure to effective treatment components.

In the worst situation, therapeutic interventions that exceed the window can harm the survivor. This occurs when the process errors are too numerous and severe to be balanced or neutralized by client avoidance or when the client is so impaired in the self domain or so cowed by the therapist that he or she cannot use self-protective defenses. In such instances, the survivor may become flooded with intrusive stimuli, may "fragment" to the point where he or she appears to be functioning at a developmentally primitive level, or may become sufficiently overwhelmed that more extreme dissociative behaviors emerge. Further, in an attempt to restore a self-trauma equilibrium, she or he may have to engage in avoidance activities such as self-mutilation or excessive substance abuse after an overstimulating session. Although these states and responses may not be permanent, they are stigmatizing or disheartening for many clients and may lead them to quit treatment or become especially defensive during subsequent sessions.

In contrast, effective therapy provides sufficient safety and containment that the client does not have to overrely on avoidance strategies. By carefully titrating therapeutic challenge and attendant distress so that neither exceeds the survivor's internal capacities, treatment in the therapeutic window allows the client to go where he or she may not have gone before without being injured in the process. As is described below under "Intervening in Abuse-Related Trauma Symptoms," this sense of safety and concomitant lower level of avoidance is an absolute prerequisite to the successful desensitization of posttraumatic stress in some individuals.

Clinical experience suggests that, at minimum, three aspects of therapeutic process should be considered in effective (window-centered) abuse-focused psychotherapy: (a) exploration versus consolidation, (b) intensity control, and (c) goal sequence. Each represents the therapist's attempt to find the appropriate point between support and opportunity for growth, with the assumption that, when in doubt, the former is always more important than the latter.

Exploration Versus Consolidation

The exploration versus consolidation aspect of the therapeutic process occurs on a continuum, with one end anchored in interventions devoted to greater exposure to potentially threatening (but therapeutically important) material and the other constrained to interventions that support and solidify previous progress or that provide a secure base from which the survivor can operate without fear. This continuum is, in many ways, similar to McCann and Pearlman's (1990) notion of the differential functions of "supportive" versus "uncovering" interventions.

Exploratory interventions typically invite the client to examine or reexperience material related to his or her traumatic history. For some abuse survivors, exploration may not involve as much consideration of cognitive material per se as a testing of the waters in the affective domain. For example, an exploratory intervention might involve asking the client to approach the possibility of using less cognitive avoidance or dissociation when describing a previously described painful subject. The key here is that the survivor—in the context of relative safety—attempts to do something new, whether it be thinking of something previously not completely considered or feeling something previously not fully experienced.

Consolidation, in contrast, is less concerned with exposure or processing than it is with safety and foundation. *Consolidative interventions* focus the client on potential imbalances between trauma and self at a given moment and invite the client to shore up the latter. An important issue here is that the survivor is not being asked to merely avoid existing traumatic states, but rather to more fully anchor him- or herself in such a way as to strengthen faltering self capacities. Interventions in this domain may involve, in one instance, "grounding" the agitated client in the "here and now." In another, it may involve reminding the client who is attempting to move too fast of how far he or she has come and of the need to honor his or her needs for safety.

The decision to explore or consolidate at any given moment reflects the therapist's assessment of which direction the client's balance between stresses and resources is tilting. The overwhelmed client, for example, typically requires less exploration and more consolidation, whereas the stable client may benefit most from the opposite. Further, this assessment of the client's internal state may vary from moment to moment: At one point, exploration may be indicated, whereas at another, consolidation may be required. From the therapeutic window perspective, exploration moves the client toward the outer edge of the window, where emotional processing and new insights may occur, whereas consolidation moves toward the inner edge, where safety is more predominant.

Intensity Control

Intensity control refers to the therapist's awareness of and access to the relative level of affect occurring within the session. Most generally, it is recommended that intensity be highest at around mid-session, whereas the beginning and end of the session should be at the lowest intensity. At the onset of the session, the therapist should be respectful of the client's need to gradually enter the therapeutic domain of trauma and self work, whereas by the end of the session the client should be sufficiently de-aroused that she or he can reenter the outside world without difficulty. In addition, the relative safety of the session may encourage some clients to become more affectively aroused than they usually would outside the therapeutic environment. As a result, it is the therapist's responsibility to leave the client in as calm an affective state as is possible—ideally, no more than the arousal level present initially—lest the client be left with more affective tension than he or she can tolerate.

Beyond the time-oriented aspects of intensity control, the therapist should appreciate what some have referred to as the survivor's *dread of affect* (Krystal, 1978). Those severely abused as children may have a fear that extreme anger will lead to violent behavior and that extreme sadness will result in self-destructiveness. For others, immersion in extreme abuse-related fear may seem to signal that childhood trauma is about to happen all over again (Krystal, 1978). Some survivors with major self difficulties may unconsciously fear that extreme affect will engulf them or destroy their sanity. For such individuals, intensity control is a mandatory aspect of good therapy.

From the perspective offered in this chapter, intense affect during treatment may push the survivor toward the outer edge of the window, whereas less intensity (or a more cognitive focus) will represent movement toward the inner (safer) edge. The need for the client, at some point, to feel seemingly dangerous feelings—not to dissociate them—during abuse-focused treatment requires that the therapist carefully titrate the level of affect the client experiences, at least to the extent that this is under the therapist's control. The goal is for the client to neither feel too little (dissociate or otherwise avoid to the point that abuse-related distress cannot be processed) nor feel too much (become so flooded with previously avoided affect that he or she overwhelms available self resources).

Goal Sequence

As noted by various authors (Courtois, 1991; Linehan, 1993; McCann & Pearlman, 1990), therapy for severe abuse-related difficulties should generally proceed in a stepwise fashion, with early therapeutic attention paid more to the development of self resources and coping skills than to trauma per se. This notion of "self before trauma" takes into account the fact that those interventions most helpful in working through major traumatic stress may overwhelm the client who lacks sufficient internal resources (Linehan, 1993). Specifically, the process of remembering and affectively processing traumatic experiences requires basic levels of affect tolerance and regulation skills. In the relative absence of such self resources, exposure to traumatic material can easily exceed the therapeutic window and lead to fragmentation, increased dissociation, and later involvement in tension-reduction activities.

Because of the need for adequate self skills prior to intensive trauma work, the choice of therapeutic goals for a client must rely on detailed psychological assessment. Whether done with the assistance of psychological tests that tap both self and trauma domains (e.g., Briere, 1995) or solely through careful attention to self and trauma dynamics during early sessions, the therapist must determine whether a given client has sufficient self functioning to tolerate relatively quick progression to trauma-focused interventions or whether she or he requires extended therapeutic attention to identity, boundary, and affect regulation before significant trauma work can be undertaken (Linehan, 1993).

Because of the complex relationship between self capacities and traumatic stress, however, assessment of readiness to do trauma work cannot be determined solely at one point in time and then assumed thereafter. Indeed, self functioning may appear sufficient early in treatment, only to emerge as far less substantial later in therapy. For example, as therapy successfully reduces dissociative symptomatology, it may become clear that what originally appeared to be good affect regulation actually represents the effects of dissociative avoidance of painful affect. Alternatively, a client who initially had superficially intact self functioning may later experience a reduction in self capacities as he or she addresses especially traumatic material. Although some of this fragmentation may be amenable to careful attention to the therapeutic window, it is also true that intense reexperiencing of traumatic events can temporarily reduce self functioning (Linehan, 1993). Given these potential scenarios, it is strongly recommended that the therapist continue to evaluate the client's current self functioning and trauma level throughout treatment so that he or she can adjust the type, focus, or intensity of intervention when necessary.

Intervening in Impaired
Self Functioning

As noted above, the availability and quality of self resources are typically major determinants of level of symptomatology and response to treatment. So important are self resources to traumatic stress and therapeutic intervention that, as mentioned, some clients may require extensive self work before any significant trauma-focused interventions can occur. For others, sufficient self skills may be available to allow some trauma-based interventions, yet continued attention to the development of further self resources will be required. In relatively few clinical abuse survivors, self issues may not require any significant intervention, and desensitization of traumatic material may occur more quickly (Linehan, 1993). Even in the latter case, however, it is possible for processing of especially painful traumatic memory to briefly overwhelm normally sufficient self capacities, thereby requiring some (typically temporary) self-level interventions.

Safety and Support

Because, for many survivors, the earliest hazard to the development of self resources was the experience of danger and the lack of support or protection, these issues must receive continuing attention in abuse-focused psychotherapy. In the absence of continual and reliable safety and support during treatment, the survivor is unlikely to reduce his or her reliance on avoidance defenses or to attempt the necessary work of forming an open relationship with the psychotherapist. Because early neglect, abuse, or both may have led to the development of an ambivalent or avoidant attachment pattern (Alexander, 1992), the client is, in some sense, being asked to go against lifelong learning and become dangerously vulnerable to a powerful figure. That he or she is willing to do so at all in such cases is testament to the investment and bravery that many abuse survivors bring to therapy.

Given the above, the clinician must work very hard to provide an environment where the survivor can "let in" therapeutic nurturance and support. Just as the chronically avoidant child may reject a loving foster parent, the survivor of severe abuse may use similar defenses that, at least initially, preclude a working relationship with his or her therapist. As many clinicians will attest, there is no shortcut to the process of developing trust in such instances. Instead, the clinician must provide ongoing, reliable data to the survivor that he or she is not in danger—not from physical or sexual assaults or from rejection, domination, intrusion, or abandonment (Courtois, 1988; Meiselman, 1994).

Beyond providing a secure base from which the client can explore his or her internal and interpersonal environment, therapeutic safety and support ideally provide a curative example of relationship per se. Long-term interactions in a safe therapeutic relationship can rework previous assumptions about the value of self in relation to others, such that the client begins to approximate a sense of personal validity. In addition, by receiving continuous support from the therapist, the client has the opportunity to internalize the possibility of benevolent others and of situations in which avoidance and defense are less required.

Facilitating Self-Awareness
and Positive Identity

In the context of sustained and reliable support and acceptance, the survivor has the opportunity to engage in the relative luxury of introspection. Looking inward may have been punished by the survivor's early environment in at least two ways: (a) It took attention away from hypervigilance and therefore safety, and (b) greater internal awareness meant, by definition, greater pain. As a result, many untreated survivors of severe abuse are surprisingly unaware of their internal processes and may, in fact, appear to have very little self-knowledge. This may present, for example, as reports of the inability to predict one's own behavior in various situations or of little insight regarding the abuse or its effects.

By facilitating self-exploration, abuse-focused therapy may allow the survivor to become more acquainted with self and thus to gain a greater sense of personal identity. Increased self-awareness may be especially fostered by *Socratic therapy* (Briere, 1992), wherein the client is asked many open-ended questions throughout the course of treatment. These include multiple, gentle inquiries about, for example, the client's early (preabuse) perceptions and experiences, the options that were and were not available to him or her at the time of the abuse, his or her feelings and reactions during and after victimization experiences, and his or her current thoughts, feelings, and self-assessments. As opposed to the overuse of therapeutic interpretations or blanket reassurance, Socratic interventions not only support the survivor's acquisition of a growing body of information regarding self but also teach the techniques of self-exploration and self-examination.

In the process of self-exploration, many opportunities arise for the reworking of cognitive distortions and negative self-perceptions. These distortions typically involve harsh self-judgments of having caused, encouraged, or deserved the abuse (Jehu, Gazan, & Klassen, 1984/85), as well as those broader self-esteem problems typically associated with child maltreatment (Janoff-Bulman, 1992). By exploring with the survivor the inadequate information and logical errors associated with such beliefs and self-perceptions, the therapist can assist in the development of a more positive model of self. The reader is referred to Janoff-Bulman, (1992), Jehu (1988), and Resick and Schnicke (1993) for further information on interventions helpful with the cognitive sequelae of interpersonal victimization.

Self-Other and Boundary Issues

As noted earlier, many survivors of severe childhood sexual abuse have difficulty distinguishing the boundary between self and others. This problem is thought to arise both from attachment disruption, wherein the child is deprived of the opportunity to learn normal self-other behaviors, and from early intrusion by the abuser into the child's bodily space (McCann & Pearlman (1990).

Effective abuse-focused therapy addresses both of these bases. The clinician is careful to honor the client's dignity, rights, and psychological integrity—even if the survivor is unaware of his or her entitlement to such treatment. Over time, the therapist's consistent regard for the client's rights to safety and freedom from intrusion can be internalized by the client as evidence of his or her physical and psychological boundaries. Some of this learning process is cognitive: During the client's recounting of his or her child abuse history and later adult experiences of violation or exploitation, the therapist actively reinforces the survivor's previous and current entitlement to integrity and self-determinism. Other aspects of this process are intrinsic: As he or she is treated with respect by the therapist and slowly develops a growing sense of personal identity, the survivor begins to assume that he or she has outside limits and that these boundaries should not be violated by others.

At the same time that the demarcation of his or her own boundaries are being demonstrated and learned, the survivor in therapy may be exposed to important lessons regarding the boundaries of others. This may occur as the client impinges on the therapist, typically through inappropriate questions, requests, or behavior. As the therapist firmly (and, hopefully, adroitly) repels such intrusions, he or she both teaches about the needs and rights of others to boundary integrity and models for the survivor appropriate limit-setting strategies that the survivor can use in his or her own life (Elliott & Briere, 1995). In this way, the interpersonal give-and-take of psychotherapy tends to replicate some of the lessons the survivor would have learned in childhood were it possible.

Affect Modulation and Affect Tolerance

Because affect tolerance and modulation are such important issues for adults severely abused as children, the self-trauma model addresses these issues in as many ways as possible. It stresses two general pathways to the development of affective competence: (a) the acquisition of an affect regulation repertoire and (b) the strengthening of inborn, but underdeveloped, affective capacities.

Skills training in this area is well outlined by Linehan (1993) in her outstanding manual on the cognitive behavioral treatment of borderline personality disorder. She notes that distress tolerance and emotional regulation both are internal behaviors that can be taught during therapy. Among the specific skills directly taught by Linehan's "dialectical behavior therapy" (DBT) for distress tolerance are distraction, self-soothing, "improving the moment" (e.g., through relaxation), and thinking of the "pros and cons" of behavior (p. 148). In the area of emotional regulation skills, Linehan teaches the survivor to (a) identify and label affect, (b) identify obstacles to changing emotions, (c) reduce vulnerability to hyper-emotionality through decreased stress, (d) increase the frequency of positive emotional events, and (e) develop the ability to experience emotions without judging or rejecting them (pp. 147-148).

Self-trauma theory makes use of these skills training approaches, although it generally avoids the formally programmatic aspects of DBT. Linehan's (1993) model, which has been shown in outcome research to be effective for borderline personality disorder (Linehan, 1993), stresses a central issue: Affect dysregulation does not reflect a structural psychological defect (as suggested by some neoanalytic theories and approaches) as much as skills deficits arising from distorted or disrupted childhood development.

Affect regulation and tolerance are also learned implicitly during self-trauma therapy. Because, as outlined in the next section, trauma-focused interventions involve the repeated evocation and resolution of distressing but non-overwhelming affect, such treatment slowly teaches the survivor to become more "at home" with some level of distress and to develop whatever skills are necessary to de-escalate moderate levels of emotional arousal. This growing ability to move in and out of strong affective states, in turn, fosters an increased sense of emotional control and reduced fear of affect.

Finally, in the process of self work, the survivor also learns to identify and describe the intrusive and repetitive cognitions that often trigger trauma-related affect. Thus, for example, the client's attention may be focused on self-talk that occurs just before an emotional reaction (e.g., "They're trying to hurt me" or "I'm so disgusting") and the cognitions occurring during strong emotion that produce panic and fears of being overwhelmed or inundated (e.g., "I'm out of control" or "I'm making a fool of myself"). As the client becomes more aware of these cognitive antecedents to overwhelming affect, he or she can also learn to forestall such thoughts through "thought stopping," by disagreeing with herself (e.g., "Nobody's out to get me," "I look/sound fine," or "I can handle this"), or merely by experiencing such cognitions as "old tapes" rather than accurate perceptions.

Intervening in Abuse-Related Trauma Symptoms

If one assumes either that the client has sufficient self skills or that these self functions have been strengthened sufficiently, the treatment of trauma symptoms is relatively straightforward. This process has at least three major steps, although they may recur in different orders at various points in treatment: (a) identification of traumatic (abuse-related) events, (b) gradual reexposure to the affect and stimuli associated with a memory of the abuse while keeping avoidance responses minimal, and (c) emotional and cognitive processing.

Identification of Traumatic Events

For traumatic material to be processed in treatment, it must be identified as such. Although this seems an obvious step, it is more difficult to implement in some cases than might be expected. The survivor's avoidance of abuse-related material may lead either to conscious reluctance to think about or speak of upsetting abuse incidents (e.g., denial) or to less conscious dissociation of such events. In the former case, the survivor may believe that a detailed description of the abuse would be more painful than he or she is willing to endure or that exploration of the abuse would overwhelm his or her self resources. Dissociation of abuse material, in contrast, may present as incomplete or absent recall of the events in question.[1]

Whether denial or dissociation, avoidance of abuse-related material by an abuse survivor should be respected because it indicates his or her judgment that exploration in that area would exceed the therapeutic window. The role of the therapist at such junctures is not to overpower the client's defenses or in any way to convince him or her that abuse occurred, but rather to provide the conditions (e.g., safety, support, and a trustworthy environment) whereby avoidance is less necessary. Because this latter step can require significant time and skill, the specific enumeration and description of abusive events is far from a simple matter (Courtois, 1995).

Gradual Exposure to Abuse-
Related Material

If, at some point, sufficient abuse material is available to the treatment process, the next step in the treatment of abuse-related trauma is that of careful, graduated exposure to various aspects of the abuse memory. According to Abueg and Fairbank (1992), *exposure treatment* can be defined as "repeated or extended exposure, either in vivo or in imagination, to objectively harmless but feared stimuli for the purpose of reducing anxiety" (p. 127). As noted earlier, the goal of exposure techniques in the current context is somewhat more ambitious than solely eradicating irrational anxiety. Instead, the intended outcome includes the reduction of intrusive (and secondarily, avoidant) symptomatology associated with unresolved traumatic events.

The exposure approach suggested here for abuse trauma is a form of systematic desensitization (Wolpe, 1958), wherein the survivor is asked to recall non-overwhelming but painful abuse-specific experiences in the context of a safe therapeutic environment. The exposure is graduated according to the intensity of the recalled abuse, with less upsetting memories being recalled, verbalized, and desensitized before more upsetting ones are considered. It should be noted that this form of exposure is self-administered: The client is asked to recall painful material, as opposed to a fear hierarchy approach in which the client is presented with a series of gradually more upsetting or frightening stimuli. The use of exposure or desensitization procedures appears to be effective in the treatment of various types of trauma survivors, including rape victims (e.g., Foa, Rothbaum, Riggs, & Murdock, 1991; Frank & Stewart, 1983) and war veterans (e.g., Bowen & Lambert, 1986; Keane et al., 1989).

In contrast with more strictly behavioral interventions, the self-trauma approach does not adhere to a strict, preplanned series of exposure activities. This is because the survivor's ability to tolerate exposure may be quite compromised and may vary considerably from session to session as a function of outside life stressors, level of support from friends, relatives, and others, and the "place" in the therapeutic window that the therapy occupies at any given moment. In addition, the immediate target for desensitization may not be a specific, discrete abuse memory, but instead the more elusive and complex phenomenon of transferentially evoked, abuse-relevant thoughts, feelings, and relational patterns.

Regarding this last point, the client may be sufficiently stressed by previous therapeutic events or aspects of the therapeutic relationship (e.g., restimulated attachment dynamics; Elliott & Briere, 1995) that his or her ability to handle any further stressful material is limited. Further exposure at such times usually leads to avoidance responses or even to some level of fragmentation. Instead of further exposure, the focus of therapy should become consolidation, arousal reduction, and the shoring up of self resources, as indicated earlier in this chapter. In addition, if previous exposure has led to enduring feelings of revulsion, self-hatred, or helplessness, the client may require interventions that interrupt or contradict cognitive distortions before he or she can move on to more exposure.

As noted by McCann and Pearlman (1990), exposure to abuse memories is complicated by the fact that there are probably at least two coding systems to address: verbal and imagery/sensorimotor. The former is more narrative and autobiographical; the latter involves the encoding and recovery of sensations. McCann and Pearlman note that material from both systems must be desensitized—the first by repeatedly exploring the factual aspects of the event (e.g., who, what, where, and when), and the second by recollection of the physical sensations associated with the abuse. In my experience, exposure to verbal memories is considerably less overwhelming for most survivors than processing of sensory memories, and therefore the former should usually be addressed before the latter.

The need to process sensory material may be especially relevant because, as indicated by van der Kolk (1994) and others, some components of posttraumatic memory are intrinsically sensory or sensorimotor. As a result, therapeutic work that operates solely on the narrative level is unlikely to allow processing of all available posttraumatic memories. Instead, self-trauma work is both cognitive and affective—addressing not only distorted cognitions and impaired self capacities but also the need for emotional exposure, expression, processing, and desensitization.

As indicated earlier, for abuse-focused therapy to work well, there should be as little avoidance as possible during the session. Specifically, the client should be encouraged to stay as "present" as he or she can during the detailed recall of abuse memories so that exposure is maximized. The very dissociated survivor may have little true exposure to abuse material during treatment—despite what may be detailed verbal renditions of a given memory. Of course, the therapist must keep the therapeutic window in mind and not interrupt survivor dissociation that is, in fact, appropriate in the face of therapeutic overstimulation. This might occur, for example, when the therapist requires or allows client access to memories whose affective characteristics exceed the survivor's self resources. It is not uncommon, however, for dissociative responses to become so overlearned that they automatically (but unnecessarily) emerge during exposure to stress. In this case, some level of reduced dissociation during treatment is not only safe but frequently imperative for significant desensitization to occur.

Emotional Processing

The last component of abuse-focused desensitization of traumatic memories involves the emotional activity that must occur during self-exposure to traumatic memories. This is an important step because, without such processing, exposure may result only in reexperienced pain, not resolution (Rachman, 1980). In other words, therapeutic interventions that focus solely on the narration of abuse-related memories will not necessarily produce symptom relief. Two aspects of abuse-related emotional processing are immediately relevant to the self-trauma model: (a) facilitation of emotional discharge and (b) titration of level of affect.

Classic exposure therapy is not especially concerned with catharsis or emotional release during therapy. Instead, it tends to involve one of two approaches. In the first approach, *exposure alone,* the client is repeatedly exposed to a stimulus (e.g., a tape recording or detailed description of a battle or assault) that triggers conditioned emotional responses (e.g., fear) until the emotional response fades away (habituates) for lack of reinforcement (because there is, in fact, no current danger). In the second approach, *exposure and relaxation* (the classic systematic desensitization paradigm), the traumatic stimulus also becomes associated with low autonomic arousal and thus is less able to produce anxiety (see Marmar, Foy, Kagan, & Pynoos, 1993, and Rothblum & Foa, 1992, for descriptions of these approaches).

Although repeated client descriptions of abuse memories during therapy, alone, often result in some habituation and counterconditioning of painful emotional responses (via the experienced safety of the therapy office), self-trauma therapy also capitalizes on the positive effects of emotional release. Specifically, the inherent biological "reason" for crying (and perhaps other forms of emotional discharge) in response to upsetting events may be that such release engenders a relatively positive emotional experience. This more positive state can then countercondition the fear and related affects initially associated with the trauma. In other words, the lay suggestion that someone "have a good cry" or "get it off of your chest" may reflect support for ventilation and other emotional activities that naturally desensitize post-traumatic dysphoria. From this perspective, just as traditional systematic desensitization pairs a formerly distressing stimulus with a relaxed (anxiety-incompatible) state and thereby neutralizes the original anxious response over time, repeated emotional catharsis during nondissociated exposure to painful memories pairs traumatic stimuli with the relatively positive internal states associated with emotional release. Thus, a "good cry" is good because, in the absence of significant dissociation, it tends to countercondition traumatic stress.

Although appropriate emotional expression may facilitate the counter-conditioning of abuse-related trauma, such activity is not equivalent to the recently rediscovered notion of "abreaction" of chronic abuse trauma. These more dramatic procedures often involve pressure on the client to engage in extreme emotional discharge, often in the context of a hypnotic state. Unfortunately, such techniques run the risk of greatly exceeding the therapeutic window, with resultant flooding of painful affects. In addition, by their very nature, such interventions encourage dissociated emotional release—a phenomenon that, though easily accomplished by many survivors, is unlikely to be therapeutically helpful. As noted by Cornell and Olio (1991), "[abreactive] techniques may appear to deepen affect and produce dramatic results in the session, but they may not result in the client's sustained understanding of, or connection to, their experience of abuse" (p. 62).

When combined with the cognitive processing outlined earlier, emotional processing changes considerably the original associations to traumatic abuse both by desensitizing abuse-related memories and by providing insight and altering the cognitive matrix in which the abuse was imbedded. In this way, the survivor who remembers her abuse (both narratively and through intrusive reexperiencing), who cries or rages about it, and who repetitively talks and ruminates about it is engaging in a natural healing response. This process may be most effective during therapy, in which the clinician can provide a safe and organized structure for the unfolding of each component and can be counted on to keep the processing well within the therapeutic window.

Access to Previously Unavailable Material

Taken together, the self-trauma approach outlined in this chapter allows the therapist to address the impaired self functioning, cognitive distortions, and posttraumatic stress found in some adults who were severely abused as children. The serial desensitization of painful memories is likely to slowly reduce the survivor's overall level of posttraumatic stress—a condition that eventually lessens the general level of dissociation required by the survivor for internal stability. This process also increases self resources; as noted earlier, progressive exposure to nonoverwhelming distress is likely to increase affect regulation skills and affect tolerance. As a result, successful ongoing treatment allows the survivor to confront increasingly more painful memories without exceeding the survivor's (now greater) self capacities.

In combination, decreasing stress levels and increasing self resources can lead to a relatively self-sustaining process: As the need to avoid painful material lessens with treatment, memories and affects previously too overwhelming to address become more available for processing. As this new material is, in turn, desensitized and cognitively accommodated, self capacity is further improved and the overall stress level is further reduced—thereby permitting access to (and processing of) even more unavailable material. Ultimately, treatment ends when traumatic material is sufficiently desensitized and integrated, self resources are sufficiently learned and strengthened, and the survivor no longer experiences significant intrusive, avoidant, or dysphoric symptoms.

This progressive function of self-trauma therapy removes the need for any so-called memory recovery techniques. Instead of relying on hypnosis or drug-assisted interviews, for example, to somehow increase access to unavailable material, self-trauma therapy allows these memories to emerge naturally as a function of the survivor's reduced need for avoidance. Whereas authoritarian memory recovery techniques might easily exceed the therapeutic window and flood the survivor with destabilizing memories and affects, the self-trauma dynamic only allows access to dissociated material when, by definition, the therapeutic window has not been exceeded. The self-trauma model reverses an assumption of those who advocate aggressive memory retrieval: It holds that clients do not necessarily get better when they remember more, but rather that they may remember more as they get better.

CONCLUSIONS

This chapter presented a synthesis of current dynamic, cognitive, and behavioral approaches that have been found helpful in the treatment of severe abuse trauma. This model suggests that postabuse "symptomatology" generally reflects the survivor's adaptive attempts to maintain internal stability in the face of potentially overwhelming abuse-related pain. It further suggests that many of these symptoms are, in actuality, inborn self-healing procedures that only fail when overwhelming stress or inadequate internal resources motivate the hyperdevelopment of avoidance responses.

I argued in this chapter that successful treatment for abuse-related distress and dysfunction should not impose alien techniques and perspectives on the survivor, but rather should help the client do better what he or she is already attempting to do. Thus, like the survivor, the therapist should be especially concerned with balancing challenge with resource, and growth with safety. The natural healing aspects of intrusion and avoidance are not countered in treatment, but instead are refined to the point that they are maximally helpful and can be abandoned once they are successful.

In this way, the self-trauma model is ultimately optimistic; it assumes that much of abuse-related "pathology" and dysfunction are solutions in the making, albeit ones intrinsically more focused on survival than recovery. At the same time, unfortunately, the inescapable implication of abuse-focused therapy is that to reduce posttraumatic pain and fear, both must be repeatedly confronted and experienced. As therapists, we must not forget what we are asking of our clients in this regard, lest we lose track of the courage and strengths that they inevitably must bring to the treatment process.

NOTE

1. Although this issue is a source of controversy, with some individuals claiming that psychological amnesia for childhood abuse is virtually impossible (e.g., Loftus & Ketcham, 1994), the last three editions of the American Psychiatric Association's diagnostic manual (*DSM-III*, *DSM-III-R*, *DSM-IV*) and recent research (see Briere, 1997, and Pezdek & Banks, 1996, for reviews) suggest that some level of dissociative amnesia for traumatic events is not especially rare.

REFERENCES

Abueg, F. R., & Fairbank, J. A. (1992). Behavioral treatment of post-traumatic stress disorder and co-occurring substance abuse. In P. A. Saigh (Ed.), *Post-traumatic stress disorder: A behavioral approach to assessment and treatment* (pp. 111-146). Needham Heights, MA: Allyn & Bacon.

Alexander, P. C. (1992). Effect of incest on self and social functioning: A developmental psychopathology perspective. *Journal of Consulting and Clinical Psychology, 60,* 185-195.

Bowen, G. R., & Lambert, J. A. (1986). Systematic desensitization therapy with post-traumatic stress disorder cases. In C. R. Figley (Ed.), *Trauma and its wake* (Vol. 2). New
York: Brunner/Mazel.

Bowlby, J. (1982). *Attachment and loss: Vol. 1. Attachment* (2nd ed.). New York: Basic Books.

Bowlby, J. (1988). *A secure base: Parent-child attachment and healthy human development.*
New York: Basic Books.

Briere, J. (1992). *Child abuse trauma: Theory and treatment of the lasting effects.* Newbury
Park, CA: Sage.

Briere, J. (1995). *Trauma symptom inventory professional manual.* Odessa, FL: Psychological
Assessment Resources.

Briere, J. (1996a). A self-trauma model for treating adult survivors of severe child abuse. In
J. Briere, L. Berliner, J. Bulkley, C. Jenny, & T. Reid (Eds.), *The APSAC handbook on
child maltreatment.* Thousand Oaks, CA: Sage.

Briere, J. (1996b). *Therapy for adults molested as children* (2nd ed.). New York: Springer.

Briere, J. (1997). *Psychological assessment of adult posttraumatic states.* Washington, DC:
American Psychological Association.

Classen, C. (Ed.). (1995). *Treating women molested in childhood.* San Francisco: Jossey-Bass.

Cole, P. M., & Putnam, F. W. (1992). Effect of incest on self and social functioning: A
developmental psychopathology perspective. *Journal of Consulting and Clinical
Psychology, 60,* 174-184.

Cornell, W. F., & Olio, K. A. (1991). Integrating affect in treatment with adult survivors of
physical and sexual abuse. *American Journal of Orthopsychiatry, 61,* 59-69.

Courtois, C. A. (1988). *Healing the incest wound: Adult survivors in therapy.* New York:
Norton.

Courtois, C. A. (1991). Theory, sequencing, and strategy in treating adult survivors. In
J. Briere (Ed.), *Treating victims of child sexual abuse* (pp. 47-60). San Francisco:
Jossey-Bass.

Courtois, C. A. (1995). Assessment and diagnosis. In C. Classen (Ed.), *Treating women
molested in childhood.* San Francisco: Jossey-Bass.

Davies, J. M., & Frawley, M. G. (1994). *Treating the adult survivor of childhood sexual abuse:
A psychoanalytic perspective.* New York: Basic Books.

Elliott, D. M. (1994). Impaired object relationships in professional women molested as
children. *Psychotherapy, 31,* 79-86.

Elliott, D. M., & Briere, J. (1995). Transference and countertransference. In C. Classen (Ed.),
Treating women molested in childhood. San Francisco: Jossey Bass.

Erickson, M., & Egeland, B. (1995). Child neglect. In J. Briere, L. Berliner, J. Bulkley,
C. Jenny, & T. Reid (Eds.), *The APSAC handbook on child maltreatment.* Thousand
Oaks, CA: Sage.

Foa, E. B., & Riggs, D. S. (1993). Post-traumatic stress disorder and rape. In R. S. Pynoos
(Ed.), *Post-traumatic stress disorder: A clinical review* (pp. 133-163). Lutherville,
MD: Sindran.

Foa, E. B., Rothbaum, B. O., Riggs, D. S., & Murdock, T. B. (1991). Treatment of post-traumatic disorder in rape victims: A comparison between cognitive-behavioral procedures and counseling. *Journal of Consulting and Clinical Psychology, 59,* 715-723.

Frank, E., & Stewart, B. D. (1983). Depressive symptoms in rape victims: A revisit. *Journal
of Affective Disorders, 7,* 77-85.

Friedrich, W. N. (1995). An integrated model of therapy for abused children. In J. Briere,
L. Berliner, J. Bulkley, C. Jenny, & T. Reid (Eds.), *The APSAC handbook on child
maltreatment.* Thousand Oaks, CA: Sage.

Holen, A. (1993). The North Sea oil rig disaster. In J. P. Wilson & B. Raphael (Eds.), *International handbook of traumatic stress syndromes*. New York: Plenum.

Horowitz, M. J. (1976). *Stress response syndromes*. Northvale, NJ: Jason Aronson.

Horowitz, M. J. (1986). Stress-response syndromes: A review of post-traumatic and adjustment disorders. *Hospital and Community Psychiatry, 37,* 241-249.

Janoff-Bulman, B. (1985). The aftermath of victimization: Rebuilding shattered assumptions. In C. Figley (Ed.), *Trauma and its wake: The study and treatment of post-traumatic stress disorder.* New York: Brunner/Mazel.

Janoff-Bulman, B. (1992). *Shattered assumptions: Toward a new psychology of trauma.* New York: Free Press.

Jehu, D. (1988). *Beyond sexual abuse: Therapy with women who were childhood victims.* Chichester, UK: Wiley.

Jehu, D., Gazan, M., & Klassen, C. (1984/85). Common therapeutic targets among women who were sexually abused in childhood. *Journal of Social Work and Human Sexuality, 3,* 25-45.

Keane, T. M., Fairbank, J. A., Caddell, J. M., Zimering, R. T., Taylor, K. L., & Mora, C. A. (1989). Clinical evaluation of a measure to assess combat exposure. *Psychological Assessment: A Journal of Consulting and Clinical Psychology, 1,* 53-55.

Koopman, C., Classen, C., & Spiegel, D. (1994). Predictors of post-traumatic stress symptoms among survivors of the Oakland/Berkeley, Calif., firestorm. *American Journal of Psychiatry, 151,* 888-894.

Koss, M. P., & Harvey, M. R. (1991). *The rape victim: Clinical and community interventions* (2nd ed.). Newbury Park, CA: Sage.

Krystal, H. (1978). Trauma and affects. *Psychoanalytic Study of the Child, 33,* 81-116.

Linehan, M. M. (1993). *Cognitive-behavioral treatment of borderline personality disorder.* New York: Guilford.

Loftus, E. F., & Ketcham, K. (1994). *The myth of repressed memory: False memories and allegations of sexual abuse.* New York: St. Martin's.

Marmar, C. R., Foy, D., Kagan, B., & Pynoos, R. S. (1993). An integrated approach for treating posttraumatic stress. In R. S. Pynoos (Ed.), *Post-traumatic stress disorder: A clinical review* (pp. 99-132). Lutherville, MD: Sindran.

McCann, I. L., & Pearlman, L. A. (1990). *Psychological trauma and the adult survivor: Theory, therapy, and transformation.* New York: Brunner/Mazel.

Meiselman, K. C. (1990). *Resolving the trauma of incest: Reintegration therapy with survivors.* San Francisco: Jossey-Bass.

Meiselman, K. C. (1994). Treating survivors of child sexual abuse: A strategy for reintegration. In J. Briere (Ed.), *Assessing and treating victims of violence*. San Francisco: Jossey-Bass.

Mendel, M. P. (1995). *The male survivor: The impact of sexual abuse.* Thousand Oaks, CA: Sage.

Murray, E. J., & Segal, D. L. (1994). Emotional processing in vocal and written expression of feelings about traumatic experiences. *Journal of Traumatic Stress, 7,* 391-405.

Paddison, P. L. (Ed.). (1993). *Treatment of adult survivors of incest.* Washington, DC: American Psychiatric Press.

Pennebaker, J. W., Kiecolt-Glaser, J. K., & Glaser, R. (1988). Disclosure of trauma and immune function: Health implications for psychotherapy. *Journal of Consulting and Clinical Psychology, 56,* 239-245.

Peterson, C., & Seligman, M. E. P. (1983). Learned helplessness and victimization. *Journal of Social Issues, 39,* 103-116.

Petrie, K. J., Booth, R. J., Pennebaker, J. W., Davison, K. P., & Thomas, M. G. (1995). Disclosure of trauma and immune response to a hepatitis B vaccination program. *Journal of Consulting and Clinical Psychology, 63,* 787-792.

Pezdek, K., & Banks, W. P. (Eds.). (1996). *The recovered memory/false memory debate.* San Diego: Academic Press.

Pynoos, R. S. (1993). Traumatic stress and developmental psychopathology in children and adolescents. In R. S. Pynoos (Ed.), *Post-traumatic stress disorder: A clinical review* (pp. 65-98). Lutherville, MD: Sindran.

Rachman, S. (1980). Emotional processing. *Behavior, Research, and Therapy, 18,* 51-60.

Resick, P. A., & Schnicke, M. K. (1993). *Cognitive processing therapy for rape victims: A treatment manual.* Newbury Park, CA: Sage.

Rothblum, B. O., & Foa, E. B. (1992). Cognitive-behavioral treatment of post-traumatic stress disorder. In P. A. Saigh (Ed.), *Post-traumatic stress disorder: A behavioral approach to assessment and treatment* (pp. 85-110). Needham Heights, MA: Allyn & Bacon.

Salter, A. (1996). *Transforming trauma: A guide to understanding and treating adult survivors of child sexual abuse.* Thousand Oaks, CA: Sage.

van der Kolk, B. A. (1994). The body keeps the score: Memory and the evolving psychobiology of post-traumatic stress. *Harvard Review of Psychiatry, 1,* 253-265.

Wirtz, P., & Harrell, A. (1987). Effects of post-assault exposure to attack-similar stimuli on long-term recovery of victims. *Journal of Consulting and Clinical Psychology, 55,* 10-16.

Wolpe, J. (1958). *Psychotherapy by reciprocal inhibition.* Stanford, CA: Stanford University Press.

9

Psychotherapy With
Sexually Abused Boys

WILLIAM FRIEDRICH

Female victims were the initial focus of sexual abuse treatment. Researchers now perceive, however, that males are abused at relatively high rates, with epidemiological research suggesting that as many as 1 boy in 8 to 10 will be sexually misused prior to adulthood (Friedrich, 1995).

Several features of male sexual abuse also warrant a separate discussion of treatment approaches. For example, physical abuse accompanies sexual abuse in males more than in females (Finkelhor, 1984). Given the documented relationship of physical abuse to subsequent aggressive acting out, preventive efforts aimed at reducing future violence are needed as part of the treatment of male victims (Malinosky-Rummell & Hansen, 1993).

Other features of male sexual abuse include gender differences in how distress is manifested, with boys more likely to exhibit externalizing behavior. This also reflects differences in the socialization process of boys as contrasted with girls (Friedrich, 1995). For these reasons, specific attention to young male victims of sexual abuse is warranted.

INTEGRATING THEORY
INTO PRACTICE

There are two predominant theories on the impact of sexual abuse: the post-traumatic stress disorder (PTSD) model (McLeer, Deblinger, Atkins, Foa, & Ralphe, 1988) and the traumagenic factors model (Finkelhor & Browne, 1985). Although useful theories, these formulations have either minimized or narrowly defined treatment implications.

The integrated model that organizes this chapter borrows from attachment theory (Alexander, 1992), behavior/emotion regulation (Dodge & Garber, 1991), and self-perception/concept (Harter, 1988; Selman & Schultz, 1990). The effects of abuse are reflected in each of these three broad domains. Of even more importance clinically is the fact that treatment approaches specific to individual, group, and family treatment can be derived from this model.

The integrated model subsumes both the traumagenic factors and PTSD models and provides an additional developmental and family context. For example, the traumagenic factor of betrayal (Finkelhor & Browne, 1985) has both psychological and behavioral effects (e.g., distrust of others, impaired ability to form close relationships) that are clearly pertinent to attachment theory.

The traumatic nature of child abuse affects the child's ability to regulate his emotions, thoughts, and behaviors, all pertinent to the PTSD model. Stigmatization and powerlessness have behavioral and psychological sequelae (e.g., reduced self-efficacy, distorted view of self) that are directly related to his self-perception.

The three elements of this integrated model—attachment, dysregulation, and self-perception—are outlined below. As needed, their specific relevance to the treatment of boy victims is elaborated.

ATTACHMENT

Attachment is a central element in contemporary theories of child psychopathology (Ainsworth, 1989). The quality of a boy's relationship with his parents governs his prosocial behavior. This governance has implications for the emergence of peer relationships, aggression, and social skills, three domains more often problematic for males than for females (Friedrich, 1995). *Attachment* is a biologically based bond with a caregiver (Alexander,

1992). Attachment behavior, which ensures the child proximity with the caregiver, is most apparent during periods of early childhood distress.

A central feature of attachment is the concept of the *internal working model,* a mental construction that forms the basis of the personality. Early experiences with the attachment figure allow the child to develop expectations about his role in relationships (e.g., worthy vs. unworthy) and the other's role in relationships (e.g. caring vs. uncaring). Because the development of this internal working model is so tied to the relationship, the boy learns caregiving while receiving care.

Attachment behavior can be sorted into four categories. The first and healthiest category is *secure attachment.* The other three categories are types of insecure or anxious attachment: *resistant, avoidant,* and *disorganized attachment* (Alexander, 1992). A securely attached boy has an internal working model of caregivers as consistent, supportive in times of stress, attuned to his needs, and reciprocal. Insecurely attached children operate from the assumption that interpersonal relationships are characterized by different levels of unpredictability, the absence of reciprocity, and punitiveness. For example, the avoidantly attached boy may eventually adopt a stance viewed as self-protective and hold back from caregivers, including therapists. The boy who exhibits disorganized attachment is inconsistent in dealing with relationships (e.g., simultaneous approach/avoidance). Parents of boys who exhibit disorganized attachment are typically characterized by unresolved trauma (Main & Cassidy, 1988).

Harsh and abusive treatment by caregivers can inhibit the development of prosocial responses in children. Main and George (1985) found that physically abused preschoolers did not show responses of concern, sadness, or empathy when a peer was distressed. In fact, physically abused children were consistently more aggressive in their social interactions, although there was between-child variability (George & Main, 1979).

Alexander (1992) identified three organizing themes relevant to attachment in sexually abusive families. The first theme is *rejection,* which is most often associated with subsequent avoidant attachment in the child. Parents' earlier attachments affect their subsequent attachment to their own child. For example, male children in the sexually abusive family may be rejected because they are viewed as potential abusers by the mother. Preoccupied or dismissive parents are subtly rejecting in that they selectively attune to the child's positive and negative expressions. Boys quickly learn that those affective experiences (e.g., distress) "fall outside the realm of shareable experience and to deny or disavow such feelings" (Alexander, 1992, p. 188).

A second organizing theme is *parentification and role reversal*. This process has been empirically documented in sexually abusive families (Levang, 1989). Elevation of a boy into a parental position may make him less likely to receive the support he needs, before and after the trauma, and more vulnerable to the subsequent sexual abuse of children in his care.

The third theme pertains to *multigenerational transmission* of fear and unresolved trauma in families with a history of abuse. This is consistent with disorganized attachment, wherein parents' anxious attachment history predisposes their son to one of anxious attachment. These themes are relevant to attachment before or after the sexual abuse. For example, a securely attached boy may become quite resistantly attached after sexual abuse.

Attachment behavior in sexually abused children has been studied minimally, but research does demonstrate the high frequency of insecure attachment in physically abused or neglected children (Egeland, Sroufe, & Erickson, 1983). The attachment model helps the therapist appreciate (a) the origin and diversity of relationships between children and their parents, (b) the role of the internal working model on the formation of all social relationships, including therapy, and (c) the need by the therapist to improve parent-child attachment.

Symptoms Reflecting Impaired Attachment

Attachment difficulties are related to the following: problems with interpersonal boundaries (e.g., indiscriminate affection seeking, poor social skills); the recapitulation of victim or victimizing behavior in relationships; distrust of others; and the sexualizing of relationships. Gender differences in psychopathology suggest that these issues are particularly relevant to boys (Friedrich, Luecke, Beilke, & Place, 1992). In the next three sections, attachment-related/derived treatment suggestions are made in the areas of individual, group, and family therapy.

Attachment-Based Individual Treatment Strategies

Formation of a therapeutic alliance is the first manifestation of attachment theory and is critical for all treatment. Literature on treatment effectiveness routinely finds the therapeutic relationship to be of critical importance (Strupp & Binder, 1984). In fact, the quality of the therapist-patient relationship may be central and more important than specific therapeutic techniques or approaches. It is the therapist's duty to determine how best to maximize the quality of the therapist-patient relationship.

The therapist also has the greatest control of factors affecting alliance with the boy and must ask the question, How can I best use myself to maximize the boy's ability to develop a good attachment relationship with me and with his caregivers? Such factors as the therapist's gender, emotional and behavioral style, ethnicity, and empathy level should be considered.

Therapeutic practices that interfere with acceptance must be avoided. Sexualized, aggressive, and physically unattractive children pull for rejection from the therapist. At times, therapists can feel that they have "lost control" of the therapy process and are playing out a script from the boy's prior relationship with a caregiver. This possibility speaks to the power of the internal working model and the need for the therapist to provide a corrective experience.

A boy's attachment history will dictate his interactions with the therapist. For example, a boy without boundaries (disorganized attachment) will need a therapist who is clear in his or her own boundaries so that he or she can tolerate and gradually alter the boy's dependency, physical proximity seeking, and variability. A boy with resistant attachment and physical abuse history will expect aggression and behave in a provocative manner. He presents a different challenge to the therapist, with his aggression used as a "boundary." The avoidant boy may be very slow in forming an alliance, always anticipating rejection, and hypersensitive to therapist unavailability.

The sooner both the boy and the therapist have a sense of "we-ness," the better. Therapists must be emotionally available in session, and consults to the school and occasional telephone calls can be very important to the process. Therapeutic triangulation allows the therapist-boy dyad to ally with each other and against a third party (e.g., nonfamilial perpetrator), thus pushing the treatment alliance along (Friedrich, 1990). Finally, a sense of connection may be facilitated by closer attention to ethnic and gender matching of child and therapist.

If the boy continues to feel unsafe at home, he cannot turn his emotional energies to the formation of a therapeutic relationship. It is important early on in the therapy process to help the boy have a "secure base" at home and know that his parents support his disclosure. Unsupervised visitation, foster placement that is nonsupportive, and continued physical abuse reduce the boy's security. One technique useful in helping create a sense of safety is to include the non-offending parent early in the therapy in order to give the boy permission to talk about his victimization regardless of the outcome.

Attachment-Based Group
Treatment Strategies

It is important that the child identify with a group and its members. Although disclosure creates a sense of universality (Yalom, 1975) and can foster a sense of connection, boys who have few social skills are likely to find the group experience a rejecting one. Screening is critical to ensuring a good mix of boys, particularly if group process is expected to be important. The creation of a group identity develops a sense of group attachment. This can be facilitated in a number of ways, such as a name for the group that implies a common bond. The use of cotherapists is also important so that the availability of potential attachment figures is higher. Finally, group treatment provides an excellent context to correct problems with empathy.

Attachment-Based Family
Treatment Strategies

Egeland and Erickson's (1983) description of psychologically unavailable caregiving characterizes a subset of families with sexually abused boys. It includes the absence of a reciprocal relationship and parental ambivalence toward the child. Goals they describe for intervention include helping the parent understand the boy's behavior; becoming better able to read the child's signals; providing peer support to the parent; and meeting the parent's emotional needs, along with helping the parent learn how his or her needs influence parental perceptions of the child. The researchers state that this approach must go beyond traditional psychological services and actively bring parents and their sons together.

These suggestions fit directly with the narrative approach to family therapy, which focuses on constructing a new set of perceptions, a new reality, or a new set of stories regarding the child and family (White, 1989). Rather than allow the family to persist in their view of the problem "inside" the child, White (1989) actively "externalizes" the problem. For example, the family of the encopretic boy needs to look for, and then acknowledge with him, those times the boy is successful at preventing the encopresis from sneaking up on him.

Positive connotations about the child's behavior are also strongly recommended (Selvini-Palazzoli, Boscolo, Cecchin, & Prata, 1978). These positive references enable the family therapist to point out the boy's strengths to the parents. It is very important to assist parents in appreciating positive aspects of their sexually abused son, such as his stopping the abuse by reporting it, his symptoms reflecting honesty rather than manipulation, and so forth.

Involvement of the parents in their own therapy at this critical time is also important and can result in their becoming less rejecting and more available for the boy (Egeland & Erickson, 1983). This can be done via parallel group treatment for non-offending parents (Mandell & Damon, 1989). Finally, therapists can demonstrate acceptance of the parent through the use of home visits. This technique facilitates a more accurate perception and validation of the family, thus adding to the developing therapeutic alliance.

In summary, parent-child relations are essential in every developmental phase of life for the sexually abused boy. The quality of these relations may predispose him to abuse, may suffer as a result of the abuse, and may detract from his ability to master the abuse. It is critical that the therapist make the parent-son relationship a focus of the treatment.

DYSREGULATION

The modulation of arousal, maintaining psychological homeostasis, and expressing a differentiated range of affects are basic developmental processes. Maltreatment interferes with a boy's developing capacity to regulate feelings, thoughts, and behaviors (Cicchetti, Ganiban, & Barnett, 1991).

Not only do traumatic features of the abuse contribute to dysregulation, but they also reflect a family characterized by numerous other stressors, including marital conflict, frequent moves and losses, and high levels of unpredictability and chaos. This is true for physically abusive families (Malinosky-Rummell & Hansen, 1993), as well as those in which children are abused in either intrafamilial or extrafamilial settings (Kendall-Tackett, Williams, & Finkelhor, 1993). In fact, for many children, the major contributors to dysregulation are not specific to abuse.

Katz and Gottman (1991) have operationalized emotion regulation "as consisting of children's ability to 1) inhibit inappropriate behavior, 2) self-soothe any physiological arousal the strong affect has induced, 3) focus attention, and 4) organize themselves for coordinated action in the service of an external goal" (p. 130). The child's ability to coordinate play and manage conflict are directly related to his ability to make friends.

Cicchetti et al. (1991) describe how the development of emotional regulation in the child occurs on both physiological (e.g., central nervous system functioning) and psychological levels (e.g., growing cognitive and representational skills). Perry (1993), for instance, found that prolonged abuse is related to physiological alterations in the stress response. How maltreated children differentiate and respond to affect is part of self-regulation. Cicchetti et al. refer to four response patterns presumably dependent on caregivers responses: (a) developmentally and affectively retarded, (b) depressed, (c) ambivalent and affectively labile, and (d) angry. These also reflect the child's internal working model of attachment.

Symptoms Reflecting Dysregulation

Specific treatment targets derived from dysregulation include the most classic constellation of symptoms of post-traumatic stress disorder (PTSD), with its features of distorted arousal and intrusion. Other symptoms, however, include anxiety and its related problems, sleep problems, and behavioral regression. In addition, victimized children may not have learned self-soothing behaviors and live in a heightened state of arousal, resulting in somatic symptoms. Other manifestations are inattentiveness/overactivity in class, akin to ADHD symptoms (Sroufe, 1989). This expression applies particularly to males, who are vastly overrepresented in the ADHD literature. In addition, sexualized behavior can add to the boy's feeling out of control and, as such, should be addressed specifically. In the next three sections, individual, group, and family therapy techniques that can be used to correct the dysregulatory effects of sexual abuse are presented.

Dysregulation-Based Individual
Treatment Strategies

Boys do not naturally associate emotionally painful therapy with support and feeling in control. This underscores the need for structure and predictability in the therapy process. Predictability can prevent dysregulation in the boy. Defining therapy for the boy, as well as the need for disclosure, provides structure and predictability. The boy may formally schedule when and how he wants to talk about his victimization experiences.

Psychoeducational techniques (e.g., safety, sexual education) are not as dysregulating and may be more useful to extremely reactive boys. It is also possible for the therapist to partition the session. The boy is provided with an agreed-on amount of time to work on issues and then is given a period during which he feels less threatened. The play portion, if placed at the end of the session, can give the boy a chance to reorganize.

The boy may never directly acknowledge having been molested, but he may talk to the therapist as if he had been or give the therapist advice for working with a similarly aged child who had a similar abuse experience. This particular technique underscores the boy's need for some control in therapy.

Cognitive-behavioral strategies can be used to ameliorate the dysregulating aspects of PTSD (Friedrich, 1995). By way of illustration, the therapist can help the boy examine and then correct his thinking about when he avoids certain stimuli that might trigger a flashback. These can be combined with relaxation and imagery strategies that also aid in correcting problems with sleep, panic, and aggression. Therapy must become a reliable and predictable process for the boy; this can prevent "spillover" from the therapy to the home and school and make the boy a more positive presence in the home.

Dysregulation-Based Group Treatment Strategies

Boys must be screened as to their appropriateness for group treatment because group therapy can be highly dysregulating. Group therapy is not a given for every sexually abused boy. Boys typically are disruptive and prone to acting out and feeling dysregulated (Friedrich, Berliner, Urquiza, & Beilke, 1988). Boys with a history of poor peer relationships and frequent victimization may benefit from pair therapy (Selman & Schultz, 1990) before being involved in group treatment. Pair therapy is a strategy that places two boys together on the basis of similar developmental levels. Allowing them to form a relationship and mature together not only is a therapeutic outcome but also assists them in being able to join a larger therapy group.

Psychoeducational techniques lend themselves to preventing dysregulation in the group setting (Cunningham & MacFarlane, 1990). The use of structured treatment modules, wherein the boy has the opportunity to work through a relevant segment (e.g., talking about feelings related to the abuse) and has a sense of closure by the end of it, can add a great deal to the child's sense of resolution and feeling in control.

Dysregulation-Based Family
Treatment Strategies

Therapists must help the families they see to realize the purpose of therapy and focus on specific behavioral targets that provide the families with both a measure of success and an opportunity to learn to be more consistent with their children. When physical abuse is present, continued aggressive behavior adds to dysregulation. Anger management and self-control in a parent must be attended to, and alternatives to physical punishment created.

A goal-setting approach to therapy can provide the necessary structure to prevent dysregulation. The *goal attainment scaling system* as described in Friedrich (1995) can be useful for families of sexually abused boys. With this goal-setting strategy, families are helped to identify specific goals that have graduated levels of accomplishment. Dysregulation-based goals could include anger management for parents, the creation of some predictable opportunities for family interaction, bedtime rituals, and learning more consistent parenting approaches.

The prescription of rituals, which can be regularly scheduled events in the family, can also measurably contribute to a sense of structure and order within the family (Friedrich, 1995). These rituals should be targeted around eating and bedtime, two naturally occurring occasions when families can become dysregulated. For example, the family can create a ritual in which the boy's safety is assured at bedtime by reminding him that the doors are locked, the parents' bedroom is next door, and so forth.

Finally, if the boy does not feel safe from further victimization, the family context itself may be upsetting and potentially dysregulating. Each family member must feel safe. The therapist must help the family realize different ways that they are potentially victimizing to each other or excitatory in one way or another. Factors contributing to the boy feeling unsafe include aggression, nudity, overt family sexuality, unsupervised contact with the perpetrator, and other potential reminders of sexuality or vulnerability to the child.

In summary, dysregulation addresses how the experience of trauma can make it difficult for the boy to modulate his thoughts, feelings, and actions. Symptoms reflecting problems with dysregulation include, but are not limited to, PTSD, dissociation, panic, ADHD-like behavior, sleep problems, eating problems, and generalized anxiety. Trauma-based treatment must address these issues while at the same time be sensitive to how dysregulating therapy can be.

SELF-PERCEPTION

Boys' understanding of their attributes and emotions follows a developmental course and includes cognitive and affective processes (Harter, 1988). Children's self-understanding has a number of developmental shifts, beginning with descriptions of one's physical self and transitioning to the active self, to the social self, and to the psychological self (the latter containing one's emotions and cognitions).

A critical component of self-perception is the accuracy with which the child views himself. Young children are highly egocentric, and their self-assumptions often reflect wishes rather than accuracy. Harter (1988) points out that environmental changes produce inaccuracies in the judgment of one's abilities. Presumably, abuse could count as an environmental change. In addition, children who consistently view themselves inaccurately, either by over- or underestimating their competence, expose themselves to less challenging problems, such as avoidant coping.

Harter's (1988) research has important clinical implications. Supportive therapists who want to strengthen an abused boy's self-esteem should concentrate on the accuracy of the self-perception, not necessarily on the optimism of the perception. In fact, Harter states that "a strategy . . . undoubtedly doomed to failure involves . . . categorically asserting . . . 'you are not dumb, you know, you really are quite smart' " (p. 135).

Numerous contributors to inaccurate self-perception exist in the world of the maltreated child. Examples of inaccuracies include all-or-none thinking, overgeneralizations, and shifts from one extreme self-perception to another. In the presence of increased stress and reduced support, an abused boy is likely to remain stuck at an immature level of self-perception.

Harter (1977) presents several clinical examples of all-or-none thinking (e.g., "all dumb") and her approach to its resolution by increasing the accuracy of self-perception. Although this approach may resemble cognitive therapy, it goes beyond it in its developmental appreciation and its simultaneous emphasis on affect.

Another phenomenon in the area of self-perception pertains to stability, or conservation of self, across settings or in the face of contradictions. Children will vary in whether they attribute changes to internal versus external forces, with internally focused children and adolescents not as likely to be bothered by these fluctuations (Harter, 1988). Because maltreatment is an external force, it takes a significant effort for the boy not to blame himself.

Despite the centrality of self-perception in the establishment of the self, boys typically have little interest in self-examination. Given the fact that children are so deeply embedded in the family matrix, they most naturally will externalize their problems. In fact, the therapist may find more fruit in working to alter the environmental influences on self-development, such as poor attachment, rather than in helping the child develop insight. Harter (1988) goes so far as to suggest developmental reasons for the use of more didactic techniques and fewer attempts at insight.

It is also very useful to consider an intrapsychic (inner) self, in addition to the interpersonally (outer) related self-perception described above. The *intrapsychic self* is manifested by the presence of defense mechanisms and its idiosyncratic understanding of intimate relationships. For example, we have all seen children whose "inner-outer" differences are significant. This is applicable to abused boys who are precociously mature superficially, but if asked will report that they feel empty inside. One boy captured this dilemma when he told me, "If I stop telling jokes, then I will start crying."

Symptoms Reflecting Problems With Self

Problems in self-perception are less tangible, and specific symptoms may not be overt, particularly with younger boys. Somatic symptoms may reflect the abused boy as being fixated at the physical self. In addition, disadvantaged boys of all ages may have more than the usual difficulties identifying their feelings or talking about how they feel about themselves. Thus, a focus on self-related symptoms may be less important than creating a therapy context in which the boy can develop greater ease and competence when talking about thoughts and feelings. Individual, group, and family therapy approaches that facilitate the development of an accurate self-perception are discussed below.

Self-Perception-Based Individual Therapy Strategies

Therapy must help a boy correct his immature and inaccurate self-perceptions. First, he must learn how to understand and describe feelings. This can be facilitated through feelings exercises, the use of a feelings list, and so on. Boys are notoriously poor at identifying feelings, and simply increasing their facility with feelings identification may have few implications for their adjustment at home. Interpersonally oriented questioning such as "What would you have to do to make Mom mad?" is a more useful strategy and reflects even more the necessary interpersonal focus in correcting sexual abuse sequelae (Benjamin, 1996).

The therapist must first understand the boy's view of himself and his world before the therapist provides blanket reassurances to the child. Reassurances such as "You are not bad" may be unbelievable and undermine his connection to the therapist. A group of sexually abused teenage boys told me they could be more honest with me than with my cotherapist about their sexual acting out. Why? I was less likely than my cotherapist to tell them how much I admired them. Focusing only on what the therapist believes is important may make it that much more difficult for the boy to feel heard. For example, a boy who was aroused by the victimization and appreciated the abuser's support may be alienated by the therapist's focus on the negative aspects of the abuse, at least at the initial stage of their relationship.

Harter (1977) described an excellent technique to deal with "good-bad" extremes, which I strongly recommend for work with abused boys. The therapist draws a circle, and the boy fills it in to reflect those aspects of himself that are "bad," "dirty," "hopeless." It helps the boy make progressive approximations to a more accurate perception of himself as having a combination of positive, neutral, and negative features.

It is also important to increase a boy's sense of efficacy. An example of this is to "contract with the child for competency"—for example, making the sexually reactive boy responsible for his sexual behavior, e.g. "you are in charge of your penis." Cognitive approaches that address the physically abused child's self-defeating cognitions are also useful to enhance a child's sense of mastery and competency (Friedrich, 1995). A sexually abused boy who feels stigmatized by the abuse he suffered will need to learn how to identify other areas of his life where he is competent. This knowledge can allow him to reduce his feelings of stigma.

For older boys, particularly those who have some mastery of their feelings, it is also useful to "externalize" the problem (White, 1989). Children are egocentric and assume automatic responsibility. Sexually abused boys will view themselves as bad, duplicitous, and guilty for the abuse. Reassurance to the boy of his goodness is not helpful. If you help the boy learn how to talk about his depression as "outside himself" and "sneaking up on him when he is unaware," however, he can learn to view himself as having the potential for a more active role in keeping negative feelings outside himself and learning to cope better with those times when he is more vulnerable to feeling poorly about himself.

The maltreated boy can be quite self-critical. This likelihood creates the potential for depression and reduced self-efficacy. Older latency and adolescent victims can be aided in the development of a "personal fable" regarding some unique aspect that helps in their overcoming the abuse. This can be done in a cognitive therapy format, complete with a chalkboard to facilitate the boy's visual perception of the important concept that thoughts create feelings and direct behavior. For example, Cunningham and MacFarlane (1990) have written about the role of "vulture thoughts" (thoughts about touching another child) in the thinking of sexually aggressive children.

Finally, in keeping with Harter's (1988) finding, the therapist would do well to avoid focusing on insight in the child and concentrate on a developmentally simpler task, such as accuracy of self-perception. It may not help an 8-year-old to know why he predictably gets upset when his mother goes out on a date, but he may respond very well to assistance in developing self-control over his feelings, and in so doing be more like his favorite superhero.

Self-Perception-Based Group Therapy Strategies

The universality present in group therapy not only helps with attachment, which was described earlier, but also helps a boy view himself more accurately (Yalom, 1975). Given that our self-perception is constructed, in part, by our understanding of other people's perceptions of us, group therapy provides an excellent opportunity for peer perspectives to be incorporated into one's sense of self. The boy is also able to see other, normal-looking sexually abused boys.

A critical component of both attachment and self-perception is the often undisclosed defect in empathy that victimized boys may have. Empathy is impossible to teach outside the context of relationships, and group treatment provides numerous opportunities in which the child can learn to feel for the other person. In addition, the group format allows the boy to hear feedback from other people about gains they have made. Finally, by the use of structured treatment models that run for a preset number of sessions, the boy can realize that he is gradually working through the victimization, achieving closure, and improving his sense of self-efficacy (Mandell & Damon, 1989).

Self-Perception-Based Family
Therapy Strategies

Non-offending parents who have been victimized in the past and who now have a son who has been abused will most likely view themselves as inept. Countering that perspective will be very difficult, but family therapy is an appropriate setting in which to confront such perceptions. This may be done by empowering the parents and allowing them to see their effectiveness at achieving small, easily attainable goals. These early goals pertain to their ability to parent their son in a less angry and nonvictimizing manner.

Some of the same "all or nothing" thinking that the boy has about himself is seen in the parents' perception of their son. Discussions between the parents and the boy about specific instances of dislike can contribute to the development of a more positive sense of connection between the parents and the child. Parents can be motivated to change if the therapist appeals to that almost universal wish to be a better parent than their own parents. Parents appreciate your recognition of their wish, and once this strength is "discovered," they are more motivated to parent effectively.

In sum, the experience of sexual abuse may cause both the boy and his parents to question their self-efficacy. Passivity, revictimization, and hopelessness may reflect this reduced self-efficacy. Boys can learn to correct their negative self-perceptions, although they may have little developmental capacity for insight. Parents also need an opportunity to recommit themselves to the parenting process.

CONCLUSION

A recent review of the impact of sexual abuse (Kendall-Tackett et al., 1993) decried the atheoretical approach to the assessment of the impact of abuse. The theoretical model suggested in this chapter combines a number of developmentally sensitive theories that can guide both the assessment and treatment of sexually abused children and their families. These treatment strategies must be empirically tested, however. Child clinicians seem to view outcome research as daunting. Shirk (1988) wrote that an average of only one child therapy outcome study has been published annually for the past 30 years, an enormous contrast with the adult treatment literature. The published research on treatment of sexually abused children must be expanded.

The efficacy of group treatment relative to individual needs must be documented. Moreover, directive therapy, including disclosure of victimization, is strongly suggested by many clinicians (Friedrich, 1990), but its relative treatment value is only now being demonstrated. Practitioners also need to know whether child treatment can be helpful with boys who are in foster care and whose parents are neither in treatment nor supportive of the boys' disclosure. Finally, it may be that changing external factors, including those of poverty, maternal depression, and use of physical punishment, are as important as any "internal" changes the boy makes. These are big questions that must be answered in addition to asking narrower questions about the utility of specific techniques.

The following guidelines seem warranted, however, in the light of the needs of this population: (a) Assess the presence of behavioral problems by using standard measures pre-, immediately after, and 3 to 6 months later; (b) document the interventions used in therapy; (c) invite other clinicians to collaborate, to expand sample size and types of interventions; and (d) share our findings. Not only will following these guidelines inform our practice, but it can also guide the treatment of other abused children as well.

Furthermore, the theories and associated techniques identified in this chapter have the added advantage of targeting specific symptoms presented by sexually abused boys. An equally valid approach determining treatment effectiveness is goal attainment scaling, discussed specifically for sexually abused boys (Friedrich, 1995). This approach can be used to determine therapy outcome for a diverse group of abused children with a broad range of presenting complaints. For example, treatment goals can be established in each of the domains suggested, such as an attachment-related goal of more positive parental interaction with the child; a dysregulation-related goal of no physical punishment; and a self-perception goal of the child achieving better in school. This technique can be both a treatment adjunct and a means of enabling the therapist to measure outcome empirically.

Developmentally sound theory can provide a useful road map for therapeutic intervention with sexually abused boys. Sexual abuse has implications for parent-child attachment, the ability of the child to modulate new and possibly overwhelming thoughts and feelings, and the accuracy and optimism with which a child views his future. It is important that treatment attempts to address these symptoms, borrowing from a range of developmentally appropriate and empirically supported techniques.

REFERENCES

Ainsworth, M. D. S. (1989). Attachments beyond infancy. *American Psychologist, 44,* 709-716.

Alexander, P. C. (1992). Application of attachment theory to the study of sexual abuse. *Journal of Consulting and Clinical Psychology, 60,* 185-195.

Benjamin, L. S. (1996). *Interpersonal diagnosis and treatment of personality disorders* (2nd ed.). New York: Guilford.

Cicchetti, D., Ganiban, J., & Barnett, D. (1991). Contributions from the study of high-risk populations to understanding the development of emotion regulation. In J. Garber & K. A. Dodge (Eds.), *The development of emotion regulation and dysregulation* (pp. 15-48). New York: Cambridge University Press.

Cunningham, C., & MacFarlane, K. (1990). *When children molest children.* Orwell, VT: Safer Society Press.

Dodge, K., & Garber, J. (1991). Domains of emotion regulation. In J. Garber & K. A. Dodge (Eds.), *The development of emotion regulation and dysregulation* (pp. 3-11). New York: Cambridge University Press.

Egeland, B., & Erickson, M. F. (1983, August). *Psychologically unavailable caregiving: The effects on development of young children and the implications for intervention.* Paper presented at the International Conference on Psychological Abuse, Indianapolis, IN.

Egeland, B., Sroufe, L. A., & Erickson, M. (1983). The developmental consequence of different patterns of maltreatment. *Child Abuse & Neglect, 7,* 459-469.

Finkelhor, D. (1984). Boys as victims: Review of the evidence. In D. Finkelhor (Ed.), *Child sexual abuse: New theory and research* (pp. 150-170). New York: Free Press.

Finkelhor, D., & Browne, A. (1985). The traumatic impact of child sexual abuse: A conceptualization. *American Journal of Orthopsychiatry, 55,* 530-541.

Friedrich, W. N. (1990). *Psychotherapy of sexually abused children and their families.* New York: Norton.

Friedrich, W. N. (1995). *Psychotherapy with sexually abused boys.* Thousand Oaks, CA: Sage.

Friedrich, W. N., Berliner, L., Urquiza, A. J., & Beilke, R. L. (1988). Brief diagnostic group treatment of sexually abused boys. *Journal of Interpersonal Violence, 3,* 331-343.

Friedrich, W. N., Luecke, W. J., Beilke, R. L., & Place, V. (1992). Psychotherapy outcome of sexually abused boys: An agency study. *Journal of Interpersonal Violence, 7,* 396-409.

George, C., & Main, M. (1979). Social interactions of young abused children: Approach, avoidance, and aggression. *Child Development, 50,* 306-318.

Harter, S. (1977). A cognitive-developmental approach to children's expression of conflicting feelings and a technique to facilitate such expression in play therapy. *Journal of Consulting and Clinical Psychology, 45,* 417-432.

Harter, S. (1988). Developmental and dynamic changes in the nature of the self-concept. In S. R. Shirk (Ed.), *Cognitive development and child psychotherapy.* New York: Plenum.

Katz, L. F., & Gottman, J. M. (1991). Marital discord and child outcomes: A social psychophysiological approach. In J. Garber & K. A. Dodge (Eds.), *The development of emotion regulation and dysregulation* (pp. 129-155). New York: Cambridge University Press.

Kendall-Tackett, K. A., Williams, L. M., & Finkelhor, D. (1993). Impact of sexual abuse on children: A review and synthesis of recent empirical studies. *Psychological Bulletin, 113,* 164-180.

Levang, C. A. (1989). Interactional communication patterns in father-daughter incest families. *Journal of Psychology and Human Sexuality, 1,* 53-68.

Main, M., & Cassidy, J. (1988). Categories of response to reunion with the parent at age 6: Predictable from infant attachment classifications and stable over a 1-month period. *Developmental Psychology, 24,* 415-426.

Main, M., & George, C. (1985). Responses of abused and disadvantaged toddlers to distress in age-mates: A study in the day care setting. *Developmental Psychology, 21,* 407-412.

Malinosky-Rummell, R. & Hansen, D. J. (1993). Long-term consequences of childhood physical abuse. *Psychological Bulletin, 114,* 68-79.

Mandell, J. G., & Damon. L. (1989). *Group treatment for sexually abused children.* New York: Guilford.

McLeer, S., Deblinger, E., Atkins, M., Foa, E., & Ralphe, D. (1988). Post-traumatic stress disorder in sexually abused children. *Journal of American Academy of Child and Adolescent Psychiatry, 27,* 650-654.

Selman, R. L., & Schultz, L. H. (1990). *Making a friend in youth.* Chicago: University of Chicago Press.

Selvini-Palazzoli, M., Boscolo, L., Cecchin, G., & Prata, G. (1978). *Paradox and counter paradox.* Northvale, NJ: Jason Aronson.

Shirk, S. R. (Ed.). (1988). *Cognitive development and child psychotherapy.* New York: Plenum.

Sroufe, L. A. (1989). Pathways to adaptation and maladaptation: Psychopathology as developmental deviation. In D. Cicchetti (Ed.), *The emergence of a discipline: Rochester Symposium on Developmental Psychopathology* (Vol. 1). Mahwah, NJ: Lawrence Erlbaum.

Strupp, H. H., & Binder, J. L. (1984). *Psychotherapy in a new key.* New York: Basic Books.

White, M. (1989). *Selected papers.* Adelaide, South Australia: Dulwich Center.

Yalom, I. (1975). *The theory and practice of group psychotherapy* (2nd ed.). New York: Basic Books.

10

The Emergence of Sexual Abuse Treatment Models Within First Nations Communities

EDWARD A. CONNORS

MAURICE L. B. OATES, JR.

Healing Ourselves

I believe that healing for us as human beings will be hard
to do unless we become humble and honest and straightforward
in all our dealings with women and children and men.
What we are searching for is harmony and balance again.
The way that it was before the strangers came to this sacred land,
and messed things up for us with their strange ways.
They came with an unbelievable greed and arrogance.
They came to a paradise and they turned it into a
living hell upon earth.
As Willfred Pelletier said many years ago in Thunder Bay;
"If there is a heaven and hell, Aboriginal people should
be able to go straight to heaven when they die,
because they have already spent a lifetime in hell."

What differentiates us from them is a difference in philosophy.
One is based on the false principle of materialism.
The other is based on the principle of the beauty,
the sacredness,
the harmony and the balance of the creation within which
we were to live.
We did not kill for sport,
we had to kill for sustenance.
We understood that we did not create the animals, the birds
and the fish.
They were created by the God of all creation.
And thus they belonged only to God
and we had to be constantly grateful for that bounty
as well as to the animals whose life we had taken.
Is it wrong for us to live that way
We have always been a simple people
but for that they have hated our guts.

Yet they had a commandment that says,
"Thou shalt love thy neighbour as thyself."
So how do we heal ourselves?
How did we get unbalanced?
Well the imperative for me is that we as men have to
go back to the old ways again to look back at how we did it
before when there was harmony
in our families and in our communities.
One of the dynamics of life that I have observed
through the years
is the dynamics of tension.
If two or more people come together
there is tension.
It is good or bad,
but there is tension.
It is either positive or negative.
We either like the other person or we are wary.

If we look back into the past we will see that women were
honoured and were respected for who they were

and what they did. There was harmony.
Our women kept the harmony and the balance in the families
and in the communities just by being there.
They taught the language and the customs and the ways
of being and doing.
They were the glue that held it all together
in the most beautiful way.

—Arthur Solomon (1994, p. 73)

To understand the process of healing social ills, such as sexual abuse, within First Nations communities, we must first understand the root causes that have promoted the development of these dysfunctional relationships. This task requires that we look at the connections between dysfunctional relationships and social structures.

Abuse of people is related to the misuse of power against vulnerable members of society. During the period of human history when people lived in tribal societies, we organized ourselves within social structures that reduced the disparity in the distribution of power, thus reducing vulnerability and the likelihood of abuse. In Judeo-Christian society, social structures have increased the disparity in the distribution of power, thus increasing the vulnerability of citizens and increasing the rates of abuse.

Gawitrha, a Traditional Chief from the Six Nations Brantford First Nation in southern Ontario, recently wrote the book *Dwanoha: One Earth, One Mind, One Path* (1991) which provides a detailed analysis of these historical developments and their relationship to increased violence and social dysfunction. The following statements are a summary of his arguments.

We know that all people on earth today are descendants of tribal societies. In fact, it would appear that, for approximately 1 million years, we lived exclusively in tribal societies. It has only been for the last 5,000 years that Judeo-Christian society has existed. The term *Judeo-Christian society* is being used to identify the lifestyle and values that evolved with this new social structure. We do not assume that either one of these social structures is superior; rather, the reader is invited to reevaluate both societies on the basis of their ability to promote health, well-being, and survival.

Exposure of North American tribal peoples to Judeo-Christian society began only 500 years ago, when the people of the Euro-Western world decided to settle on this land. To date, a significant portion of the world's human population lives in tribal societies.

Gawitrha believes it is not a coincidence that we chose to maintain our tribal lifestyles for most of the time that we have existed on this planet. He argues that considerable evidence supports his belief that tribal societies in their natural state offer healthier environments than Judeo-Christian societies. He suggests that tribal societies offer an organizational structure that promotes supportive, mutually protective relationships based on the values of respect, sharing, and caring. These environments ensure that all members of the tribal group are part of an interdependent system of relationships that provides maximum protection for its members. These communities, usually numbering fewer than 1,000 members, value all their members equally and recognize the unique contributions of all their members toward the survival of the group. Their values support respectful relationships in which no one uses power to interfere with the choices an individual makes regarding her or his own life. In this regard, Gawitrha believes that the structure of the tribal society evolved, in part, to provide socialization of the male members. This socialization is meant to subdue the innate aggressive tendencies of males and to enhance their nurturing qualities within the tribal groups. Tribal societies create totems and taboos that promote prosocial behaviors, thus enhancing the viability of the community by encouraging supportive caring and sharing behaviors within the community and allowing for the expression of male aggression outside the community. This socializing of the male is mainly directed by the female members of the community during the early years of development. They also monitor and guide the behavior of the males within the community during later years. Gawitrha offers the Mohawk society as an example of this form of social organization. It is his belief that tribal societies maintained this structure during our first 45,000 years because it promoted the optimum healthy environment for people. He also states that the women of tribal societies inherently recognized the dangers of adopting social structures that would not keep the male aggressive tendencies in check. They have therefore resisted these changes to the best of their abilities.

From what we know about tribal societies, it would appear that self-destructive behaviors and aggression toward other members of the tribal group are minimized by the social structures that are designed to ensure the survival of the group. Obviously, within interdependent communities, any uncontrolled aggressive behavior expressed within the community is viewed by all members as a threat to the entire community and is therefore checked by the community.

Approximately 10,000 years ago, Judeo-Christian society was born when the idea to cultivate and farm some particularly fertile regions began. This led to the settlement of populations larger than 1,000 people in certain geographic regions and accompanying changes in the social structures within which these people lived. Initially, families became more self-reliant than they had been in tribal societies because they were able to produce food for their family unit independent of the community. In addition, the development of the concept of property ownership was a central part of the new social structure and value system.

It appears as though the influence of women in socializing males to check their aggressive tendencies declined as the evolving social structures began to support and promote male dominance on the basis of their greater aggressive tendencies. These social structures tended to be hierarchical in design and to allow for males to exert power and control over woman, children, and all other life forms that are viewed as lesser beings. The accompanying value system supports competition, independence, and the accumulation of property. In turn, the amount of property accumulated is an indication of one's position in the hierarchy and thus determines the degree of power and control one can exert. The principles from tribal society of sharing, caring, and equality were replaced in Judeo-Christian society with accumulation of property, independence from the group, and dominance by the most powerful members.

Obviously, the social organization provided within Judeo-Christian society does not offer the degree of protection and safeguards from internal violence that tribal society once did. In fact, it is easy to see how the level of human violence directed toward other social groups and within one's own social group has escalated within Judeo-Christian societies during the 5,000 years of its development. It is apparent that we have caused more destruction to ourselves and our environment in the 5,000 years that Judeo-Christian society has existed than in the preceding 1 million years of tribal history. In comparison with Judeo-Christian societies, tribal societies that have remained untouched, or relatively so, by Judeo-Christian society have remained comparatively nonviolent and protective of their members.

When Judeo-Christian society emerged, a completely new way of thinking and behaving evolved. This created at least two lifestyle options for the humans on this earth. One is to think in a holistic manner and to live as if everything in creation is interdependent and of equal importance; the other is to think in a reductionistic manner and to live as if the world is ordered in hierarchies based on one's ability to exert control over lesser beings. The former thinking represents the pervasive conceptual framework of tribal societies (Ross, 1992), and the later of Judeo-Christian societies. In the past 500 years since the tribal peoples of North America have come into contact with the peoples of Euro-Western Judeo-Christian society, the process of colonization has involved converting tribal peoples to the Judeo-Christian view of the world and/or annihilation. It is apparent at this point in history that we must reevaluate all the former assumptions about Judeo-Christian society that have led to the belief that it offers a superior and healthier lifestyle over tribal society. History shows that tribal societies of North America experienced lower levels of internal violence and violence between tribal societies than Euro-Western Judeo-Christian societies. Prior to contact with Europeans, North American tribal societies had relatively low levels of abuse of self and others (e.g. suicide, family violence, sexual abuse). Reports range from no known incidence of internal violence to relatively low levels. Since contact, those First Nations communities that have demonstrated a rise in internal violence are those that have had the greatest amount of contact with Judeo-Christian societies (Westlake Van Winkle & May, 1986).

Berry's (1990) model of acculturation offers a framework for examining changes in health standards when two different cultures come into contact. He suggests that several responses are possible when different cultures collide. These responses include integration, assimilation, separation, and marginalization. Figure 10.1 shows how a minority culture's response to contact with a dominant culture can be determined from answers to two questions.

The highest rates of self-destructive behavior and violence toward others appear to occur within minority communities that can be described as marginalized or that are lost between minority and dominant society. In a study of the New Mexico Pueblos' suicide rates between 1954 and 1962, Levy (1965) found that the acculturated communities had the highest rates, whereas the traditional (separated) communities recorded the lowest rates.

Many First Nations communities have reached the conclusion that the rise of violence within our communities is related to the acculturation experience or the disconnection from tribal thinking and behavior.

Extensive discussions among community members and senior service staff point to a gradual erosion of the community ideals, moral behaviour, standards and social controls. Such erosion is traced ultimately to the broader conditions

ISSUE 1

Is it considered to be of value to
maintain cultural identity and
characteristics?

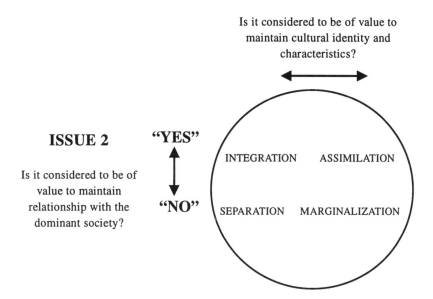

ISSUE 2   "YES"

Is it considered to be of
value to maintain
relationship with the   "NO"
dominant society?

INTEGRATION   ASSIMILATION

SEPARATION   MARGINALIZATION

Figure 10.1. Four Modes of Acculturation

of government policy, socioeconomic conditions, alcohol abuse and other
societal influences. (Maidman, 1991, p. 6)

In a recent community workshop about sexual abuse (Maidman, 1991,
p. 6), members of our communities identified the following as causes of the
high rates of sexual abuse in First Nations communities:

- *The breakdown of the native traditional values and practices related to
  sexuality, which contributed to the loss of community standards as communities lost control of their governments and were forced to follow the ways of
  Judeo-Christian society. The do's and don'ts of sexual behavior are confused
  or missing, and the natural community controls against unacceptable behavior are weak or nonexistent. This state evolved as the tribal norms for sexual
  behavior were replaced by the norms of Judeo-Christian society that were
  unclear and confusing. Many of the newcomers did not practice the values
  they espoused. Consequently, the new standard for sexual behavior became
  "It is important to appear good but not to act good."*

- *Previous experiences in residential schools and foster homes in which some people were sexually abused and all people were denied a sexual identity through role modeling experiences with natural parents. Many people who sexually abused children in these environments were considered by Judeo-Christian society to be teachers of their moral codes and, as such, were supposed to be fine examples of appropriate moral behaviour. This is where many First Nations people learned their values regarding sexual behavior. As a result, many were taught to justify sexually abusive behavior with their new values.*

- *The mass media, which convey an ideal of sexual attractiveness and uncommitted sexuality, often in conjunction with alcohol consumption, and teach values that support sexual exploitation and oppression.*

- *Poverty in which multiple families are living together in crowded conditions and in which children or teenagers are lured into sexual activities for money or gifts.*

- *Alcohol abuse, which lessens the inhibitions against sexually inappropriate behavior or is used as an excuse after the fact; alcohol and expected sexual activity are seen to go hand-in-hand during partying and gang rape.*

- *Blended family situations in crowded circumstances that provide sexual abuse opportunities between stepfathers and teenage daughters and generally give mixed messages to young children concerning appropriate sexual behaviour.*

- *Family and other male-female structures in which men in positions of power are able to exercise dominance over women and children, who are treated as objects. This new hierarchical structuring of relationships was introduced into First Nations communities when we were forced to adopt Judeo-Christian society's structure of government under the Indian Act.*

- *Sexual behavior among young children in which extremely young, powerless children are coerced into sexual acts, thus contributing to early learning of sexual abuse as a norm.*

- *Barriers against open discussions of positive sexuality or sexual abuse, thus limiting a healthy exchange of sexual information, as well as an initiation of concern and action against sexual abuse. The Euro-Christian teachings regarding sexuality instilled values that linked shame and guilt to sex. This led to a repression of healthy discussions about sex.*

- *Inadequate or insufficient information about sexuality, resulting in poor parental teaching and inappropriate sex role learning within the peer group.*

- *Urbanization of natives in which people become involved in off-community events, such as hockey tournaments, where alcohol and relaxed controls sometimes lead to sexually inappropriate behavior.*

All these factors can be seen as consequences of the acculturation process that has disconnected many tribal communities from the beliefs and values that had formerly guided healthy behavior.

To counter the negative effects of the acculturation process, many of our communities are attempting to reestablish elements of tribal thinking (values and beliefs) and behavior within the healing processes that we are developing. The steps in this acculturation process have involved providing a definition of health/mental health from a tribal/holistic conceptual framework (Mussel, Nicholls, & Adler, 1991), articulating the values that are characteristic of tribal society, and developing treatment programs that operate from these perspectives and that are consistent with tribal healing processes. In the area of sexual abuse healing, several community programs have been established during the past 15 years that have employed the above steps—for example, Biidaaban Sexual Abuse Healing Program (1996), Circle of Harmony Healing Society (Oates, 1992), Gwa'Sala-'Nakwaxda'xw Family Violence and Sexual Abuse Intervention Program (1993), the Hallowater First Nation Sexual Abuse Program (1993), and the Prince George Native Friendship Centre Sexual Abuse Treatment Services (1992). None of these programs have been documented within the existing health literature, but all have extensive written documentation available for training purposes.

Efforts to structure the healing process so that it is consistent with tribal thinking and behavior provide these programs with approaches that are unique to First Nations. In other words, the core tribal values including sharing, caring, and respect tend to guide the process of healing that is structured to use the holistic/interdependent organization of the tribal community. These programs recognize that the process of healing must begin from the point that a disclosure of sexual abuse is made. Therefore, the healing models involve each community in conducting its own investigations, systems of justice, and treatment/healing programs. In most cases, these community processes replace those of the external society. Healing or sentencing circles, which have received considerable media attention recently, are good examples of this approach to healing. These models essentially involve the extended family members, along with victims and offenders, in a process of determining what injustices have occurred and a process for correcting the harm. Central to this process is the belief that harm to one community member affects the health and harmony of the entire community. Because *health* is defined as a state of harmony and balance among all community members, reestablishing health requires that relationships are set back into a state of balance. Because all community members have a vested interest in reestablishing balance, the extended family takes an active role in supporting, assisting, encouraging, and guiding the victim and the offender to restore balance in the relationships.

Across Canada and the United States, many First Nations communities are using sentencing circles as part of their efforts to reestablish tribal healing processes. Consequently, many First Nations communities are following the example set by the Hallowater First Nation Sexual Abuse Program (1993) and are resuming the responsibility to correct such social ills as sexual abuse. These community programs include all steps, from investigation and judgment to the completion of treatment, correction, and reconciliation.

While reviewing a variety of First Nations healing programs, including Hallowater's sexual abuse program, Ross (1996) identified the following seven differences between aboriginal and Western justice processes. These principles demonstrate how healing is more significant within the aboriginal system of justice than it is in the dominant culture's justice process.

> First, western law seems to believe that it can effectively deal with offenders as individuals, whether for rehabilitative or for deterrent purposes. Traditional wisdom, by contrast, seems to suggest that people must be seen not primarily as individuals but as products of all their relationships. Traditional law thus seems to require that justice processes involve all the people who operate within the webs of relationships which surround and, in a real sense, 'define' every offender and every victim.
>
> Second, western law seems to believe that each of us is equally capable of moving out of anti social behaviour on our own; all we have to do is decide to behave differently than we have been. Traditional wisdom, by contrast, suggests that each of us is confronted on a daily basis by a multitude of waves, some stretching back centuries, all of which push us in various directions. Some of us face only small waves and have been given both good health and superior skills in riding them. Others, however, must confront far more powerful and destructive waves, and with almost no skills or health at all. Because it is understood that none of us can fundamentally change the waves which come our way, that they will still be there tomorrow, the challenge for a justice system involves not punishing people for their incapacities, but helping them to develop greater capacities instead. In short, justice involves healing injuries which have already occurred, and helping people develop the skills they will need to avoid further injury in the future, both to themselves and to others.
>
> Third, western law focuses very narrowly on particular acts. It is acts which must be alleged and proven in court, and it is the criminal act itself which substantially controls the court's response under the principle that "the punishment must fit the crime." Traditional understandings, by contrast, seem to suggest that acts are no more than signals of disharmonies in the relationships between individuals and between the physical, mental, emotional and

spiritual dimensions of each individual. Traditional law thus requires that the investigations and interventions of a justice system must focus on these disharmonies instead, instead of just the acts which erupt out of them.

Fourth, western law puts people through adversarial processes which add to whatever feelings of antagonism exist between them. Traditional wisdom, by contrast, suggests that antagonistic feelings within relationships are the very cause of antagonistic acts. Traditional law thus requires that justice processes must be structured to reduce, rather than escalate, that antagonism. Only then is there a chance of bringing health, understanding and respect back to those relationships, and reducing the harmful, angry acts between them.

Fifth, western law seems to insist upon labelling and stigmatizing offenders, both to themselves and to the community at large. Traditional wisdom seems to suggest that we are very complex beings who cannot be captured by such simplistic labels, that we are constantly re-forming within ever-changing relationships. Traditional law thus requires that justice processes be structured to help people begin to believe that they are more than their anti social acts, that they too are capable of learning how to cope with the forces which surround them. In short, while our punitive law treats offenders as enemies of the community, traditional wisdom suggests that such alienation is part of the problem, and traditional law commands that every effort be made to overcome that conviction, not add to it.

Sixth, western law seems to believe that "taking responsibility for your crime" means little more than admitting the physical things you did and paying a proportionate price in punishment. Traditional wisdom suggests that crimes are important primarily because of their impact on the mental, emotional, spiritual and physical health of all those affected, including all those within the offender's relationships. Traditional law thus seems to require that justice processes "hold people responsible" by doing two things:

(a) specifically involving all of those other people who have been affected, and creating respectful, dignified and "non blaming" processes for them to express and deal with their "felt" responses to what the offender has done to them; and

(b) helping the offender come to a "felt" awareness of the true extent of the impact of his act on the lives of all of those people.

Seventh, western law seems to believe that "solutions" are best provided by relying on professional experts like judges, psychiatrists, probation officers and the like, all of whom come as "strangers" to each case. Traditional wisdom seems to suggest that the only people who can be fully aware of the complexities of their relationships are the people actually involved. What they need is assistance in solving the problems which are getting the better of them. While stranger-experts can bring such assistance, they must be careful to restrict themselves to:

(1) creating and regulating respectful processes within which the parties themselves can come together in non blaming and non adversarial ways;

(2) helping people to confront and discharge incapacitating feelings like alienation, grief, anger, guilt, fear and the like;

(3) showing people how respectful relationships can be developed, and that they are possible for them as well; and

(4) demonstrating in their every word and deed that they too are striving to attain such ideals as honesty, kindness, sharing and respect. The responsibility for actual problemsolving, however, remains with the parties themselves, for only then will they need to avoid such problems in the future. (Ross, 1995, pp. 431-435)

First Nations sexual abuse treatment models also vary according to the degree of acculturation experienced by the community from which they emerge. These models can be categorized according to Berry's (1990) acculturation matrix. Urban programs, such as the Prince George Native Friendship Center Sexual Abuse Treatment Service and the Circle of Harmony Healing Society, offer treatment models that appear to have been developed to serve the needs of individuals whom Berry (1990) refers to as assimilated and integrated. In contrast, reserve programs, such as the Hallowater First Nation Sexual Abuse Program and the Biidaaban Sexual Abuse Healing Program, have been created for people who tend to fall into Berry's integrated category.

Programs serving a largely assimilated native population in urban centers tend to offer programs that are consistent with the child welfare, legal, and treatment practices of the dominant Canadian society. In these instances, the only things that identify these programs as being specific to First Nations are the native clients, native staff, and some cultural practices.

The First Nations communities that exist near nonnative urban centers tend to opt for sexual abuse treatment models that reflect their integrated state of acculturation. In these situations, communities like Mnjikaning First Nation have evolved program models that incorporate their traditional beliefs and values along with the child welfare, legal, and treatment practices of the dominant Canadian society. The community has developed a program that enables them to offer their own child welfare investigations, sentencing circles, and treatment program as alternatives to the dominant culture's model. This community's model offers a range of options for investigation, sentencing, and treatment that reflects the diverse needs of its members. Integrated communities tend to exhibit a wider range of cultural identities among their membership, and it is therefore necessary to provide a range of justice and treatment options that best matches the needs of all community members. For example, treatment options in this community include a variety of therapies offered by the dominant society and traditional healing ceremonies (e.g., sweat lodge ceremonies). Each course of therapy is designed to match the cultural identity of the person receiving treatment. Also, all therapies used in this program are selected according to how well they match with the tribal/holistic conceptual framework (Mussel et al., 1991).

In the more remote First Nations communities, the programs have developed relatively independently of the dominant culture's system. These models have relied heavily on traditional beliefs and practices to reform a system of justice and healing for addressing sexual abuse. According to Berry's (1990) model of acculturation, these communities can best be described as in a state of separation.

In the next section, we describe a sexual abuse treatment model that was developed by Oates (1992) for reserves in the northern interior of British Columbia. These communities are isolated from nonnative settlements and have retained much of their traditional practices and beliefs. Therefore, this treatment model has been developed from their traditional healing practices and has formed the basis for the development of the Hallowater model, which has had a major influence on the development of other First Nations sexual abuse programs.

DEALING WITH NATIVE SEXUAL ABUSE IN A TRADITIONAL MANNER: A COMMUNITY PROCESS OF HEALING

The Traditional Process

1. Disclosure

At the moment of disclosure, the Sexual Abuse Coordinator is contacted. This coordinator must be well trained in the dynamics of sexual abuse, both as they apply to white society, and in a native context. This coordinator is responsible for seeing that all 18 steps (see Figure 10.2) are followed in the proper sequence.

2. Protecting the Child

Throughout this entire process, the protection and support of the victim takes priority. The coordinator will be responsible for the removal of the

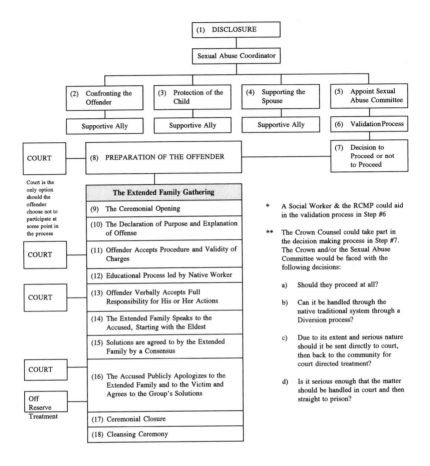

Figure 10.2. Summary: A Community Process of Healing

victim from the home, if necessary, either by direct intervention or by appointing an appropriate person. Because of the intrafamily dynamics on reserves, it may not always be best for the coordinator to be the one to remove the child. It is recommended that when there is a perceived conflict of interests, the coordinator should appoint an elder in the family affected to be involved in the removal and placement of the victim with a non-offending member of the extended family or clan. The removal of the child should take place as quickly as possible after the disclosure to avoid pressure from the alleged offender or other family members, unless the alleged offender is immediately removed from the home and it is believed that the child would be safe.

It is important that the victim not be isolated with strangers. The structure of an extended native family is such that it may range up to more than 100 individuals living within close proximity to the victim. It is usually possible to find a sympathetic, non-offending relative to act as a "supportive ally" to the child, who can provide a place to stay, protection from the offender (with community support), and psychological support. Once the band members become aware of this system and believe that the community supports their actions, emergency placement will become less and less of a problem.

3. Confronting the Alleged Offender

The alleged offender should be approached by an appropriate leader of the community (e.g., chief, elder) or the Sexual Abuse Coordinator. This person explains that the child has been removed because of the disclosure and will be staying with a non-offending relative until he or she leaves the home or until the community resolves the situation. The alleged offender should be told that he or she will be contacted by the coordinator after a decision is made within a 5-day period. The alleged offender should be told of the real possibility (depending on the severity of the offense and his or her willingness to cooperate) that the matter could be handled within the community or through court diversion or, after court, by way of a suspended sentence. It should be made clear that any such option depends largely on how *the offender responds* to the situation. It should also be made clear that any attempt made by the offender to interfere with the process or to pressure the victim will result in the immediate notification of off-reserve authorities, or band police where they exist.

A non-offending elder or friend whom the alleged offender respects should be assigned to give the offender support during this period to avoid a possible suicide attempt or an attempted violent act or threat to other village members. Strong denial and anger can be expected on the part of the accused. This supportive ally should offer caring, nonthreatening, and nonjudgmental support but should try not to reinforce the alleged offender's denial system.

4. Supporting the Spouse

A non-offender elder or friend whom the spouse respects should be assigned to give him or her support during this period to avoid a possible suicide attempt, violent act, or threat to other village members. Strong denial and anger may occur on the part of the spouse at this point. The spouse's supportive ally should offer caring, nonthreatening, and nonjudgmental support but should try not to reinforce the spouse's denial system. It should be gently emphasized to the spouse how important it is to support the victim and where the responsibility lies for the offense (with the offender).

5. Appointing the Sexual Abuse Committee

Once the child has been protected and the basic facts gathered, a meeting should be called by the coordinator. This could include a social worker, RCMP or Crown representative (where appropriate), elders, and clan or band members. This group will be considered a "Sexual Abuse Committee," whose membership is determined by the coordinator, who will be the chairperson. With the exception of the coordinator, the membership of the Sexual Abuse Committee can be flexible and specific to each case.

6. Validation Process

The validation process in this system, though similar, is not as rigid and demanding as that imposed by nonnative society, as the results are to be used by the community, not the courts. If handled through court, the standard approach must be used. The offender, to be treated through the community, especially if diversion is used, must admit to the offense and accept responsibility. We are not working with the "adversary" system, but rather are developing a healing process for all those involved in or affected by the offense. If the offense is deemed to be beyond that which the village can handle, even if the offender is willing to cooperate, then the appropriate off-reserve authorities will be notified by the Sexual Abuse Committee in Step 7. Some guidelines should be developed by the community (in concert with the Crown Counsel) to determine which offenses can be handled by the village and which should be handled by off-reserve authorities.

Sgroi (1982) provides an excellent discussion of a validation process that can be used as is or be modified somewhat to meet the needs of the community.

In the village validation process, the coordinator, the child's supportive ally, and perhaps one or two supportive, appropriate elders question the child as to the nature and extent of the offense. This is independent of the validation process carried out by the social worker and RCMP, which is court oriented. One advantage of this community validation is that the people involved know the offender and family well and, properly trained ahead of time, can be very accurate in determining the validity of the charges.

In this system, the threat of incarceration to an extended family or community member, if not removed, is at least somewhat within the community's control. Punishment or treatment is largely dependent on the willingness of the alleged offender to cooperate. Under these conditions, the committee can concentrate on a *healing* process, seeking methods to bring the family and individuals back into a healthy, nonabusive balance.

7. Decision to Proceed or Not to Proceed

At this point, the traditional system can be synchronized with the non-native legal system. A combined report from the village Sexual Abuse Committee and the RCMP/social worker is provided to the local Crown Counsel, explaining the offense and asking permission to proceed through the village system by way of diversion. This report may lengthen the process considerably while awaiting a reply, and a noncooperative Crown Counsel could lay down conditions that would negate the purpose of this community approach. It could provide a serious block where the Crown Counsel was not inclined to work with the village. Diversion as practiced by most Crown Counsels is on the assumption that should the admitted abuser fail to take part in the treatment process, the matter would proceed to court. This is most effective when the Crown knows that it does not have enough evidence to proceed but some leverage can still be applied to the abuser.

The other legal approach is by way of court, and a guilty plea, or judgment of guilt being determined through the court process, followed by a suspended sentence. Thus the court, once offender guilt has been established, could order the offender to either take part in the treatment process or go to jail. If the offender refuses to take part in the process anywhere along the line, his or her suspended sentence is revoked, and he or she is sent to prison.

Following the validation process, a decision must be made as to the course of action to be taken. There are three possibilities:

1. There does not appear to be reasonable grounds for the alleged abuse.
2. The charges of abuse are valid and should be dealt with within the native community.
3. The charges hold true but are so serious that they must be dealt with by nonnative, off-reserve authorities.

8. Preparation of the Offender

At this point, a decision has been made by the Sexual Abuse Committee to proceed with the matter within the village social structure either through diversion or after sentencing. If diversion is the decision, the offender is told that he or she must, within 3 days, either admit to the allegations and accept treatment or deny the charges.

Should the offender decide to deny the allegations or should she or he fail to inform the committee of the decision by a set time, the matter is then turned over to the off-reserve authorities for disposition. The committee will then focus on providing treatment and support for the victim and extended family.

If the offender admits to the allegations and is willing to accept the community process, he or she is then told to appear before a special gathering of his or her extended family, clan, or community and must accept the gathering's decisions as to treatment and reparations. The coordinator and the offender's supportive ally will prepare the offender for appearing before this gathering, explaining the procedure and what will be expected of the offender. This is the first time the offender is asked to accept responsibility for her or his offense(s).

The Extended Family Gathering

Steps 9 through 18 take place at an extended family gathering. The Sexual Abuse Committee arranges to have the agreed-on members of the extended family, clan, or community meet with the offender and others involved in the offense. A place is agreed on, the time is set, and notifications are sent out explaining the purpose of the gathering. Steps 9 to 13 should take place in one session, and Steps 14 to 17 in another. This schedule leaves adequate time in the first session for the educational component. It is best not to let more than 1 day elapse between the sessions. Seating arrangements will vary from group to group, depending on the traditional beliefs and preferences. *The important element is that the abuser is brought face-to-face with the extended family or community group to answer for his or her misconduct and that all affected immediate family members are present.*

9. The Ceremonial Opening

The ceremonial opening will vary from group to group. This may be a traditional opening, with drum, song, and/or prayer, or a Christian prayer.

This can be determined by the Sexual Abuse Committee or the extended family involved with the offense. Some sort of ceremonial gesture should be made to mark the event as important, as distinctly native, and to announce the beginning of the gathering and the closing of the gathering.

10. The Declaration of Purpose and Explanation of the Offense

Either the coordinator or a capable leader of the people that are gathered (e.g., elder, traditional chief, elected chief) will address the abuser and the people and explain to those present the purpose of the meeting:

To hear the details of the offense from a member of the Sexual Abuse Committee

To publicly speak to the offender about the offense

To decide on how best the community can deal with this offense to heal all members of the family and to reunite the community

To show their support for the offender (as a member of the community in need of help), the spouse, and the victim and to demonstrate that such behaviour is unacceptable by the community as a whole

To learn something about sexual abuse in general through an educational process

To accept the responsibility for supervising any conditions placed on the offender by the whole group

After the purpose of the gathering has been explained to the participants, the Sexual Abuse Coordinator explains the findings of the Sexual Abuse Committee.

11. Offender Accepts Procedure and Validity of Charges

Following the reading or explanation of the offense, the offender is asked whether he or she accepts the charges as true and is willing to participate in the proceedings. If the offender accepts the proceedings and agrees on the charges, the meeting can continue. This is the second time the offender is asked to accept responsibility for his or her offense(s). If the offender rejects either or both conditions, the coordinator explains to the group that the meeting must be brought to a close and the matter will be turned over to off-reserve authorities and that *the responsibility for this decision rests on the shoulders of the offender.* At this point, it is the responsibility of the community to support the action of the Sexual Abuse Committee.

12. Educational Process Led by Native Worker

This part of the process is extremely important in that it sets the stage for the rest of the proceedings. It helps educate all the people present about the seriousness and dynamics of the offense. It sets the emotional stage necessary for changes in attitudes to occur.

13. Offender Verbally Accepts Full Responsibility for His or Her Actions

After this educational process has been completed and the offender and the people present have a clearer idea of what they are treating, the coordinator again asks the offender to accept full responsibility for the offense, without rationalization, justifications, or reservations. If the offender fully accepts the responsibility for the offense, the meeting can continue. If not, it is turned over to outside authorities. This is the third time the offender is asked to accept responsibility for the offense.

14. The Extended Family Speaks to the Accused, Starting With the Eldest

The family members speak to the offender, telling him or her how they feel about the offense, counseling him or her as to how to deal with the problem effectively, and encouraging him or her to accept full responsibility for his or her behavior.

The family members speak to the spouse about his or her responsibility in helping in the healing process, or perhaps talking to the spouse about his or her part in the abusive situation.

The family members speak to the victim, relieving the victim of any guilt he or she may feel and reassuring the victim that he or she is not responsible for the offense; the extended family members offer community support to help the victim cope with the aftereffects of the abuse.

When the offender, spouse, and victim are willing, the gathered people can encourage and offer support to the concept of the family reuniting in the future, *after* the healing process has taken place enough to ensure that such behavior will not be repeated.

Members of the group are free to relate to all present their own experiences in the past of being abused or being an abuser and the emotional and social problems they incurred as a result of their experience. This takes place in a context of shared experiences for the purpose of helping in the healing process.

In some tribal groups, it is appropriate for the eldest to speak first, standing and speaking freely, followed by anyone else who wishes to speak to the matter.

There are some strong, positive aspects to the community showing group support for the victim and spouse, as well as demonstrating the desire to heal the abuser. The feelings of shame and stigmatization on the part of the victim are minimized, and guilt over what happens to the offending parent is relieved by the group's positive actions. No amount of individual counseling will protect a victim in a native community from verbal and emotional abuse by extended family members or other community people who believe that the child has turned on his or her people. A community approach, however, can protect and heal that child. The same is true for the spouse.

15. Solutions Are Agreed to by the Family Through Consensus

Having addressed the offender about the offense, the group now seeks possible solutions to the problem. This can include, but is not limited to, the following:

Community service work
Restricted access to children thought to be in danger for a specified period of time
Taking part in a native-oriented treatment program for this or related problems, such as alcohol abuse or spousal abuse
Attendance at support groups in the community
Some combination of the above

Remember that solutions are only limited by the imagination of the group and the willingness of the offender to participate. Those solutions proposed by the group during this part of the program should have at least three components:

1. Some limited degree of punishment that enhances the community and the offender's self-esteem
2. Protection against any further victimization
3. A treatment aspect over a specified period of time for all members of the affected family

Martens (1988) established a very comprehensive community-oriented plan for dealing with sexual abuse in the least punitive manner possible under present circumstances. His program, or variations thereof, could be considered to be part of the treatment process.

After a period of discussion by the group, leading to various suggestions as to what should be done, and such suggestions are recorded by the coordinator, the group is asked to decide on the treatment plan by consensus. The matter is discussed until the entire group agrees. This tactic ensures solid support for the community's decision.

It is the duty of the coordinator to record the final treatment plan, to notify the Crown Counsel as to the results and the conditions agreed on, and then to see that they are carried out as intended. Failure on the part of the offender to fulfill the conditions should result in the matter going back to the Crown Counsel. It is important to realize that the committee's responsibility does not end with this session. The community must be involved in any treatment approach from beginning to end. Whatever system they agree to establish to handle sexual abuse in the community, they must support it 100%, regardless of which family member or relative goes before the community group.

16. The Accused Publicly Apologies to the Victim, the Extended Family, and Agrees to the Group's Solutions

At this point, it is the responsibility of the accused, when asked to do so by the coordinator or group leader, to publicly apologize to the gathering for his or her offensive behavior. He or she starts by apologizing to the victim and the spouse and then to the group at large. The offender must publicly agree to the conditions read to him or her by the coordinator and state that he or she understands that any failure to comply with the conditions will immediately result in the matter going to court. This is the fourth and final acceptance by the accused of full responsibility for the abusive actions. The number four has spiritual significance in most native beliefs.

17. Ceremonial Closure

Like the ceremonial opening, the ceremonial closing will vary from group to group. This may be a traditional closing, with drum, song, and prayer, or a Christian prayer. This will be determined by the leadership of the group.

18. Cleansing Ceremony

The cleansing ceremony is an important ceremony that marks the completion of the tasks assigned to the offender and/or the end of his or her treatment. This ceremony will vary from tribe to tribe. On the Pacific Coast, a public cleansing often takes place at a feast, where Juniper, Devil's Club, or False Hellebore is used in liquid form. The offender is washed down, symbolizing a cleansing of the spirit. For many groups, this ceremony would also include a feast given for the extended family of the victim and perhaps gifts given to all those affected by the offense.

This ceremony is important in that it breaks the system of *stereotyping offenders and victims* and labeling them for life. At the end of this ceremony, the offense is laid aside, never to be spoken of again in anger. It is over and deliberately forgotten. The offender is no longer an "offender," and the victim is no longer a "victim." Balance is now restored to the individuals involved, the extended family, the clan, and the village. The only place that these memories may be revived are in a treatment gathering.

CONCLUSION

It is apparent that sexual abuse programs serving First Nations clients have begun to make efforts to match their program models with the acculturation experiences of the communities. Although no large, controlled studies have been conducted to assess the effectiveness of these programs, some observations reported by these communities regarding the outcomes related to their programs are available. For example, the community of Hallowater reported as follows:

> In nine years, 52 offenders have been enrolled in the healing program, along with 94 victims and 260 relatives of offenders and victims. In the same period, five sexual offenders have gone to jail after their offenses were disclosed, mainly because they refused to acknowledge what they had done. Only two sex offenders have reoffended. Both were given penitentiary terms. ("Native Healing Program," 1995, p. 1A)

The Circle of Harmony Healing Society has reported similar findings. It indicates that 5 years after completing treatment, none of the 23 offenders from its program has been involved in further sexual offenses.

Although these results are not based on controlled studies of the effectiveness of the program, they do suggest that these programs are producing positive changes in First Nations communities.

These treatment models are growing in number very quickly and are part of larger efforts by First Nations communities to reestablish the components of tribal society that have supported and promoted healthier environments than those experienced within Judeo-Christian society. These components are related to the organizational structures of tribal society that create interdependent, close relationships in which prosocial and dysfunctional behaviors are both guided and monitored by all community members. It is believed that this process decreases the likelihood that dysfunctional behavior will be demonstrated and severely limits recidivism ("Native Healing Program," 1995).

In contrast with the sexual abuse correction and treatment models offered by Judeo-Christian society, the tribal society approach appears to be more successful at stopping the cycle of violence that has become too familiar to First Nations communities. As part of the process of self-empowerment, our communities have begun to realize that much within the structure of tribal societies afforded greater health than that experienced within Judeo-Christian society. Many of our communities are now looking into our tribal pasts and bringing forward the information that will make it more likely that our children will have healthier futures. How far we return to tribal thinking, behavior, and organization will be determined by the degree of increased health that our communities experience as a result of our reinvolvement in tribal thinking and behavior.

One has to wonder whether Judeo-Christian society might also, sometime in the future, return to a form of tribal society as the dysfunctional effect of this oppressive lifestyle continues to mount and pose increasing threats to the survival of all creation.

REFERENCES

Berry, J. (1990). Acculturation and adaptation: Health consequences of cultural contact among circumpolar peoples. *Arctic Medical Research, 49,* 142-150.
Biidaaban Sexual Abuse Healing Program. (1996). (Rama Health Centre, Box 35, Rama, Ontario L0K 1T0 Canada).
Gawitrha. (1991). *Dwanoha: One earth, one mind, one path.* (Available from Pine Tree Publication Group Six Nations, Grand River, R.R. #6, Hagersville, Ont. N0A 1H0 Canada).
Gwa'Sala-'Nakwaxda'xw Family Violence and Sexual Abuse Intervention Program. (1993). Unpublished document (Gwa'Sala-'Nakwaxda'xw Council, Box 998, Port Hardy, British Columbia V0N 2P0 Canada).
Hallowater First Nation Sexual Abuse Program. (1993). Unpublished report (Hallowater First Nation, Wanipigow, Manitoba R0E 2E0 Canada [204/363-7426]).
Levy, H. E. (1965). Navajo suicide. *Human Organization, 24,* 308-318.

Maidman, F. (1991). *Ojibway Tribal Family Services Sexual Abuse Workshop.* Unpublished document. (Ojibway Tribal Family Services, 512-1st Avenue South, Kenora, Ontario P9N 1W5 Canada).

Martens, T. (1988). *The Spirit Weeps: Characteristics and dynamics of incest and child sexual abuse with a Native perspective.* (Neechi Institute, Box 3884, Postal Station D, Edmonton, Alberta T5L 4K1 Canada).

Mussel, W. T., Nicholls, W. M., & Adler, M. T. (1991). *Making meaning of mental health in First Nations: A Freirian perspective.* Unpublished document. (Available from Salishan Institute, Box 242, Chilliwack, B.C. V2P 6J1 Canada).

Native healing program helps abusers. (1995, April 8). *Globe & Mail,* pp. A1, A8.

Oates, M. L. (1992). *Native treatment programs: Circle of Harmony Healing Society.* Unpublished document. (Terrace Mental Health Centre, 202-3412 Kalum St., Terrace, B.C., V8G 4T2 Canada).

Prince George Native Friendship Center Sexual Abuse Treatment Services. (1992). Unpublished document. (Prince George Native Friendship Healing Center, 144 George St. Prince George, B.C. V2L 1P9 Canada).

Ross, R. (1992). *Dancing with a ghost: Exploring Indian reality.* Markham, Ontario: Octopus Publishing.

Ross, R. (1995). Restorative justice: Exploring the aboriginal paradigm. *Saskatchewan Law Review, 59*(2).

Ross, R. (1996). *Returning to the teachings: Exploring aboriginal justice.* Toronto: Penguin.

Solomon, A. (1994). *Eating bitterness: A vision beyond the prison walls.* Toronto: N.C. Press.

Sgroi, S. M. (Ed.). (1982). *Handbook of clinical intervention in child sexual abuse.* Lexington, MA: Lexington.

Westlake Van Winkle, N., & May, P. (1986). Native American suicide in New Mexico, 1957-1979: A comparative study. *Human Organizations, 45,* 22-30.

11

Sexually Abused Children
as Witnesses

PROGRESS AND PITFALLS

LOUISE SAS

Over the last 15 years, the topic of childhood sexual abuse has received increased attention by both the public, who have been shocked by its widespread nature, and by professionals whose research efforts and clinical practices have endeavored to explicate the factors underlying the sexual victimization of children and to treat its traumatic aftermath. As we have become more receptive to children's disclosures, an increase has occurred in the number of children reporting incidents of sexual abuse. These disclosures, in turn, have led to an increase in the number of criminal prosecutions of offenders as society displays its collective outrage. What has this trend meant for individual child victims?

Unfortunately, the clandestine nature of child sexual abuse and the general absence of physical signs or injury mean that the external corroboration of children's reports is rare (Sas, Cunningham, & Hurley, 1995). This lack of corroboration has had direct forensic implications. In most cases of child sexual abuse, conviction is only possible if a child can testify in court in front of the accused and in a manner that is not only credible but also leaves no room for doubt.

The phenomenon of secondary victimization of child witnesses by the criminal justice system has been well documented (Berliner & Barbieri, 1984; Runyan, Everson, Edelsohn, Hunter, & Coulter, 1988; Goodman et al., 1992; Sas, Wolfe, & Gowdey, 1996). As increasingly younger children are forced to relive their abusive experiences on the witness stand, we are forced to consider whether, in our endeavor to punish and deter child abusers, we are further victimizing children.

The year 1998 marks the 10-year anniversary of Bill C-15, legislation enacted by the Canadian Parliament in 1988 amending the Canadian *Criminal Code* (CCC) in respect of child sexual abuse prosecutions and modifying the Canada Evidence Act (1987) dealing with the reception of testimony by child witnesses. Many professionals working with child victims of sexual and physical abuse had great expectations of these reforms and a renewed hope for a criminal justice system that was long seen as potentially traumatic and generally insensitive to children.

This chapter reviews, with a critical "clinical" eye, some recent legal advances in the prosecution of child sexual abuse. The overall effectiveness of legal amendments to the CCC, designed to improve children's experiences in court, and the extent to which these changes are routinely implemented are discussed. A clinical case presentation, as well as recent research findings, are presented to illustrate some continuing difficulties.

HISTORICAL PERSPECTIVES
ON CHILD WITNESSES

Children Should Be Seen, But Not Heard

Until 1988, the laws of evidence contained in the Canada Evidence Act were premised largely on the notion that children were inherently unreliable and not credible as witnesses in a court of law. Two significant obstacles impeded the reception of their evidence: (a) the need for corroboration for unsworn testimony by children (under 14 years) and (b) the requirement that children under 14 years swear an oath before being permitted to give their testimony. No clear guidelines existed for courts on the nature of the questions that should be asked as part of an inquiry into the competency of the child to testify under oath. Therefore, judicial inquiries to determine whether children were of sufficient intelligence to understand the implications of swearing an oath varied in difficulty and content across jurisdictions. Many young children, in particular those 7 years and under, were often barred from testifying because they did not meet the "test" of the particular judge hearing their case in court. Even if children had previously given a coherent account of their abuse to a social worker, the police, and the prosecutor, their inability to satisfy the court of their understanding of the oath prevented them from being heard.

A further example of discriminatory practices against children's testimony was described by Bala (1993), who noted the courts' reluctance to hear the testimony of children and to convict in cases of child sexual abuse. In his review of case law in this area, Bala referred to the "duty" of judges to warn jurors about the "frailties of children and the dangers of convicting an adult on the word of a child" (*Regina v. Kendall,* 1962). The courts routinely advised jurors to be wary of children's accounts of abuse when the allegations were denied by the accused. As a result of this ruling, even when children were permitted to testify in court under oath, their testimony was viewed with great skepticism.

Legislative Reforms

Following extensive research on the incidence and prevalence of sexual offenses against children and on the response to the problem by mandated agencies, the Badgley Royal Commission on Sexual Offenses Against Children and Youth (1984) made more than 52 recommendations regarding the handling of child sexual abuse in Canada. Proposed reforms to the criminal justice system included revisions to the *Criminal Code* and the Canada Evidence Act (1987) so that children could speak more directly for themselves at legal proceedings.

Reception of Children's Evidence

In response to the Badgley Commission of 1984, two sets of amendments to the CCC and the Canada Evidence Act were approved by Parliament (Bill C-15 in 1988; Bill C-126 in 1993). These amendments made it possible for young children to testify in the absence of corroboration and for convictions to occur in cases that had unsworn testimony by children. More than any other reforms, these amendments opened the door to the testimony of younger children (Sas et al., 1996) and mirrored similar changes in other countries (Myers, 1996).

In 1993, another hindrance to the reception of children's testimony was addressed by Parliament. Legislation was enacted preventing the judiciary from warning jurors about the dangers of convicting solely on the evidence of a child under 14 years. With this reform, it was hoped that a gradual change in attitude on the part of the courts toward child witnesses would develop.

Modifications to Court Procedure

Another avenue for legislative reform has been to change how children's evidence is heard. In recognition of the potential negative impact on children of testifying in court, Bill C-15 contained several modifications to court process, codifying special procedural rules for the giving of testimony by child victims of sexual assault. For example, specific sections of Bill C-15 could allow a child witness to testify behind a screen in the courtroom or to testify by using a closed-circuit television link-up in another room outside the actual courtroom. This legislation to modify Canadian courtroom procedure is similar to legislation enacted in other countries such as the United States (Whitcomb, 1992), Australia (Cashmore, 1992), and England and Wales (Davies & Noon, 1991).

The use of these modifications, however, has depended on a complex interaction of system factors: (a) the geographic location of the courtroom (in many small communities, the courts do not have access to screens, and very few courtrooms have been retrofitted for the use of closed-circuit television equipment), (b) the skills of the prosecutor and the defense lawyer, (c) the availability of an expert witness to explain the phenomenon of child sexual abuse, and (d) the sensitivity of the judiciary to the special needs of the child witness.

A survey by Schmolka (1992) found that modifications to court procedures were being used very sparingly across Canada, with the screen employed more frequently than closed-circuit television. One obstacle has been that, to obtain a modification of court procedures, the prosecutor must make a successful application for the screen under Section 486 (2.1), CCC. In the absence of consent by the defense lawyer, an intricate "dance" occurs between two reluctant partners—the prosecutor and the defense lawyer. In some cases, expert testimony is offered to the court on the potential secondary trauma to the child of facing the accused and the negative impact on the child's testimony.

Defense arguments are presented to the judge regarding whether the standard of proof required to satisfy the court that a child cannot give a full and candid account of the sexual assault on the witness stand has been met. These arguments can range from the reasonable to the ridiculous.

The Supreme Court of Canada, in its ruling in *Regina v. Levogiannis* (1993), upheld the constitutionality of Section 486 for child victims, basing its decision on the premise set out in the legislation "to better get at the truth by young victims." The problem remains, however, that even though attention is given to the fact that children are particularly vulnerable to fears of the accused, the test in Section 486 is high and the court's concern is misplaced. It appears that only the quality of the product (the completeness of the testimony), and not the child's emotional well-being, remains the central concern.

Why is it that courts are only interested in hearing about the extent to which a child's fear will prevent her or him from giving a full and candid account and are not really concerned about the negative emotional impact on the child complainant in the court process? Perhaps the answer lies in the fact that the criminal justice system has historically been uncomfortable with children's disclosures of sexual abuse. Support for this hypothesis is evident in the court's continued reluctance to modify procedures to make it easier for children and in its hesitancy to accept expert testimony by social scientists on such topics as the phenomenon of delayed disclosure and the insidious nature of "grooming" and "accommodation" (Sas et al., 1995).

The Impact

The last 9 years have seen an influx of children testifying in courtrooms everywhere. As a result, the judiciary has been exposed to a clinical reality that has been known to health care professionals for years: There are a multitude of cases of child sexual abuse, and young children are often the most vulnerable victims of sexual predators.

The underlying motive for legislative changes in respect of child witnesses is based on the notion that allowing children into courtrooms to talk about their victimization experiences would result in more offenders being brought to justice, thereby promoting a general deterrent in society against child sexual abuse. In 1993, the Canadian Department of Justice prepared an evaluation of Bill C-15 to determine whether it was being successfully implemented. Indeed, the results suggested that more cases involving younger complainants (4 to 9 years) were being prosecuted and that more younger complainants were being allowed to testify (Beisenthal & Clements, 1992). Anecdotal reports by child victim advocates, however, suggest that many children are experiencing harsh cross-examinations by defense lawyers and that the cases often result in acquittals.

Our own observations over the last decade of children in the witness stand indicate that many children do find themselves under attack, their credibility challenged, and their emotions manipulated. Figure 11.1, taken from a 3-year follow-up study on child witnesses referred for court preparation (Sas, Hurley, Hatch, Malla, & Dick, 1993), contains revealing quotes by a sample of child witnesses of their memories of testifying. One child described it as the hardest thing she had ever done in her life.

Despite legislative amendments, attitudes toward the veracity of children's accounts of sexual abuse have not changed much, and media coverage of child sexual abuse prosecutions often overdramatize such issues as children's suggestibility, children's memory, and most important, children's credibility. What are our expectations of child witnesses?

Current Expectations of Child Witnesses in Court

In general, the court's expectation of children who testify as complainants is often based on unrealistic assumptions about their understanding of the adversarial system. It does not take into account children's level of social comprehension, cognitive abilities, or emotional immaturity. As well, despite the best intentions of the prosecutors, few cases are expedited. Cases can be adjourned for months. Sometimes they drag on for years before there is any resolution; such delays force children onto an emotional roller-coaster ride.

The Surroundings

Being a child witness requires great fortitude. Children are expected to walk into a large formal courtroom filled with strangers, some of whom are even robed for the solemn occasion. Usually, children are not accompanied by their parents because the parents have been subpoenaed as well, and there is almost always a court order excluding witnesses.

Child witnesses must walk past the accused on their way up to the witness stand (several feet away), where they must testify in full view of everyone in attendance in the courtroom.

What Do You Remember About Testifying?

"Misleading questions and trickery."

"Sometimes I went blank but most of the time I was scared seeing my father. I was scared he might do something because he made me promise not to tell."

"I told the story. I wasn't thinking about what I was saying. I wanted to do a good job."

"All I remember is that it had to be the hardest thing in my life to do."

"The only thing I remember was the defense lawyer—he grilled me, twisted everything I said, made me feel like a criminal and as if [my stepfather] was the victim."

"I remember everything. I was horrified, scared. I kept looking down at him [the defendant]. The Crown attorney kept giving me signs to look up at him."

"I got really scared because he [the defendant] was so close and I had to look at him and he gave me a very threatening look."

"I remember crying a lot."

Figure 11.1. Child Witnesses' Recollections of Testifying

The Test

If under age 14, child witnesses must demonstrate testimonial competency. Their testimony must be preceded by an inquiry, during which the court determines whether they can give sworn testimony (an oath) or promise to tell the truth and whether they have the necessary skills to communicate the evidence.

The Burning Question

Child witnesses are expected to respond to two rounds of questions in a controlled and articulate manner. Although the examination-in-chief conducted by the prosecutor may be fairly straightforward, the defense cross-examination can be extremely challenging and hurtful: Why didn't you tell someone? Why did you go back to his classroom? Why didn't you scream?

Unrealistic demands are often placed on child witnesses to explain on the witness stand why they delayed telling or why they went back to an abuser's home after being assaulted. These challenges occur despite our current knowledge of the power balance that exists between an adult abuser and a child victim (Sauzier, 1989; Sorenson & Snow, 1991), the level of fear and intimidation that can be used to secure compliance and secrecy (Haugaard & Reppucci, 1988; Sgroi, 1982), and the nature of psychological entrapment (Summit, 1983).

Understanding the Terminology

The language and terminology employed in court can be highly technical and, therefore, hard for children to understand (Flin, Stevenson, & Davies, 1989; Melton et al., 1992). Children can become easily confused by misleading or difficult questions. Brennan and Brennan (1988), Cashmore (1991), and Saywitz (1989) have all drawn attention to the frequent use of age-inappropriate questions and the resulting misinterpretations by children of questions put to them.

Recently, in response to the observed need to prepare children better for cross-examination, Saywitz, Nathanson, Snyder, and Lamphear (1993) developed a training technique in which children are trained to identify misleading questions and to resist suggestion. Overall, the experimental program is designed to improve children's communication, memory, and emotional resiliency. If these techniques are used in clinical settings, will they assist child witnesses in real-life cases?

Remembering the Abuse Details

One of the most demanding expectations of children by the court is that they must remember every detail of their victimization, even if months or years pass before they testify. Many children experience intrusive thoughts and flashbacks of the abuse because of post-traumatic stress (Mcleer, Deblinger, Atkins, Foa, & Ralphe, 1988). The requirement that they intentionally keep these memories alive for court involves a punishing paradigm of preparation. Not many children can tolerate reviewing their statements over and over again and talking about the circumstances of their abuse to a prosecutor, only to find out on the morning of court that the matter has been adjourned and that they must wait until another day to relive their abuse on the witness stand.

Facing the Accused

Last, and probably most important, is the fear of testifying in front of the accused (Goodman et al., 1992). Facing the accused has been described by the majority of child witnesses in our research sample to be their most salient fear (Sas et al., 1993). In fact, 95% of child witnesses reported, on the evening prior to the hearing, that they were afraid to testify. This was found to be particularly true when the sexual abuse had been intrusive or violent, of long duration, or within the context of a highly manipulative emotional relationship with someone who was close to the child. The inherent power imbalance that naturally exists between children and adults can undermine the children's confidence in court. Stares and frowns, or just the presence of the accused in the courtroom, can inhibit a child victim's ability to testify. This is particularly true in intrafamilial cases, in which confused feelings of fear and loyalty for an abusive parent can exist, making full and candid accounts by children difficult to obtain.

CAN PREPARATION REDUCE CHILDREN'S FEARS SO THAT THEY CAN TESTIFY?

Court Preparation

As previously mentioned, secondary victimization arising out of court involvement has been documented in early studies on child witnesses (Berliner & Barbieri, 1984; Bulkley, 1982; Jaffe, Wilson, & Sas, 1987; Runyan et al., 1988; Weiss & Berg, 1982; Wolfe, Sas, & Wilson, 1987). As well, the need for court preparation for child witnesses is well supported in the literature (Goodman et al., 1992; Sas, Austin, Wolfe, & Hurley, 1991; Sas et al., 1996; Whitcomb et al., 1991). In response to this concern, innovative child witness and victim witness programs in many communities now assist children and their families who become entangled in the court process as complainants. One such program is the Child Witness Project (CWP) at the London (Ontario) Family Court Clinic.

The Child Witness Project (CWP)

The preparation protocol for the CWP was developed in 1987 as part of a demonstration grant by Health and Welfare Canada (see Sas et al., 1991, for a full description). The CWP includes an educational component designed to teach children about court procedures, court etiquette, and legal terminology (see Figure 11.2), and a stress reduction component (see Figure 11.3), which can include deep muscle relaxation exercises, development of a fear

Objective	Medium
Teach Child Courtroom Procedures and Roles of Key Persons	Court Tour
	Courtroom Model
	Booklets
	Review Checklist Terms
	Roleplay Scenes (Judge's Gown)
Familiarize Child With Legal Terms and Concepts	Repetition & Review
	Homework Assignments
	Activity Book
	Court Tour
Teach Child Meaning of Oath Taking	Review Terms
	Generate Vignettes
	Provide Real Life Examples
	Homework Assignments
Develop in Child Good Techniques of Testifying	Roleplay Practices:
	– speaking loudly
	– answering yes or no
	– speaking slowly
	– clear articulation
Help Child Understand Adversarial Nature of Criminal Justice System	Provide Explanation of System
Explain Court Outcomes to Child	Review "Reasonable Doubt" and Range of Dispositions
Make Child Comfortable With Physical Layout of Courtroom	Court Tours

Figure 11.2. Summary of Educational Components

hierarchy related to testifying in court, a systematic desensitization component, and a cognitive restructuring approach.

The overall goal of the court preparation protocol is to (a) demystify the courtroom experience through education, (b) reduce the fear and anxiety related to testifying, and (c) empower children through emotional support and system advocacy. Prior to court preparation, children's knowledge of the court process, feelings about the sexual abuse, concerns about having to testify, and presence of postabuse sequelae are assessed. More than 700 child witnesses have received preparation services to date.

In 1991, the efficacy of the preparation protocol was evaluated in a study funded by Health and Welfare Canada (Sas et al., 1991). The results were very promising. Children's psychological adjustment postabuse and court involvement was assessed, and a regression analysis was conducted of their

Audience	Objective	Medium
All Child Witnesses	Breathing Relaxation Exercises	Instruction: Script of technique—to be used in court while on the stand
All Children Who Present With Significant Fears	Deep Muscle Relaxation Training	Imagery based relaxation script (ages 5-10) Regular deep muscle relaxation script (ages 11-17)
All Child Witnesses	Development of Fear Hierarchy	Five most salient fears—least to most anxiety-provoking generated by child
All Child Witnesses	Cognitive Restructuring and Empowerment	Positive reasons for attending court List of strengths Concept of a team going to court
Child Witnesses With Extreme Fears Who are Able to Use Imagination	Systematic Desensitization	Pairing of fears with deep muscle relaxation exercises
All Child Witnesses	Therapeutic Support	Words of encouragement Advocacy

Figure 11.3. Stress Reduction Components

postcourt adjustment scores on their precourt psychological adjustment. Results indicated that their sexual abuse fears and their total fears postcourt were mediated significantly by two aspects of their court experience: (a) the number of days they were involved in the criminal justice system and (b) their participation in the CWP court preparation program. Preparation reduced their fears. Furthermore, prosecutor ratings of child witnesses' performances on the witness stand were significantly higher for prepared versus nonprepared children. Parent and child feedback on the court preparation was also very positive. As shown in Table 11.1, over 90% of parents who responded found the preparation helpful for their children, and all the parents believed that their children's fears were reduced. Children who received preparation reported feeling understood and supported by project staff (see Table 11.2). For example, 82% of child witnesses reported that the preparation helped them understand what happens in court.

TABLE 11.1. Parent Feedback Questionnaire Responses
% Responding in Affirmative

Questions	Prelim.	Trial
Preparation was very helpful for your child	98	92
The project was very supportive of your child	98	94
The project was very supportive of the parent	76	86
Child received a lot of individual attention	93	90
The project served to reduce your child's fears	100	91
The project affected the disposition	N/A	73

TABLE 11.2. Child Feedback Questionnaire Responses
% Responding in Affirmative

Questions	Prelim.	Trial
The project was very helpful	78	90
The person you talked to understood your feelings a lot	76	86
The project helped you understand what happens in a courtroom	76	82
Will you be a good witness?	76	86

Overall, the CWP was found to assist child witnesses in four distinct ways: (a) educating them about the court process, (b) dealing with their stress and fears, (c) helping them be good witnesses, and (d) advocating for them and their families within the criminal justice system.

MELINDA: A CASE EXAMPLE OF
SECONDARY TRAUMATIZATION

Melinda, age 7, was referred to the CWP by the police for court preparation in anticipation of her role as a complainant in the prosecution of her paternal uncle for sexual assault. Following assessment, she attended five sessions of individual court preparation over a period of 6 weeks prior to the preliminary hearing. In addition, she met with her prosecutor on two occasions and had a court tour. These meetings with the prosecutor were facilitated by a procedure known as "red flagging," in which child sexual abuse cases are flagged for special attention by the prosecutors in our jurisdiction.

Melinda's Clinical Sequelae Related
to Her History of Sexual Abuse

Assessment results indicated that Melinda was experiencing behavioral and emotional sequelae related to the sexual abuse. Her symptomatology included feelings of depression and guilt, nightmares, intrusive thoughts of the sexual abuse, fear, and general anxiety. In particular, Melinda was very fearful of the accused and, as time wore on, dreaded facing him in court. Being only 7 years old, she knew very little about the criminal justice system or her expected role as a witness. Pressure from her extended family to withdraw the complaint was obvious, and her parents, though supportive, were clearly upset by her disclosure. Her extended family members were angry over her disclosure, and her paternal grandparents supported her uncle in his denial.

Court preparation for Melinda included several strategies. One goal of the preparation was to familiarize her with the legal terms and court procedures that she needed to know. Two videos showing the role of child witnesses were shown to Melinda: *Kids in Court* (Victims Assistance Committee, 1992) and *Taking the Stand* (Victim Witness Assistance Program, 1989). One session was devoted to role playing with puppets and a miniature courtroom. She reviewed the manual *What's My Job in Court?* (Ontario Ministry of the Attorney General, 1989), and she was given homework assignments from the booklet. In the last session, she was allowed to wear a judge's gown to desensitize her to the formal robes worn by the judge and the lawyers.

Stress reduction was employed to help her cope with her fears of her uncle. Melinda was taught to control her symptoms of stress by using imagery-based relaxation therapy (Koeppen, 1974). In her fear hierarchy, Melinda's most salient fear was seeing her uncle in court. Her second fear was that he would hurt her after court. Her third fear was that no one would believe her. During the five sessions, the therapist was successful in teaching her about the court process but made little headway in reducing her level of fear related to the accused.

Melinda was a highly anxious and frightened child who was displaying a range of symptomatology consistent with post-traumatic stress subsequent to sexual abuse (Wolfe, Sas, & Wekerle, 1994). She was afraid of the accused and clearly stated that she could not talk about the sexual abuse with him present in the courtroom. Her parents described night terrors, crying jags, and clingy behavior on the part of their daughter, which worsened as she approached the day she had to testify about the sexual abuse. As a result, it was recommended to the prosecutor that he consider an application under Section 486 (2.1) of the CCC, to have Melinda testify from behind a screen.

Melinda's Day in Court

In Melinda's case, because of her young age and the fact that no one had witnessed her sexual abuse at the hands of her uncle, she clearly benefited from the changes to the Canada Evidence Act. She was able to respond adequately to questions during the voir dire about truth and lies but was unable to satisfactorily define the meaning of an oath to the court. There were no witnesses to her abuse, and therefore no corroboration. In the past, prior to 1988, she would not have been able to testify, but because of the amendments, she was permitted to testify on a promise to tell the truth.

The defense lawyer did not consent to the use of the screen or the closed-circuit television provision; therefore, prior to the preliminary hearing, a voir dire was held to consider the Crown's application. Expert testimony was called by both the Crown and the defense, with arguments centering around one issue: Was Melinda's emotional trauma sufficiently severe to prevent her from talking openly in court in front of her uncle? The voir dire continued for 1½ days, and the court decision was that Melinda should attempt to testify without the benefit of the screen, but failing to do so, consideration would be given to offering her the screen later.

The next day, Melinda was escorted (*dragged* would be a better term) into the courtroom, past her uncle, and was placed in the witness stand. Although every attempt was made to encourage her to look at her support person, the defense lawyer often positioned himself directly in front of her uncle during the cross-examination. Her eyes were drawn to him. Melinda was very frightened, especially after having to identify her uncle by looking directly at him and pointing him out. Melinda gave few details about the sexual abuse and cried pitifully the entire time on the stand. During the cross-examination, the defense lawyer suggested to her that she had made up the allegations because her uncle had not taken her to the movies with her other cousins. Melinda reacted very strongly to this line of questioning and had to be removed from the courtroom twice. At the end of a long day, Melinda was taken home by her parents, a little heap of sobs and tears. Three weeks of nightmares, bed-wetting, and crying followed her day in court. The matter was committed to trial, but at what cost? For Melinda, retraumatization by the court system was an ugly reality.

Child Characteristics
>   CDI level of depression at time of referral
>   Feelings of personal vulnerability at referral
>   Feelings of empowerment at referral
>   Age of the child
>   Sex of the child
>   History of family violence
>   History of sexual victimization
>   Length of time to follow-up

Abuse Characteristics
>   Duration
>   Relationship of child to abuser
>   Coercion used
>   Intrusiveness

Moderator Variables
>   Maternal reaction to the disclosure
>   Maternal action following disclosure
>   Court preparation

Criminal Justice System Characteristics—Court Outcome
>   Testifying
>   Time in the system

Figure 11.4. Theoretical Model for Predictors of Child Psychological and Social Adjustment at Follow-Up.

IS THERE A LONG-TERM NEGATIVE IMPACT OF TESTIFYING?

On the basis of our theoretical model (outlined in Figure 11.4), our research team attempted to predict positive adjustment in child witnesses referred to the CWP.

Our 3-year follow-up study on the long-term emotional and social adjustment of child witnesses who testified in court (Sas et al., 1993) used a therapist rating of global adjustment as the criterion and chose the best predictors from each set of (a) child victim and abuse characteristics, (b) reactions to disclosure, and (c) criminal justice system variables (length of time in the system, testifying, court outcome). A stepwise multiple regression analysis was carried out by using the following five variables: (a) the child's initial level of depression at referral, (b) any history of family violence, (c) the relationship between the abuser and the victim, (d) the level of mother's

TABLE 11.3. Regression of Case Characteristics on Therapists' Global
Clinical Ratings

	Mult R	R^2	*Adj R^2*	*F*	*p*
Block 1 Mother Support	.602	.362	.350	30.05	p<.0001
Block 2 Depression	.690	.477	.456	23.71	p<.0001
Block 3 Violent History	.722	.521	.493	18.55	p<.0001

support following disclosure, and (e) the court outcome. The results are
presented in Table 11.3.

A regression analysis indicated that mother's support was the most significant factor relating to positive adjustment in child witnesses at follow-up
($N = 61$, $R = .60$, $F = 30.05$, $p < .0001$). Notably, outcome in court, though
previously found to be correlated with adjustment, did not enter into the
regression equation. Neither did relationship of abuser to victim, which
previously was found to be related to adjustment. These results suggest that
although court outcome and identity of the abuser are important factors in
whether or not children are well adjusted after their abusive experiences and
subsequent court involvement, having mother support moderates the negative impact. Even in the worst scenarios, in which the abuser is a significant
person in the life of the child (e.g., a father figure) and the outcome in court
is an acquittal, unfailing mother's support and protective action enables
children to rise above their experiences.

Two other child/family characteristics added significantly to the prediction model in Blocks 2 and 3, respectively: level of depression at time of
referral, and history of violence in the family. It is noteworthy that these three
variables were all correlated with each other. Mother's ability to be supportive was related to history of family violence in the home, suggesting that
the mother's own history of protecting herself and her feelings of empowerment affected her ability to provide support for her child. As well, children
who were seriously depressed at the time of referral were more likely not to
have received mother's support. Although court process variables such as
outcome were important factors influencing the adjustment of the children
at follow-up, their effect was not as powerful as the support and behavior of

TABLE 11.4. Children's Recollection of Most Helpful Measure Undertaken
by a Parent Before Court

	Number	*Percent*
Emotional Support/Listening	31	57.4
Protective Measure (locks)	1	1.9
Gave Space/Did Not Pry	4	7.4
Forced Child to Testify	1	1.9
Nothing Helpful Done	10	18.5
No Recollection	7	13.0
TOTALS	54	100.0

the children's mothers who, by their actions, were able to "soften to blow"
and strengthen their children's resolve.

Despite these encouraging findings in the follow-up interviews, many
children had a bleak impression of their family as a support network during
the wait for court. Only 29% indicated that a parent was their greatest source
of support, and as mentioned earlier, the mother provided this support in the
majority of these cases. Emotional support and listening were rated most
often as a helpful measure (see Table 11.4). These results suggest that
mobilizing family support for child witnesses is crucial to their recovery.

My colleagues and I were not able to isolate any effect of testifying on
overall long-term adjustment even though some children recounted bitter
memories of testifying. It appears that testifying had its most negative effect
on the short-term emotional state of the children but that this effect either
dissipated over time or was mediated by other factors.

As part of the 3-year follow-up, children were asked about their experiences in court from their arrival at the courthouse to hearing the verdict. They
recalled a great deal of anticipatory anxiety in the days before scheduled
court dates, and parents reported that this anxiety was manifested in behavioral and mood changes. Those children who had testified described the
experience in largely negative terms. The passage of several years had not
diminished in their minds the memory of feeling scared and vulnerable. Most
saw the experience as difficult and often frightening, with few immediate
benefits.

- Not having to see the defendant
- Receiving preparation before the court
- Closing the courtroom to the public
- Having support people in the courtroom
- Having judges and lawyers use easier language

Figure 11.5. Child Witnesses' Suggestions to Make Testifying Easier for Children

Testifying remains traumatic for most children. With our present under-standing of the impact of child sexual abuse and recent research on the vulnerabilities of child witnesses, many suggestions can be offered on how to improve children's experiences in court so that they can speak about their victimization without being further traumatized. In our study, child witnesses identified five ways to make it easier for children who have to testify (see Figure 11.5).

As Myers (1996) clearly pointed out in his review of a decade of interna-tional reforms in respect of child witnesses, "Reforming the legal system is no mean feat. Many judges and lawyers are reluctant to tinker with traditional courtroom practices" (p. 419). It is time that we move on. We must change our attitudes toward child witnesses and the handling of these cases by the criminal justice system. Perhaps we need to listen more carefully to the child witnesses themselves.

REFERENCES

Badgley Royal Commission on Sexual Offenses Against Children and Youth. (1984). *Report of the Committee on Sexual Offenses Against Children and Youth* (Vols. 1 & 2). Ottawa: Ministry of Supply and Services Canada.

Bala, N. (1993). *Child sexual abuse prosecutions: Children in the courts.* Paper presented at the Canadian Judicial Council Seminar, Aylmer, Quebec.

Beisenthal, L., & Clements, J. (1992). *Canadian statistics on child sexual abuse* (Technical report). Ottawa: Department of Justice.

Berliner, L., & Barbieri, M. K. (1984). The testimony of the child victim of sexual assault. *Journal of Social Issues, 40,* 125-137.

Brennan, M., & Brennan, R. (1988). *Strange language: Child victims under cross-examina-tion.* Wagga Wagga, NSW: Riverina-Murray Institute of Higher Learning.

Bulkley, J. (1982). *Recommendations for improving legal intervention in intrafamilial child sexual abuse cases.* Washington, DC: American Bar Association.

Canada Evidence Act. R.S.C. (1987). c. 24, s.16(1).

Cashmore, J. (1991). Problems and solutions in lawyer-child communication. *Criminal Law Journal, 15,* 193-202.

Cashmore, J. (1992). *The use of closed-circuit TV for child witnesses in the court.* Sydney: Australia Law Reform Commission.

Davies, G., & Noon, E. (1991). *An evaluation of the live link for child witnesses* (Report to the Home Office). London: Home Office.

Flin, R. H., Stevenson, Y., & Davies, G. M. (1989). Children's knowledge of court proceedings. *British Journal of Psychology, 80,* 285-297.

Goodman, G. S., Pyle-Taub, E., Jones, D. P. H., England, P., Port, L. K., Rudy, L., & Prado, L. (1992). Testifying in criminal court: The effects on child sexual assault victims. *Monographs of the Society for Research in Child Development, 57*(5), Serial No. 229).

Haugaard, J. J., & Reppucci, N. D. 1988). *The sexual abuse of children.* San Francisco: Jossey-Bass.

Jaffe, P., Wilson, S. K., & Sas, L. (1987). Court testimony of child sexual abuse victims: Emerging issues in clinical assessments. *Canadian Psychology, 28,* 291-295.

Koeppen, A. J. (1974). Relaxation training for children. *Elementary School Guidance and Counseling,* pp. 14-21.

Mcleer, S. V., Deblinger, E., Atkins, M. S., Foa, E. B., & Ralphe, D. L. (1988). Post-traumatic stress disorder in sexually abused children. *Journal of the American Academy of Child and Adolescent Psychiatry, 27,* 650-654.

Melton, G. B., Limber, S. P., Jacobs, J. E., Oberlander, L. B., Berliner, L., & Mamamoto, M. (1992). *Preparing sexually abused children for testimony: Children's perceptions of the legal process.* Final report to the National Center on Child Abuse and Neglect. Lincoln, NE: Center for Children and Families and the Law.

Myers, J. (1996). A decade of international reform to accommodate child witnesses. *Criminal Justice and Behavior, 23,* 402-422.

Ontario Ministry of the Attorney General. (1989). *What's my job in court?* [Activity book]. Toronto: Author.

Regina v. Kendall (1962). 132 C.C.C. 216, at 220 (S.C.C.).

Regina v. Levogiannis (1993), 25 C.R. (4th) 325, 85 C.C.C. (3d) 327 (S.C.C.), affirming (1990), 2 C.R.(4th), 355, 62 C.C.C. (3d) 59 (Ont. C.A.).

Runyan, D. K., Everson, M. D., Edelsohn, G. A., Hunter, W. M., & Coulter, M. L. (1988). Impact of legal intervention on sexually abused children. *Journal of Pediatrics, 118,* 647-653.

Sas, L., Austin, G., Wolfe, D., & Hurley, P. (1991). *Reducing the system-induced trauma for child sexual abuse victims through court preparation, assessment, and follow-up* (Project No. 4555-1-125). Ottawa: National Welfare Grants Division, Health and Welfare Canada. (Available from the author at the London Family Court Clinic, 254 Pall Mall St., Suite 200, London N6A 5P6 Canada)

Sas, L., Cunningham, A., & Hurley, P. (1995). *Tipping the balance to tell the secret: The public discovery of child sexual abuse* (FVDS No. 4887-05-92-017). Final report prepared for the Family Violence Prevention Division, Health and Welfare Canada.

Sas, L., Hurley, P., Hatch, A., Malla, S., & Dick, T. (1993). *Three years after the verdict: A longitudinal study of the social and psychological adjustment of child witnesses referred to the Child Witness Project* (FVDS No. 4887-06-91-026). Final report prepared for the Family Violence Prevention Division, Health and Welfare Canada.

Sas, L., Wolfe, D. A., & Gowdey, K. (1996). Children and the courts in Canada. *Criminal Justice and Behavior: An International Journal, 23,* 338-357.

Sauzier, M. (1989). Disclosures of child sexual abuse: For better or for worse. *Psychiatric Clinics of North America, 12,* 455-469.

Saywitz, K. (1989). Children's conceptions of the legal system: "Court is a place to play basketball." In S. Ceci, M. Toglia, & D. Ross (Eds.), *Perspectives on children's testimony* (pp. 13-157). New York: Springer-Verlag.

Saywitz, K., Nathanson, R., Snyder, L., & Lamphear, V. (1993). *Preparing children for the investigative and judicial process: Improving communication, memory, and emotional resiliency* (Grant No. 90CA1179). Washington, DC: National Center on Child Abuse and Neglect.

Schmolka, V. (1992). *Is Bill C-15 working? An overview of the research on the effects of the 1988 child sexual abuse amendments*. Ottawa: Supplies and Services Canada.

Sgroi, S. M. (Ed.). (1982). *Handbook of clinical intervention in child sexual abuse*. Lexington, MA: Lexington.

Sorenson, T., & Snow, B. (1991). How children tell: The process of disclosure in child sexual abuse. *Child Welfare, 70,* 3-15.

Summit, R. C. (1983). The child sexual abuse accommodation syndrome. *Child Abuse & Neglect, 7,* 177-193.

Victims Assistance Committee. (1992). *Kids in court* [Videotape]. Yellowknife, NWT: Department of Justice, Government of Northwest Territories.

Victim Witness Assistance Program. (1989). *Taking the stand* [Videotape]. Greenville, SC: 13th Judicial Circuit, Solicitor's Office.

Weiss, E. H., & Berg, R. F. (1982). Child victims of sexual assault: Impact of court procedures. *Journal of the American Academy of Child Psychiatry, 21,* 513-518.

Whitcomb, D., Runyan, D. K., Devos, E., Hunter, W. M., Cross, T. P., Everson, M. D., & Peeler N. A. (1991). *Child victim as witness research and development program.* (Final report, Grant No. 87-MC-CX0026). Washington, DC: U.S. Department of Justice.

Whitcomb, D. K. (1992). *When the victim is a child* (2nd ed.). Washington, DC: U.S. Department of Justice, National Institute of Justice, Office of Justice Programs.

Wolfe, D. A., Sas, L., & Wekerle, C. (1994). Factors associated with the development of post-traumatic stress disorder among child victims of sexual abuse. *Child Abuse & Neglect, 18,* 37-50.

Wolfe, V. V., Sas, L., & Wilson, S. K. (1987). Some issues in preparing sexually abused children for courtroom testimony. *Behavior Therapist, 10,* 107-113.

Index

About the Editors

David A. Wolfe, Ph.D., FAClinP, is Professor of Psychology and Psychiatry at the University of Western Ontario in London, Canada, and a founding member of the Centre for Research on Violence Against Women and Children in London. His interests in empowering youth as a means to prevent personal violence derive from 20 years of research on child abuse and neglect and his view that these phenomena are preventable. His numerous articles and books on the broad topics of child abuse and domestic violence include *Children of Battered Women* (with P. Jaffe and S. Wilson, 1990); *Working Together to End Domestic Violence* (with N. Lemon, P. Jaffe, & J. Sandler, 1996), and *Alternatives to Violence: Empowering Youth to Develop Healthy Relationships* (with C. Wekerle & K. Scott, 1997).

Robert J. McMahon, Ph.D., is Professor and Director of the Child Clinical Psychology Program in the Department of Psychology at the University of Washington, Seattle. His primary research and clinical interests concern the assessment, treatment, and prevention of conduct disorders in children. He is a principal investigator on the Fast Track Project, a large, multisite, collaborative study on the prevention of serious conduct problems in school-age children. His primary responsibilities on that project concern the development and implementation of the family-based intervention components. He is also a principal investigator on the Early Parenting Project, a longitudinal study examining the development of children of adolescent mothers from infancy into elementary school. He is the author (with R. Forehand) of *Helping the Noncompliant Child: A Clinician's*

Guide to Parent Training and of a number of scientific articles, chapters, and reviews. He has also coedited (with R. Peters and others) several volumes emanating from the Banff International Conferences on Behavioural Science.

Ray DeV. Peters, Ph.D., is Professor of Psychology at Queen's University in Kingston, Ontario, Canada, and is Research Director of the Better Beginnings, Better Futures Project, a large, multisite, longitudinal study in Ontario on the prevention of mental health problems in young children from birth to 7 years of age. He was a Visiting Scientist with the Oregon Social Learning Center in 1979-1980 and with the Mental Health Division of the World Health Organization in Geneva, Switzerland, in 1986-1987. His primary research interests are in the areas of children's mental health and developmental psychology. Since 1982, he has served on the Executive Committee of the Banff International Conference on Behavioural Science.

About the Contributors

Sandra T. Azar, Ph.D., is Associate Professor at the Frances L. Hiatt School of Psychology at Clark University in Worcester, Massachusetts. She has published numerous papers and chapters dealing with theory, research on treatment and assessment work with abusive families, and legal issues. She is conducting a NIMH-funded research study testing the validity of a cognitive model of the etiology of child abuse.

Lucy Berliner, MSW, is Clinical Associate Professor at the University of Washington School of Social Work and Director of Research for the Harborview Center for Sexual Assault and Traumatic Stress. She is Associate Editor for the *Journal of Interpersonal Violence* and *Child Maltreatment* and serves on the Editorial Board for *Child Abuse & Neglect* and *Sexual Abuse: A Journal of Research and Treatment.* She has published the results of a randomized clinical trial of treatments for sexually abused children and a review of the treatment outcome literature for sexually abused children. Research interests include aspects of clinical and social interventions with victims and offenders.

John Briere, Ph.D., is Associate Professor in the Departments of Psychiatry and Psychology at the University of Southern California School of Medicine, and a clinical psychologist at the Department of Emergency Psychiatric Services of LAC-USC Medical Center. He is on the editorial boards of several journals, is a member of the Board of Directors of the International Society for Traumatic Stress Studies (ISTSS), and is on the Advisory Board of the American Professional Society on the Abuse of

Children (APSAC). The author of numerous research papers, chapters, and books in the areas of child abuse, psychological trauma, and interpersonal violence, his books include *Therapy for Adults Molested as Children: Beyond Survival; Child Abuse Trauma: Theory and Treatment of the Lasting Effects;* and *Psychological Assessment of Adult Posttraumatic States.* He is also coeditor of *APSAC Handbook on Child Maltreatment* and author of two standardized psychological tests: the Trauma Symptom Inventory (TSI) and the Trauma Symptom Checklist for Children (TSCC). He provides consultation on clinical and forensic issues to various groups and agencies and is a frequent workshop presenter.

Edward A. Connors, Ph.D., is a psychologist registered in the Provinces of Ontario, Manitoba, and Saskatchewan, Canada. Of Mohawk ancestry and a band member of Kahnawake First Nation, he has worked with First Nations committees across Canada during the past 10 years in both urban and rural centers. His work during the past 12 years includes positions as Clinical Director for an infant mental health center in the city of Regina and Director for the Sacred Circle, a suicide prevention program developed to serve First Nations communities in Northwestern Ontario. Currently, he is Vice President of the Canadian Association of Suicide Prevention. His practice incorporates traditional knowledge about healing, along with his training as a psychologist. He directs Onkwatenro'shon:'a Health Planners, which is a health consulting firm for First Nations communities. He has published book chapters in the areas of suicide, family therapy, and healing in First Nations.

E. Mark Cummings, Ph.D., is Professor of Psychology at the University of Notre Dame, Notre Dame, Indiana. He is the author of numerous research papers and chapters on family emotional functioning and children's adjustment and is the coauthor or coeditor of several books, including *Children and Marital Conflict: The Impact of Family Dispute and Resolution; Attachment in the Preschool Years: Theory, Research, and Intervention;* and *Altruism and Aggression: Biological and Social Origins.* In addition, he is an Editor with *Child Development* and is on the editorial boards of *Developmental Psychology* and *Journal of Emotional Abuse.*

Cynthia Dopke, M.A., is a doctoral candidate in Clinical Psychology at Northern Illinois University, DeKalb. She is working on an intervention program for high-risk mothers, which is supported by a grant from the Illinois Department of Children and Family Services. The coauthor of several book chapters in the areas of child abuse and human sexuality, her research interests include the relationship among child physical abuse, social information processing, and stress.

William Friedrich is Professor and Consultant in the Department of Psychology and Psychiatry at the Mayo Clinic and Mayo Medical School, Rochester, Minnesota. His interests in sexually abused boys derive from 22 years of research and clinical practice in child abuse and neglect. He has written numerous articles and books, including *Psychotherapy With Sexually Abused Children and Their Families* (1990).

Carolyn Grasley, M.A., is a doctoral candidate in Clinical Psychology at the University of Western Ontario, London. She has a special interest in the long-term repercussions of child sexual abuse for the development of adult intimate relationships.

Peter Jaffe, Ph.D., C.Psych., is Director of the London Family Court Clinic in London, Ontario, Canada, and a member of the Clinical Adjunct Faculty for the Department of Psychology and Department of Psychiatry at the University of Western Ontario. His clinical work and research concern children and adolescents involved with police or the courts, either as delinquents or as victims of family violence or custody disputes.

Andrea MacEachran, B.A., is the coauthor of a chapter on child abuse and neglect in *Assessment of Childhood Disorders* (1997). She is currently a research assistant for a study on depression.

Joel S. Milner, Ph.D., is Professor of Psychology, Distinguished Research Professor, and Director of the Family Violence and Sexual Assault Research Program at Northern Illinois University, DeKalb. He has received funding for family violence and sexual assault research from federal agencies such as the National Institute of Mental Health, the National Center on Child Abuse and Neglect, and the Department of Defense. The author or coauthor of more than 130 book chapters and articles, most in the area of family violence, his current research interests include the description and prediction of intrafamilial child sexual abuse and the testing of a social information processing model of child physical abuse.

Maurice L. B. Oates, Jr., M.A., is a psychologist who has created innovative native programs in British Columbia that have spread widely. Of mixed native/Scottish background and a member of the Eagle Clan of the Nisgha village of Kincolith, his background includes some 15 years involved in the legal system (Probation Officer, Parole Agent, Auxiliary RCMP) and another 17 years working as a psychologist with aboriginal peoples both on and off reserves. His other interests include the environment, backpacking, and the study of plants and their uses.

David Olds, Ph.D., is Professor of Pediatrics, Psychiatry, and Preventive Medicine at the University of Colorado Health Sciences Center, Denver, where he directs the Prevention Research Center for Family and Child Health. He has devoted his career to investigating methods of preventing health and developmental problems in children and parents from low-income families. He has conducted a series of randomized clinical trials that examined the effects of prenatal and postpartum nurse home visitation on the outcomes of pregnancy, infant caregiving, and maternal life-course development and determined the impact of those services on government spending. His numerous awards include the Charles A. Dana Award for Pioneering Achievements in Health, the Lela Rowland Prevention Award from the National Mental Health Association, and a Research Scientist Award from the National Institute of Mental Health. His publications have appeared in numerous journals, including *Pediatrics, Journal of Community Psychology, Medical Care,* and the *American Journal of Public Health.*

Anna-Lee Pittman, MLIS, is Project Manager for the Youth Relationships Project and coauthor of a chapter in *Handbook on Research and Treatment in Child Abuse and Neglect* (1997).

Deborah Reitzel-Jaffe, Ph.D., has published several journal articles and chapters on the topic of woman abuse and teen violence and has worked as a youth counselor and facilitator of groups for youth that address violence in relationships.

Louise Sas, Ph.D., is a clinical child psychologist and Director of the Child Witness Project at the London Family Court Clinic in London, Ontario, Canada. She is also Adjunct Clinical Professor at the University of Western Ontario in London, Ontario. The author of research papers, journal articles, and chapters in the areas of child sexual abuse, legislation pertaining to child witnesses, and the impact of criminal justice system involvement in the lives of young victims, her most recent publication is a coauthored article entitled "Children and the Courts in Canada," which appeared in *Criminal Justice & Behavior.*

Marlies Sudermann, Ph.D, C.Psych., is a clinical psychologist, researcher, and Director of Violence Prevention Services at the London Family Court Clinic in London, Ontario, Canada. In addition, she serves as Adjunct Clinical Professor with the University of Western Ontario, Department of Psychology. She has published numerous scholarly articles, chapters, and evaluation reports on the topic of violence in relationships.

Christine Wekerle, Ph.D., is Assistant Professor of Psychology at York University in Toronto and Co-Investigator of the Youth Relationships Project. Her research interests range across areas related to children and families (e.g., parenting problems, child abuse, child maladjustment). She has published articles and chapters pertaining to the link between child maltreatment and adolescent outcomes and is coauthor of the book *Alternatives to Violence: Empowering Youth to Develop Healthy Relationships* (1997) and the accompanying text *The Youth Relationships Manual.*